胡適文選

做學問要在不疑處有疑待人要在有疑處不疑

胡適

"In research one should always doubt what (appears) doubtless (but) in relationships with people, never doubt even when there is room for doubt."

Hu Shi's calligraphic inscription published in the **Hu Shi Wen Xuan**.

The Hu Shi Reader

An Advanced Reading Text for Modern Chinese

Compiled and Annotated by

**Sharon Shih-jiuan Hou
and
Chih-p'ing Chou**

Far Eastern Publications
Yale University

Copyright ©1990 by Far Eastern Publications. Printed in the United States of America at Yale University, New Haven, Connecticut. All rights reserved. This book may not be reproduced in whole or in part, in any form (except by reviewers for the public press), without written permission from the publishers.

This book is dedicated to

TA-TUAN CHEN

Professor Emeritus
Princeton University
and Former Director of the Chinese School
Middlebury College
for his contributions
to the field of Chinese language instruction

ACKNOWLEDGMENTS

The compilation of the *Hu Shi Reader* has greatly benefited from the assistance of Der-lin Chao and Cecilia Chang of Princeton University and Li-na Hsieh of St. Catherine's School, Richmond, Virginia. When the text was first completed during the summer of 1986, Prof. Vivian Ling Hsu of Oberlin College was kind enough to read part of the manuscript and offered many valuable suggestions. The award of a research grant from the National Endowment for the Humanities in 1987 enabled a further revision with the able assistance of Paul O. Stern of Pomona College. We extend our deep appreciation to all the above-named persons and institutions. Above all, we wish to thank the Language Schools of Middlebury College for financial support for the preparation of this reader during the summers of 1985 and 1986. Our special thanks go to Dr. Edward C. Knox, Vice-President and Director of the Language Schools at Middlebury, without whose generosity and understanding this project could not have been completed.

February, 1989
S.S.J.H.
C.P.C.

CONTENTS

Dedication v
Acknowledgments vii
Introduction xi

我的兒子 1
My Son (a poem)
我答汪先生的信
My Reply to Mr. Wang

我們對於西洋近代文明的態度 19
Our Attitude Toward Modern Western Civilization

信心與反省 79
Confidence and Self-Examination

再論信心與反省 112
Further Discussion on Confidence
and Self-Examination

問題與主義 149
Problems and -Isms

愛國運動與求學 171
The Patriotic Movement and Scholarly Pursuits

領袖人才的來源 199
The Sources of Leadership Talent

不朽 233
On Immortality

文學改良芻議 273
A Preliminary Discussion of Literary Reform

Selected Bibliography 286

INTRODUCTION

Hu Shi (1891-1962), Chinese historian, philosopher and diplomat, was one of the most influential and controversial figures in modern Chinese intellectual history. For the past half century criticism of him has been characterized by a polarity: he has either been hailed as a first-rate scholar or condemned as an enemy of society.

On the positive side, he has been regarded by some, in both China and the West, as the father of the Chinese literary renaissance, the champion of the vernacular language movement and a vigorous supporter of the values of science and democracy. In addition, he has been credited with launching the effort to "reorganize the national heritage" (整理國故, *zhengli guogu*), which rejuvenated classical learning through the application of the scientific method.

Still others, especially Chinese, have viewed him in less favorable light. Hu's image as an enemy of the people was largely the result of the campaign to criticize Hu Shi's thought which took place in China during the mid-fifties. At that time and later Hu was branded not only as a "running dog of imperialism," but also accused of being the "foremost enemy of Marxist-Leninist thought." In the *Critique of Hu Shi's Thought*, published in eight volumes in 1955, Hu was condemned as the greatest enemy of Chinese Communist ideology and as the public enemy of the people.[1]

Since the beginning of the eighties, this negative image of Hu Shi, which has largely conditioned the way he is viewed in China, has taken a turn for the better. The Chinese Academy of Social Sciences, a leading scholarly association, has decided to collect, collate, and eventually publish Hu Shi's letters and diaries.[2] Additionally, more objective appraisals of Hu Shi have been gradually appearing in Chinese periodical literature.[3] All this seems to indicate the intention of the Chinese Communists to re-evaluate Hu Shi's position in history and scholarship.

As a scholar and political activist, Hu Shi demonstrated the intellectual's concern for culture, society, government and current affairs. He lived through a period of radical transformation of Chinese thought and culture and he himself was an important part of that process of change and tumult.

In 1910, at the age of nineteen, Hu Shi went to the United States for study. He entered Cornell University and received his A.B. degree in 1914. Later he entered

Columbia University to study philosophy and received his doctorate in 1917. Returning to China in that same year he taught philosophy at National Peking University. Less than two years later he published in Chinese *A History of Chinese Philosophy (Ancient Period)*. This seminal work opened up new vistas for Chinese philosophical studies, established new models and introduced a new methodology.

The vernacular language movement, which had been initiated by Hu Shi, and sought the establishment of the spoken language as the only suitable medium for writing, also reached its climax at this time. The movement eventually succeeded in substituting the spoken language for classical writing but did not stop there. It went on, in the so-called New Culture Movement, to a re-evaluation and reorganization of China's entire cultural tradition. This ignited the interest of scholars and others in China's vernacular literature, the study of which, at least up to that time, had been regarded as unworthy of scholarly endeavor. In 1919, following the famous May Fourth Movement, the vernacular language effort and the New Culture Movement fused into one and together exerted a profound influence on every facet of Chinese culture.

As far as methodology of scholarship was concerned, Hu Shi was much influenced by the pragmatism of John Dewey (1859-1952), who, in general, advocated skepticism of all unproven theories. Briefly put, this would hold that everything should be doubted until scientifically proven.[4] In academic circles in China, this triggered a wave of "doubting antiquity" (疑古, *yi gu*), which sought to subject all Chinese systems and values to the test of critical "reappraisal."[5] Many beliefs hitherto regarded as sacred and inviolable were shaken to their very foundations by the raging tide of "skepticism." Hu Shi had no little hand in this.

In the process of China's Westernization, Hu Shi's contribution was not the mere introduction of Western ideas to China but rather his effort to elevate "Western Learning" (西學, *xixue*) from the level of mere technology to the higher levels of thought and culture. In concrete terms, "Western Learning" for Hu Shi not only meant the acquisition and construction of battleships and cannon but also the application of the scientific method and the institution of democracy in China. Rather than adopting the attitude of "Chinese learning for substance, Western learning for application" (中學爲體, 西學爲用, *zhongxue wei ti, xixue wei yong*), a theory first propounded by the late Qing reformer Zhang Zhidong (1833-1909),[6] Hu Shi opted for "wholesale cosmopolitanization,"[7] that is, complete westernization.

Hu Shi's thought was part of an attempt by the Chinese intelligentsia of the early twentieth century to find a way out for traditional Chinese culture. It is our hope that the following selections, which represent some of the most important writings of Hu Shi, will show the reader the suffering, sorrow, struggle and conflict that Hu Shi and others experienced when the Chinese and Western worlds were colliding and the new threatened to engulf the old.

* * *

Hopefully the above remarks concerning the significance of Hu Shi will convince the student of his importance in Chinese intellectual history. But the student of Chinese language can reap a double benefit. By reading Hu Shi the language student can not only be rewarded with important cultural insights but, because the language used by Hu Shi is so suitable for language study, the student gains in this aspect as well. His clarity of expression, logical development of argument and understandable content make his essays ideal instructional materials. The controversy that is so much a part of his writings encourages student enthusiasm and classroom debate, and stimulates exchange of opinion and argument. This text has been used in draft form at Middlebury College and Princeton University for some time and our experience confirms the views expressed above.

We have arranged the selections in this *Hu Shi Reader* by subject rather than by degree of language difficulty. This will facilitate, we expect, classroom discussion of the themes of the pieces. Vocabulary lists are given for each piece. In addition to vocabulary notes, we also provide notes on Chinese sentence structure, illustrative sentences, and suggested discussion topics. Although this book is called a "Reader" we suggest to the teacher that the texts serve as stimuli for oral exchanges leading, we hope, to the development of increased student proficiency in presentation of argument in Chinese.

Notes

1. Chinese Communist criticism of Hu Shi began in 1953. Zhou Yang declared in December 8, 1953: "He [Hu Shi] is the earliest, firmest and most irreconcilable enemy of Chinese Marxist and socialist thought." For details, see Hu Shi, "Sishinian lai Zhongguo wenyi fuxing yundong de kangbao xiaodu liliang" (The power of opposing tyranny and eliminating poison as the repercussions of the Chinese renaissance movement in the past forty years), with the subtitle "Zhongguo Gongchandang qingsuan Hu Shi sixiang de lishi yiyi" (The historical significance of the Chinese Communists' criticism of Hu Shi's thought), collected in *Hu Shi shougao* (Handwritten manuscripts of Hu Shi), vol. 9, p. 493 (Taipei: Hu Shi jinianguan, 1970). One may also consult *Hu Shi sixiang pipan* (Critique of Hu Shi's thought), 8 vols. (Beijing: Sanlian Shudian, 1955).

2. *Hu Shi laiwang shuxin xuan* (Selected collection of correspondence from and to Hu Shi), 3 vols. (Hong Kong: Zhonghua shuju, 1983); *Hu Shi de riji* (The Diary of Hu Shi), 1 vol. (Hong Kong: Zhonghua shuju, 1985).

3. For instance, Wang Jiwu maintained that Hu Shi's promotion of individualism as an outlook on life has proven very inspiring to the Chinese youth, who were prompted by it to break their bonds of feudalism. Therefore, "Hu Shi," Wang stated, "is worthy of the title of a warrior against feudalism during the May Fourth period." For details, see Wang's article "Lun Wusi xinwenhua yundong zhong de Hu Shi" (On Hu Shi in the new cultural movement of the May Fourth period) in *Jilin Daxue shehui kexue xuebao* (Journal of Social Sciences, Jilin University), 2 (1981), 28-37. Zhu Defa also acknowledged that the criticism in the fifties of Hu Shi's thought at one point showed a tendency toward simplicity. It was, he said, overly subjective and arbitrary, and did not tally with the historical facts. For details, see Zhu's article "Ping Wusi shiqi Hu Shi de wenxue zhuzhang" (A critique of Hu Shi's literary ideas during the May Fourth period), in *Wenxue pinglun congkan* (Literary critic), February 1982, vol. 11, p. 250.

4. Concerning Hu Shi's pragmatism, see Hu Shi, "Shiyan zhuyi" (On pragmatism), in *Hu Shi wencun, yiji* (Collected writings of Hu Shi, first collection), 2, pp. 75-145 (Shanghai: Yadong tushuguan, 1921). One may also consult "Lushan youji" (Travel notes on Lu Mountain), in *Hu Shi wencun, sanji* (Collected writings of Hu Shi, third collection), 2, p. 273 (Shanghai: Yadong tushuguan, 1930).

5. See Hu Shi, "Xinsichao de yiyi" (The meaning of the new thought), in *Hu Shi wencun, yiji*, 4, p. 153.

6. See Yu Yingshi (Yü Ying-shih), "Zhongguo jindai sixiangshi shang de Hu Shi" (Hu Shi in the modern intellectual history of China), in Hu Songping, ed., *Hu Shizhi xiansheng nianpu changbian chugao* (The first draft of Hu Shi's comprehensive chronological biography), 10 vols., preface, pp. 9-16 (Taipei: Lianjing chuban shiye gongsi, 1984).

7. See Hu Shi, "Chongfen shijiehua yu quanpan xihua" (Sufficient cosmopolitanization and total Westernization), in *Hu Shi lunxue jinzhu* (Hu Shi's recent writings on scholarship), pp. 558-561 (Shanghai: The Commercial Press, 1935).

胡適文選

My Son (a poem)
我的兒子

My Reply to Mr. Wang
我答汪先生的信

Hu Shi's poem, "My Son," which was composed in vernacular Chinese, interests modern readers more for its content than its style. The views expressed in this short poem and in the following related piece represent a powerful criticism of the traditional Chinese conception of filial devotion (*xiao* 孝), a central feature of Chinese moral beliefs. Indeed, *xiao* headed the list of the basic values governing all human relationships. Hu Shi's challenge to such traditionally held beliefs shocked his contemporaries. His basic point seems to say that the parent-child relationship is a two-way street, each side nurturing the other. His words were aimed at the Chinese of the early twentieth century but they reverberate in our time as well.

The poem was first published in *Weekly Critic* (Měizhōu pínglùn 每週評論), 33 (August 3, 1919), and was later included in *Collection of Experiments* (Chángshì jí 嘗試集; Taipei, 1971, 177-79). The letter was written in June 1919, and was included in *Collected Essays of Hu Shi* (Hú Shì wén cún 胡適文存; Shanghai, 1921), iv, 99-103.

我的兒子

我實在不要兒子,
兒子自己來了。
「無後主義」的招牌,
於今掛不起來了!

譬如樹上開花,
花落偶然結果。
那果便是你,
那樹便是我。

樹本無心結子,
我也無恩於你。

但是你既來了,
我不能不養你教你,
那是我對人道的義務,
並不是待你的恩誼。

將來你長大時,
莫忘了我怎樣教訓兒子:
我要你做一個堂堂的人,
不要你做我的孝順兒子。

七年五月

My Son

無後	wúhòu	無後, 沒有後代, to lack posterity
主義	zhǔyì	-ism (used jokingly here)
招牌	zhāopái	the signboard of a store or any other business concern
於今	yújīn	到現在, up to the present
譬如	pìrú	比方
落	luò	to fall
偶然	ǒurán	by chance, accidentally, incidentally
結果	jiéguǒ	to bear fruits; result; consequently
便是	biànshì	是, 就是
本	běn	本來, 原來
無心	wúxīn	having no intention
子	zǐ	seed, fruit
恩	ēn	favor, benevolence, benignity
A...於 B	yú	A with regard to B
既	jì	既然, in as much as, because, since
人道	réndào	humanitarianism, philanthropy, humanity
義務	yìwù	obligation
恩義	ēnyì	favor, benevolence, benignity
莫	mò	別 (an imperative)
教訓	jiàoxùn	to admonish, to exhort
做(作)人	zuòrén	to be a person, to behave as a person
堂堂	tángtáng	to be dignified, venerable (of personality or appearance)
孝順	xiàoshùn	of or having to do with filial piety or devotion; to show filial piety or devotion (for one's parents)

我答汪先生的信

前天同太虛和尚談論，我得益不少。別後又承先生給我這封很誠懇的信，感謝之至。

「父母於子無恩」的話，從王充孔融以來，也很久了。從前有人說我曾提倡這話，我實在不能承認。直到今年我自己生了一個兒子，我纔想到這個問題上去。我想這個孩子自己並不曾自由主張要生在我家，我們做父母的不曾得他的同意，就糊裏糊塗的給了他一條生命。況且我們也並不曾有意送給他這條生命。我們既無意，如何能居功？如何能自以為有恩於他？他既無意求生，我們生了他，我們對他只有抱歉，更不能「市恩」了。我們糊裏糊塗的替社會上添了一個人，這個

My Reply to Mr. Wang

答	dá	回答
同	tóng	跟, together with
太虛	Tàixū	name of a Buddhist priest
和尚	héshang	Buddhist monk
得益	déyì	得到益處
別後	biéhòu	分別以後
承	chéng	to be obliged, much indebted to
誠懇	chéngkěn	sincere, cordial
感謝之至	gǎnxièzhīzhì	感謝到了極點, 非常感

		謝
		感: to feel, to respond to;
		感謝: to feel grateful;
		之 (lit.): 到;
		至 (lit.): extreme, extremely, used to indicate a superlative degree — the most
王充	Wáng Chōng	27-100 A.D., a philosopher of the Eastern Han period
孔融	Kǒng Róng	153-208 A.D., a scholar of the Eastern Han period
曾	céng	once had, to have had the experience of
提倡	tíchàng	to promote (a cause, etc.)
承認	chéngrèn	to confess, to admit, to concede
纔	cái	才, only then, not until
主張	zhǔzhāng	to advocate (an opinion or idea)
得	dé	得到
條	tiáo	*numerary adjunct* for lives, dogs, roads, snakes, fishes, and long narrow things
(況)況且	kuàngqiě	moreover, furthermore
有意	yǒuyì	to intend; purposeful, intentional
既...如何	jì ... rúhé ...	既然 ... 怎麼(能)... ?
		既: 既然, inasmuch as, because, since;
		如何: 怎麼(能), how can ... ? (an interrogative for a rhetorical question)
無意	wúyì	to have no intention
居功	jūgōng	to take credit (for success, etc.)
求生	qiúshēng	to seek to live
抱歉	bàoqiàn	to feel apologetic, to regret
市恩	shìēn	賣恩, to distribute favors for some personal gain, to parade one's goodness

人將來一生的苦樂禍福,這個人將來在社會上的功罪,我們應該負一部分的責任。說得偏激一點,我們生一個兒子,就好比替他種下了禍根,又替社會種下了禍根。他也許養成壞習慣,做一個短命浪子;他也許更墮落下去,做一個軍閥派的走狗。所以我們「教他養他」,只是我們自己減輕罪過的法子,只是我們種下禍根之後自己補過彌縫的法子。這可以說是恩典嗎?

我所說的,是從做父母的一方面設想的,是從我個人對於我自己的兒子設想的,所以我的題目是「我的兒子」。我的意思是要我這個兒子曉得我對他只有抱歉,決不居功,決不市恩。至於我的兒子將來怎樣待我,那是他自己的事。我決不期望他報答我的恩,因為我已宣言無恩於他。

先生說我把一般做兒子的抬舉起來,看做一

苦樂禍福	kǔlè huòfú	苦樂: sorrows and joys, discomfort and comfort; 禍福: misfortune and fortune, calamity and blessing
功罪	gōngzuì	merits and demerits
偏激	piānjī	extreme
好比	hǎobǐ	好像, to be just like
種	zhòng	to plant, to sow
禍根	huògēn	the seeds of calamity or mis-

		fortune
		根: the root of a plant — the beginning, cause or source of something
短命	duǎnmìng	to die early, short-lived
浪子	làngzi	a prodigal, debauchee, a loafer
墮落	duòluò	to sink in moral standard, to degenerate, to indulge in evil ways
軍閥	jūnfá	warlord, the militarists
派	pài	a faction
走狗	zǒugǒu	running dog, lackey, a servile follower
罪過	zuìguò	sin, fault, mistake
補過	bǔguò	to make up for a fault, mistake
		補: to mend, repair
彌縫	míféng	to fill cracks, to cover up mistakes
		彌: to fill;
		縫: a crack, an opening, a crevice, a fissure, a chink
恩典	ēndiǎn	favor, grace
設想	shèxiǎng	to imagine, to hypothesize
個人	gèrén	the individual, oneself
題目	tímù	the title (of a composition)
曉得	xiǎode	知道
期望	qīwàng	to hope, expect; hope, expectation
報答	bàodá	to repay (another's kindness)
已	yǐ	已經
宣言	xuānyán	to announce, to declare; declaration, manifesto
一般	yìbān	common, general; commonly, generally
抬舉	táijǔ	to favor somebody
		抬: to lift, to raise;
		舉: to lift, to raise, to hold up
看作	kànzuò	to view as

個「白吃不還帳」的主顧。這是先生誤會我的地方。我的意思恰同這個相反。我想把一般做父母的抬高起來，叫他們不要把自己看做一種「放高利債」的債主。

先生又怪我把「孝」字驅逐出境。我要問先生，現在「孝子」兩個字究竟還有什麼意義？現在的人死了父母都稱「孝子」。孝子就是居父母喪的兒子，（古書稱為「主人」）無論怎樣忤逆不孝的人，一穿上蔴衣，戴上高梁冠，拿著哭喪棒，人家就稱他做「孝子」。

我的意思以為古人把一切做人的道理都包在孝字裏，故戰陣無勇，涖官不敬，等等都是不孝

白	bái (V.)	to (V.) without payment, to (V.) for nothing
還帳	huánzhàng	to pay in order to clear an account, to pay a bill or debt 帳：賬, accounts, bills
主顧	zhǔgù	a customer
誤會	wùhuì	to misunderstand, misinterpret 誤：to err; 會：to understand, to realize
恰	qià	by coincidence
相反	xiāngfǎn	to be contrary, to be opposed to each other

放高利債	fànggāolìzhài	to practise usury 利: interest (distinct from principal); 債: a debt
債主	zhàizhǔ	a creditor
驅逐出境	qūzhúchūjìng	to expel, to deport 境: region, territory
孝子	xiàozǐ	a bereaved son (as in obituary)
究竟	jiūjìng	到底, after all, in the end
稱	chēng	叫, to be called
居喪	jūsāng	to be in mourning 居: to dwell, to reside, to inhabit; 喪: of death; funeral
稱為	chēngwéi	叫作, to name as, to call
忤逆	wǔnì	stubbornly defiant, disobedient (especially to one's parents)
麻衣	máyī	hempen clothes (worn at funerals)
高梁冠	gāoliángguàn	a hat with a high crown (worn at funerals)
哭喪棒	kūsāngbàng	a staff held by the chief mourners 哭喪: to wail for the dead; 棒: a club, a stick, a staff
一切	yīqiè	所有的
道理	dàolǐ	the right way, the proper way
包	bāo	to include, to contain, to comprise
故	gù	所以
戰陣無勇	zhànzhèn wúyǒng	在戰場上不勇敢 戰陣: battlefield, battlefront; 勇: bravery, courage
蒞官不敬	lìguān bùjìng	作官的時候不恭敬 蒞官: to take office, to arrive at one's post; 敬: respect
等等	děngděng	and so forth, *et cetera*

。這種學說，先生也承認他流弊百出。所以我要我的兒子做一個堂堂的人，不要他做我的孝順兒子。我的意思以爲「一個堂堂的人」決不致於做打爹罵娘的事，決不致於對他的父母毫無感情。

但是我不贊成把「兒子孝順父母」列爲一種「信條」。易卜生的羣鬼裏有一段話很可研究：（新潮第五號頁八五一）

（孟代牧師）你忘了沒有，一個孩子應該愛敬他的父母？

（阿爾文夫人）我們不要講得這樣寬泛。應該說：「歐士華應該愛敬阿爾文先生（歐士華之父）嗎？」

這是說，「一個孩子應該愛敬他的父母」是耶教一種信條，但是有時未必適用。即如阿爾文

| 學說 | xuéshuō | a theory |
| 流弊百出 | liúbìbǎichū | 很多壞處(害處)都出現了
弊: harm, damage;
流弊: long accumulated evil effects, corrupt practices, abuses |

意想	yìxiǎng	意思跟想法
致於	zhìyú	至於, to reach as far as, to the extent of
爹	diē	父親
娘	niáng	母親
毫無	háowú	一點都沒有, not at all, not in the least
列爲	lièwéi	to list as ...
信條	xìntiáo	a creed or dogma
易卜生	Yìbǔshēng	Ibsen, Henrik (1828-1906), Norwegian playwright and poet
羣鬼	Qúnguǐ	*Ghosts*, a play by Henrik Ibsen
可	kě	值得
研究	yánjiù	to study and research, to examine
新潮	*Xīncháo*	the name of a magazine
頁	yè	a page (in books), a sheet (of paper)
孟代牧師	Mèngdài mùshī	Pastor Manders (in *Ghosts*)
寬泛	kuānfàn	general, not particular, not specific 泛: to float, to drift
阿爾文夫人之	Āěrwén fūrén zhī	Mrs. Alving (in *Ghosts*) 的
歐士華	Ōushìhuá	Oswald Alving (in *Ghosts*), the son of Mrs. Alving
耶教	yējiào	Protestant Christianity 耶 or 耶穌: Jesus; 教: a religion
未必	wèibì	不一定,不見得
適用	shìyòng	fit or suitable for use, applicable
即如	jírú	就譬如,就比方

一生縱淫，死於花柳毒，還把遺毒傳給他的兒子歐士華，後來歐士華毒發而死。請問歐士華應該孝順阿爾文嗎？若照中國古代的倫理觀念自然不成問題。但是在今日可不能不成問題了。假如我染着花柳毒，生下兒子又聾又瞎，終身殘廢，他應該愛敬我嗎？又假如我把我的兒子應得的遺產都拿去賭輸了，使他衣食不能完全，教育不能得着，他應該愛敬我嗎？又假如我賣國賣主義，做了一國一世的大罪人，他應該愛敬我嗎？

　　至於先生說的，恐怕有人扯起幌子，說，「胡先生教我做一個堂堂的人，萬不可做父母的孝順兒子」。這是他自己錯了。我的詩是發表我生平

縱淫	zòngyín	to abandon oneself to carnal desire 縱: to indulge, to give free rein to; 淫: things related to sexual desire and behaviors; lascivious, lewd
花柳毒	huāliǔdú	venereal disease, V.D. 毒: poison, toxin, venom
遺毒	yídú	poison left behind by somebody 遺: to leave behind (either intentionally or unintentionally)

傳	chuán	to transmit, to pass along (a disease), to hand down to others by heredity
發	fā	發作, (of illness) to have a relapse
若	ruò	要是, 如果
照	zhào	按照, according to, in accordance with
倫理	lúnlǐ	ethics, moral principles
觀念	guānniàn	a concept, an idea or view
自然	zìrán	naturally
不成問題	bùchéng wèntí	beyond question, without any doubt
假如	jiǎrú	要是, 如果
染	rǎn	to get infected, to catch a disease
聾	lóng	耳朵聽不見
瞎	xiā	眼睛看不見
終身	zhōngshēn	一輩子, till death, throughout life 終: to come to the end
殘廢	cánfèi	physically disabled
遺產	yíchǎn	property left behind by a deceased person, bequest 產: properties, estate
賭輸	dǔshū	賭: to gamble; 輸: to lose (here as a *resultative verb* ending)
完全	wánquán	complete and thorough
扯起幌子	chěqǐ huǎngzi	扯: to hoist, to lift; 幌子: a flag sign for a wineshop or store; something to dazzle or cheat another with
萬不可	wànbùkě	not by any means, under no circumstances, in no event
發表	fābiǎo	to make public, to make known, to publish (an article)
生平	shēngpíng	in one's course of life

第一次做老子的感想,我並不曾教訓人家的兒子!

　　總之,我只說了我自己承認對兒子無恩,至於兒子將來對我作何感想,那是他自己的事,我不管了。

　　先生又要我做「我的父母」的詩。我對於這個題目,也曾有詩,載在每週評論第一期和新潮第二期裏。

感想	gǎnxiǎng	one's intellectual and emotional response to something
總之	zǒngzhī	in short, in a word, to sum up, in sum 總: to assemble, to gather
何	hé	(lit.) 甚麼
管	guǎn	to control, to manage, to take care of, to interfere with
載	zǎi	to record, to publish, (of vehicles) to carry (loads)
每週評論	Měizhōu pínglùn	the name of a magazine
期	qī	a period, a date, a limit of time, a fixed date (used for identification of issues of periodicals)

句型

1. ...直到...才... — not until

■從前有人說我提倡這話,我實在不能承認.直到今年我自己生了一個兒子,我才想到這個問題上去.

例 (1): 我們本來一直是租房子住,直到去年我找到工作以後才買了現在這所房子.

例 (2): 他常常肚子疼,可是因為工作忙一直沒注意,直到有一次疼的非常厲害,到醫院去看過了以後才知道得了癌症[1].

[1] 癌症　　aizhèng　　cancer

2. 況且 — moreover, furthermore

■我們做父母的不曾得他的同意,就糊裏糊塗的給了他一條生命,況且我們也並不曾有意送給他這條生命.

例 (1): 這棟房子太舊了,前後院也太小,況且只有一個房間,我們還是再看看別的房子吧.

例 (2): 你為甚麼不接受這份工作呢?不但薪水高,老板人也很和氣,況且上班的地方又離你家很近.
(...何況上班的地方又離你家很近.
...再說上班的地方又離你家很近.)

3. 既...如何... — since (or as, because) ... how can ... ? (used in rhetorical question)

■我們既無意,如何能居功?

例 (1): 你既不懂,如何能教?

例 (2): 你既不喜歡他,如何能跟他結婚?

4a. 至於 — as for (starting a new topic)

■我的意思是要我這個兒子曉得我對他只有抱歉,決不居功,決不市恩.至於我的兒子將來怎麼樣待我,那是他自己的事.

例(1):你放心去唸書吧,至於錢的問題,我會替你想辦法的.

例(2):我對歷史很有興趣,所以我打算學歷史;至於將來找的到找不到工作以後再說.

4b. 不至於 (不致於) — not as (bad) as

■ 我的意思以為『一個堂堂的人』決不至於做打爹罵娘的事.

例:我們家雖然窮可是還不致於沒飯吃.
不致於…連…都(也)…
我們家雖然窮可是還不致於連飯都沒的吃.
我雖然笨可是還不致於連~ON自己的名字都看不出來.

5a. 白 V — to V without payment (e.g. 白吃,白喝,白住,白拿, etc.)

■ 我把一般做兒子的抬舉起來,看做一個『白吃不還帳』的主顧.

例:他常到別人家去白吃,所以大家都不歡迎他.

5b. 白 V 了 — to V in vain (e.g. 白吃了,白唸了,白看了,白拿了,白跑了一趟, etc.)

例(1):我去看朋友可是他不在家我白跑了一趟.

例(2):我預備了第六課的課文,可是老師要講第五課,我白預備了.

6. A 同 B 相反 (A 跟 B 相反) — A is opposite to B

■ 我的意思恰同這個相反.(我的意思恰跟這個相反.)

例(1):我的意見同他相反.(我的意見跟他相反.)

例(2):中國人吃飯的時候先吃飯後喝湯,可是美國人同中國人相反,他們先喝湯後吃飯.

7. 未必 (不見得,不一定) — not necessarily

■ …是耶教一種信條,但是有時未必適用.

例 (1): 美國的教育制度在中國<u>未必</u>適用.
　　　...<u>不一定</u>適用.
　　　...<u>不見得</u>適用.

例 (2): "我想他一定考的上大學." "我看<u>未必</u>. 他的功課並不好, 況且他一點也不用功."

8. 生平第一次　— the first time in one's course of life

■ 我的詩是發表我<u>生平第一次</u>做老子的感想.

　例 (1): 這是我<u>生平第一次</u>出國所以我非常興奮.

　例 (2): 這是我<u>生平第一次</u>用筷子吃飯.

討論

1. "我的兒子"這首詩的主題是什麼?
2. "做一個堂堂的人"跟"做一個孝順兒子"有沒有衝突[1]?
3. "父母於子無恩"是胡適答汪先生信裏的主要論點[2]; 你同意嗎?
4. 孩子是不是應該無條件的[3]敬愛父母?
5. 在你看來, 什麼是父母跟子女理想的[4]關係?

[1] 衝突	chōngtū	conflict, clash
[2] 論點	lùndiǎn	argument, point of discussion
[3] 無條件的	wútiáojiànde	unconditionally, without preconditions
[4] 理想的	lǐxiǎngde	ideal

Our Attitude Towards Modern Western Civilization
我們對於西洋近代文明的態度

This selection epitomizes many of the issues that were hotly debated in Hu Shi's time, especially the controversy surrounding the virtues of Chinese civilization as contrasted with Western civilization. In this seminal essay Hu denounced the view that China was superior to the West because of the supposed spiritual nature of China, and exhorted the Chinese people to strive for change in China. His views were, at that time, unprecedented and initiated fervent debate between the conservative and liberal elements among the educated elite. In many respects the debate is still going on.

This essay was first published in *Modern Critic* (Xiandai pinglun 現代評論), 4.83:3-11 (July 10, 1926). It is included in *Collected Essays of Hu Shi* III (Hu Shi wencun, di san ji 胡適文存, 第三集; Shanghai, 1930), i, 3-13.

我們對於西洋近代文明的態度

今日最沒有根據而又最有毒害的妖言是譏貶西洋文明為唯物的(Materialistic)，而尊崇東方文明為精神的(Spiritual)。這本是很老的見解，在今日却有新興的氣象。從前東方民族受了西洋民族的壓迫，往往用這種見解來解嘲，來安慰自己。近幾年來，歐洲大戰的影響使一部分的西洋

Our Attitude Toward Modern Western Civilization

對於	duìyú	對, to, as to, with regard to, regarding, with respect to, in relation to
西洋	Xīyáng	西方, the West, European or American nations 洋: 大海
近代	jìndài	modern ages, recent times 代: era, generation, dynasty
文明	wénmíng	civilization
根據	gēnjù	basis, grounds, foundation; on the strength of, in line with
而	ér	and yet
毒害	dúhài	poison, harm; to poison (one's mind)
妖言	yāoyán	heresy, deceptive, misleading or false talk 妖: evil and fraudulent,

		bewitching; goblin, demon, monster, evil spirit
譏貶	jībiǎn	譏: to ridicule, to jeer, to sneer; 貶: to disparage, to censure, to depreciate
爲	wéi	to be, to act as, to serve as
唯物	wéiwù	"only material" — materialistic 唯: only, alone; 物: thing, matter, material
尊崇	zūnchóng	尊: 尊敬, to respect; 崇: 崇拜, to worship, to adore, to revere
東方	Dōngfāng	the East, Oriental
精神	jīngshén	spirit, mind, consciousness; vivacity, spirit; gist, essence
本是	běnshì	本來是, 原來是
見解	jiànjiě	one's views, ideas or observation about something
却 (卻)	què	but, yet, however
新興	xīnxīng	newly risen, rising 興: to rise, to thrive, to prosper, to flourish
氣象	qìxiàng	(prevailing) spirit (or atmosphere) and scene; meteorology, weather, climate
民族	mínzú	people, nation, nationality
壓迫	yāpò	to press hard, to oppress, to pressure; oppression, pressure
解嘲	jiěcháo	to explain things away when ridiculed 解: to untie, to solve (problems), to relieve, to alleviate; 嘲: ridicule, deride
戰	zhàn	war, warfare, battle, fighting
影響	yǐngxiǎng	influence, impact, effect; to influence, to affect
使	shǐ	to cause, to make, to enable

人對於近世科學的文化起一種厭倦的反感，所以我們時時聽見西洋學者有崇拜東方的精神文明的議論。這種議論，本來只是一時的病態的心理，却正投合東方民族的誇大狂；東方的舊勢力就因此增加了不少的氣燄。

我們不願「開倒車」的少年人，對於這個問題不能沒有一種澈底的見解，不能沒有一種鮮明的表示。

現在高談「精神文明」「物質文明」的人，往往沒有共同的標準做討論的基礎，故只能作文

近世	jìnshì	modern ages, recent times 世: age, era
科學	kēxué	science
起	qǐ	to rise, to grow
厭倦	yànjuàn	to be tired of, weary of
反感	fǎngǎn	antipathy; to have an antipathy to, to have an aversion to, to be disgusted with
時時	shíshí	常常
學者	xuézhě	scholar, learned man
議論	yìlùn	argument, debate, discussion, comment; to discuss, to comment
一時	yìshí	for a short while, temporary, momentary, accidentally
病態	bìngtài	morbid, abnormal; morbid or abnormal state

心理	xīnlǐ	psychology, mentality
正	zhèng	just, right, exactly, precisely
投合	tóuhé	to be in rapport, to agree, to get along
誇大狂	kuādàkuáng	megalomania; megalomaniac 誇大: to exaggerate, to overstate; 狂: crazy, mad, mentally deranged
因此	yīncǐ	因為這, because of this
增加	zēngjiā	to increase, to add (to)
氣燄	qìyàn	arrogance, *hauteur* 氣: air, bearing, manner; 燄: flame, blaze
開倒車	kāidàochē	"to drive a car backward" — to be old-fashioned or anachronistic, to turn back the clock
澈底 (徹底)	chèdǐ	thorough, complete; thoroughly 澈: clear water; 底: bottom
鮮明	xiānmíng	(of color) bright; (of theme, literary style, political stand) clear-cut, distinct, distinctive
表示	biǎoshì	expression, indication, reaction; to express, to show, to indicate
高談	gāotán	to talk freely, to talk in a lively atmosphere; (sometimes derogatory) to indulge in loud and empty talk, to talk volubly or bombastically
共同	gòngtóng	common, together, jointly
標準	biāozhǔn	standard, criterion; typical
討論	tǎolùn	to discuss; discussion
基礎	jīchǔ	foundation, base, basis
故	gù	所以
文字	wénzì	written language, script, characters; writing (regarding form or style)

字上或表面上的爭論,而不能有根本的了解。我想提出幾個基本觀念來做討論的標準。

第一,文明(Civilization)是一個民族應付他的環境的總成績。

第二,文化(Culture)是一種文明所形成的生活的方式。

第三,凡一種文明的造成,必有兩個因子:一是物質的(Material),包括種種自然界的勢力與質料;一是精神的(Spiritual),包括一個民族的聰明才智,感情和理想。凡文明都是人的心思智力運用自然界的質與力的作品;沒有一種文明是精神的,也沒有

...上	... shàng	in ... , as far as ... is concerned
表面	biǎomiàn	surface, face, outside appearance
爭論	zhēnglùn	debate, dispute; to argue, to dispute 爭: to contend, to compete, to vie; 論: 討論
根本	gēnběn	basic, essential, cardinal; root, base; radically, thoroughly; (before negative) at all, simply
了解	liǎojiě	understanding, comprehension; to understand, to acquaint oneself with

提出	tíchū	to put forth, to raise, to advance
基本	jīběn	basic, fundamental, main, essential; base, root, foundation
觀念	guānniàn	concept, sense, idea
應付	yìngfù	to deal with, to cope with, to handle, to do something perfunctorily, to do something after a fashion
環境	huánjìng	environment, surroundings
總	zǒng	all, general, overall, total
成績	chéngjī	records established or set, results
形成	xíngchéng	to form, to produce as a result; to take shape; formation
方式	fāngshì	way, fashion, mode, pattern
凡...	fán...	every (any, all) ...
造成	zàochéng	形成, formation; to form, to produce as a result
因子	yīnzǐ	factor
包括	bāokuò	to include, to comprise, to consist of
自然界	zìránjiè	natural world, nature 界: domain, territory, world, scope, extent, circles
與	yǔ	跟, 和
質料	zhíliào	raw material; quality
才智	cáizhì	ability and wisdom
理想	lǐxiǎng	ideal, dream
心思	xīnsī	thinking, thought, idea, intention, state of mind, mood
智力	zhìlì	intelligence, intellect
運用	yùnyòng	to employ, to make use of, to wield, to put to use
質	zhí	質料, raw material; quality
力	lì	勢力, power, influence
作品	zuòpǐn	works (of literature and art) 品: article, product

一種文明單是物質的。

　　我想這三個觀念是不須詳細說明的，是研究這個問題的人都可以承認的。一隻瓦盆和一隻鐵鑄的大蒸汽鑪，一隻舢板船和一隻大汽船，一部單輪小車和一輛電力街車，都是人的智慧利用自然界的質力製造出來的文明，同有物質的基礎，同有人類的心思才智。這裏面只有個精粗巧拙的程度上的差異，却沒有根本上的不同。蒸汽鐵鑪固然不必笑瓦盆的幼稚，單輪小車上的人也更不配自誇他的精神的文明，而輕視電車上人的物質的文明。

單	dān	only, merely, singly, alone, one
須	xū	must, have to
詳細	xiángxì	in every detail and particular, with nothing omitted; detailed, minute
說明	shuōmíng	to explain, to illustrate, to show; explanation, direction, description, caption
研究	yánjiù	to study and research, to consider, to discuss, to deliberate; research, study
承認	chéngrèn	to admit, to acknowledge, to recognize, to give diplomatic recognition

瓦盆	wǎpén	clay pot
		瓦: earthen, of clay, earthenware, pottery, tile;
		盆: basin, tub, pot
鐵鑄的	tiězhùde	cast iron
		鑄: to melt or cast metal, to coin or mint
蒸汽鑪	zhēngqìlú	steam furnace
舢板船	shānbǎnchuán	sampan
汽船	qìchuán	steamship, steamer
單輪	dānlún	one (or single) wheel
車輛	chēliàng	車, vehicle, car
電力	diànlì	electric power
智慧	zhìhuì	wisdom, intelligence
利用	lìyòng	to make use of, to use, to take advantage of, to exploit
製造	zhìzào	to make, produce or manufacture; to create, mould or fabricate (trouble, tension, rumor); production, product
同	tóng	一樣
精	jīng	refined, exquisite, fine and delicate
粗	cū	coarse, crude, indelicate, rough
巧	qiǎo	skillful, artful, clever, ingenious
拙	zhuō	clumsy, awkward, dull
程度	chéngdù	level, degree or extent; general academic achievement
差異	chāyì	不同
固然	gùrán ...	no doubt, it is true, certainly, or admittedly ...
幼稚	yòuzhì	naiveté; immature, unsophisticated
配	pèi	to be qualified, to be worthy of, to deserve
自誇	zìkuā	to sing one's own praises
輕視	qīngshì	看不起
		視: 看

因為一切文明都少不了物質的表現，所以「物質的文明」(Material Civilization) 一個名詞不應該有什麼譏貶的涵義。我們說一部摩托車是一種物質的文明，不過單指他的物質的形體；其實一部摩托車所代表的人類的心思智慧決不亞於一首詩所代表的心思智慧。所以「物質的文明」不是和「精神的文明」反對的一個貶詞，我們可以不討論。

　　我們現在要討論的是①什麼叫做「唯物的文明」(Materialistic Civilization)，②西洋現代文明是不是唯物的文明。

　　崇拜所謂東方精神文明的人說，西洋近代文明偏重物質上和肉體上的享受，而略視心靈上與精神上的要求，所以是唯物的文明。

　　我們先要指出這種議論含有靈肉衝突的成見

一切	yīqiè	所有的, all, everything
少不了	shǎobuliǎo	cannot do without, cannot dispense with; be bound to, or be unavoidable
表現	biǎoxiàn	expression or manifestation; performance, or the way one does something; to show, display, or manifest, to show off
名詞	míngcí	term; (in grammar) noun
涵義	hányì	meaning, implication

摩托車	mótuōchē	motorcycle
指	zhǐ	to point to, to refer to
形體	xíngtǐ	body, form, shape, physique
人類	rénlèi	mankind, the human species, the human race
決	jué	(used before negative) definitely, certainly, under any circumstances
不亞於	búyàyú	not worse than, as good as, as well as
貶詞	biǎncí	expression of censure, derogatory term 貶: 譏貶, to ridicule and disparage; 詞: 名詞, term
所謂	suǒwèi	so-called, what is called
偏重	piānzhòng	to lean heavily toward, to give undue emphasis to, to give particular emphasis to, to lay particular stress on 偏: inclined to one side
肉體	ròutǐ	the body of blood and flesh, the human body 肉體上的: carnal, sensory, physical
享受	xiǎngshòu	enjoyment, treat; to enjoy
略視	lüèshì	to neglect, to overlook, to lose sight of, to ignore 略: to omit, to leave out
心靈	xīnlíng	heart, soul, spirit
要求	yāoqiú	demand, request; to demand, to request, to ask, to require
指出	zhǐchū	to point out
含有	hányǒu	to contain
衝突	chōngtú	conflict, clash; to conflict, to clash
成見	chéngjiàn	preconceived idea, prejudice

，我們認為錯誤的成見。我們深信，精神的文明必須建築在物質的基礎之上。提高人類物質上的享受，增加人類物質上的便利與安逸，這都是朝着解放人類的能力的方向走，使人們不至於把精力心思全拋在僅僅生存之上，使他們可以有餘力去滿足他們的精神上的要求。東方的哲人曾說：

衣食足而後知榮辱，倉廩實而後知禮節。

這不是什麼舶來的「經濟史觀」；這是平素的常識。人世的大悲劇是無數的人們終身做血汗的生

認為	rènwéi	to think, to consider, to hold, to deem
錯誤	cuòwù	wrong, mistaken, erroneous; mistake, error, blunder
信	xìn	相信, to believe
建築	jiànzhú	to build, construct or erect; building, structure, edifice; architecture
建築在... 之上	jiànzhú zài ... zhīshàng	to build ... on ... 之: 的
提高	tígāo	to raise, to heighten, to enhance, to increase, to improve
便利	biànlì	convenience; convenient, easy; to facilitate
安逸	ānyì	ease and comfort; easy and comfortable
朝	cháo	向, 對, facing, toward
解放	jiěfàng	to liberate or emancipate; liberation, emancipation
能力	nénglì	ability, capacity, capability
方向	fāngxiàng	direction, orientation

不至於	bùzhìyú	cannot go so far as, to be unlikely
拋	pāo	丟, to throw, to toss, to fling
僅僅	jǐnjǐn	只, 就, only, merely, barely
生存	shēngcún	to live, to exist, to subsist; existence
餘力	yúlì	strength or energy to spare 餘: surplus, excess
滿足	mǎnzú	to satisfy, to meet; satisfied, content, contented
哲人	zhérén	philosopher, sage
曾	céng	once, ever, to have had the experience of
衣食足	yīshízú	(lit.) 衣服跟吃的東西都夠了
知	zhī	知道
榮辱	róngrǔ	honor or disgrace
倉廩實	cānglǐnshí	(lit.) 倉廩裏存着很多東西 倉廩: granary; 實: substantial, abundant, rich in contents
禮節	lǐjié	etiquette, courtesy, ceremony, protocol
舶來	bólái	從外國來的 舶: ocean-going ship
經濟史	jīngjìshǐ	economic history
觀	guān	看法, view, concept, outlook
平素	píngsù	usual, common, ordinary
常識	chángshì	general (elementary) knowledge, common sense
人世	rénshì	人的世界
悲劇	bēijù	"sad play or drama" — tragedy
無數	wúshù	countless, innumerable 無: 沒有; 數: number, figure
終身	zhōngshēn	一輩子, all one's life, lifelong
血汗	xiěhàn or xuèhàn	"blood and sweat" — hard toil

活，而不能得着最低限度的人生幸福，不能避免凍與餓。人世的更大悲劇是人類的先知先覺者眼看無數人們的凍餓，不能設法增進他們的幸福，却把「樂天」「安命」「知足」「安貧」種種催眠藥給他們吃，他們自己欺騙自己，安慰自己。西方古代有一則寓言說，狐狸想吃葡萄，葡萄太高了，牠吃不着，只好說「我本不愛吃這酸葡萄」！狐狸吃不着甜葡萄，只好說葡萄是酸的；人們享不着物質上的快樂，只好說物質上的享受是不足羨慕的，而貧賤是可以驕人的。這樣自欺自

得着	dezháo	得到
限度	xiàndù	limit, limitation
幸福	xìngfú	happiness and well-being, bliss
避免	bìmiǎn	to avoid, to shun from, to avert
凍	dòng	to feel very cold, to freeze, to be frostbitten
先知先覺	xiānzhīxiānjué	比別人先知道（或覺得）— to have foresight
者	zhě	(lit.) those who, he who
設法	shèfǎ	想法子
增進	zēngjìn	to increase, to improve, to advance
樂天	lètiān	to be content with one's lot, to be carefree and easygoing, to be optimistic
安命	ānmìng	to be content with one's lot, to accept one's lot
知足	zhīzú	to be content with what one has had

安貧	ānpín	to be content with poverty, to be happy to lead a poor and simple life
催眠	cuīmián	to lull to sleep, to hypnotize, to mesmerize
		催: to hasten, to urge, to press, to speed up;
		眠: 睡覺
藥	yào	medicine, drug, remedy
欺騙	qīpiàn	騙, to deceive, to cheat
古代	gǔdài	古時候
則	zé	Numerary Adjunct for fables, parables, etc.
寓言	yùyán	fable, allegory, parable
		寓: to reside, to contain, to imply;
		言: speech, word
狐狸	húli	fox
葡萄	pútáo	grape
吃不着	chībuzháo	吃不到
只好	zhǐhǎo	to have to, cannot but, to have no alternative but
酸	suān	sour, tart
甜	tián	sweet, luscious
享不着	xiǎngbuzháo	享受 (to enjoy) 不到
不足	bùzú	do not deserve, to be not worth; not enough, insufficient, inadequate
羨慕	xiànmù	to envy, to admire
貧賤	pínjiàn	to be poor and lonely, to be in destitute and humble circumstances
		貧: 沒有錢;
		賤: 沒有地位
驕人	jiāorén	to try to impress people, to show off

慰成了懶惰的風氣，又不足為奇了。於是有狂病的人又進一步，索性回過頭去，戕賊身體，斷臂，絕食，焚身，以求那幻想的精神的安慰。從自欺自慰以至於自殘自殺，人生觀變成了人死觀，都是從一條路上來的：這條路就是輕蔑人類的基本的欲望。朝這條路上走，逆天而拂性，必至於養成懶惰的社會，多數人不肯努力以求人生基本欲望的滿足，也就不肯進一步以求心靈上與精神上的發展了。

西洋近代文明的特色便是充分承認這個物質

懶惰	lǎnduò	懶
風氣	fēngqì	general mood, atmosphere, common (or established) practice, custom, tradition
不足為奇	bùzúwéiqí	to be not worth being regarded as something strange or extraordinary; there is nothing strange, extraordinary or remarkable about it
進一步	jìnyíbù	to go a step further 步: step, pace
索性	suǒxìng	straightforward; simply, just
戕賊	qiāngzéi	to injure or harm, to undermine or ruin 戕: to kill; 賊: to injure, to harm, to murder

斷	duàn	to break, to break off, to cut off
臂	bì	arm
絕食	juéshí	to fast, go on a hunger strike 絕: to sever, to cut off
焚	fén	燒, to burn, to destroy by fire
以	... yǐ ...	... in order to (or so as to) ...
幻想	huànxiǎng	illusion, fancy, fantasy, reverie; to daydream, to be lost in reverie
自欺	zìqī	自己欺騙 (to deceive) 自己
自慰	zìwèi	自己安慰 (to console) 自己
以至於	yǐzhìyú	to such an extent as to ..., so that ...; down to, up to
自殘	zìcán	to injure (or damage) oneself 殘: to injure, to damage
人生觀	rénshēngguān	對人生 (human life) 的看法 觀: 看法
輕蔑	qīngmiè	輕視,看不起 蔑: to slight, disdain
欲望	yùwàng	desire, wish, lust
逆天	nìtiān	to oppose or defy nature, natural instincts, or heavenly principles
拂性	fúxìng	to go against human nature
必	bì	一定
養成	yǎngchéng	to form, to acquire, to develope, to cultivate
努力	nǔlì	to make great efforts, to strive, to exert oneself, to endeavor; hard-working, laborious, assiduous
發展	fāzhǎn	development; to develop
特色	tèsè	special feature, distinguishing quality
便是	biànshì	就是
充分	chōngfèn	fully, sufficient, ample, full

的享受的重要。西洋近代文明，依我的鄙見看來，是建築在三個基本觀念之上：

第一，人生的目的是求幸福。
第二，所以貧窮是一樁罪惡。
第三，所以衰病是一樁罪惡。

借用一句東方古話，這就是一種「利用厚生」的文明。因為貧窮是一樁罪惡，所以要開發富源，獎勵生產，改良製造，擴張商業。因為衰病是一樁罪惡，所以要研究醫藥，提倡衛生，講求體育，防止傳染的疾病，改善人種的遺傳。因為人生的目的是求幸福，所以要經營安適的起居，便利的交通，潔淨的城市，優美的藝術，安全的社會

依	yī	according to, in light of, judging by
鄙見	bǐjiàn	my humble opinion
目的	mùdì	purpose, aim, goal, objective, end
樁	zhuāng	Numerary Adjunct
罪惡	zuìè	crime, evil
衰病	shuāibìng	decrepit and beset by illness
借用	jièyòng	to borrow for use
古話	gǔhuà	old saying
利用厚生	lìyònghòushēng	to serve the requirements and to enrich the lives of the people
開發	kāifā	to open up, to develope, to exploit
富源	fùyuán	natural resources
獎勵	jiǎnglì	to encourage and reward, to award, to reward; award, reward

生產	shēngchǎn	production; to produce, to manufacture
改良	gǎiliáng	to improve, to better
擴張	kuòzhāng	to expand, extend, enlarge, or spread
醫藥	yīyào	medicine
提倡	tíchàng	to advocate, to prompt, to encourage, to recommend
衛生	wèishēng	hygiene, sanitation, health
講求	jiǎngqiú	to be particular or elaborate about, to pay special attention to
體育	tǐyù	physical culture, physical training, sports, physical education
防止	fángzhǐ	to guard against, to prevent, to avoid, to forestall
傳染	chuánrǎn	to infect, to be contagious; infection
疾病	jíbìng	illness, disease
改善	gǎishàn	改良, to improve; improvement
人種	rénzhǒng	human race
遺傳	yíchuán	heredity; hereditary; to transmit (to later generations)
經營	jīngyíng	to manage or operate, to run, to engage in
安適	ānshì	quiet and comfortable
起居	qǐjū	one's everyday life at home
交通	jiāotōng	transportation, communication, traffic
潔淨	jiéjìng	清潔乾淨, clean, stainless, spotless, untarnished
優美	yōuměi	fine, graceful, exquisite, anything that inspires a sense of joy
藝術	yìshù	art; artful, conforming to good taste
安全	ānquán	safe, secure; safety, security

，清明的政治。縱觀西洋近代的一切工藝，科學，法制，固然其中也不少殺人的利器與侵略掠奪的制度，我們終不能不承認那利用厚生的基本精神。

這個利用厚生的文明，當真忽略了人類心靈上與精神上的要求嗎?當真是一種唯物的文明嗎?

我們可以大膽地宣言：西洋近代文明絕不輕視人類的精神上的要求。我們還可以大膽地進一步說：西洋近代文明能夠滿足人類心靈上的要求的程度，遠非東洋舊文明所能夢見。在這一方面看來，西洋近代文明絕非唯物的。乃是理想主義的(Idealistic)，乃是精神的(Spiritual)。

我們先從理智的方面說起。

西洋近代文明的精神方面的第一特色是科學。科學的根本精神在於求真理。人生世間，受環

清明	qīngmíng	clean and just (administration); clear and bright (moonlight); sober and calm (mind or conscious)
政治	zhèngzhì	politics, political affairs
縱觀	zòngguān	to look freely and extensively, to take a free, wide look, to

		take a sweeping look
		縱: to allow to move or work freely, to let go, to indulge;
		觀: 看
工藝	gōngyì	technology, craft
法制	fǎzhì	legal system, legal institutions; legality
其中	qízhōng	among (which, those, them, etc.), in (which, it, etc.)
利器	lìqì	sharp weapon, good tool, efficient instrument
侵略	qīnlüè	to invade, to intrude; invasion, aggression
掠奪	lüèduó	to plunder, to pillage, to rob
制度	zhìdù	system, institution, regulation
當真	dāngzhēn	真的, really, truly
忽略	hūlüè	to neglect, to overlook, to ignore
大膽	dàdǎn	bold, daring, audacious
宣言	xuānyán	to declare, to proclaim; declaration, manifesto
絕	jué	(used before a negative) absolutely, in the least, by any means, on any account
非	fēi	(lit.) 不是
夢見	mèngjiàn	to see in a dream, to dream about
方面	fāngmiàn	respect, aspect, side, field
乃是	nǎishì	是, 就是
理想主義	lǐxiǎngzhǔyì	idealism
		理想: ideal
理智	lǐzhì	reason, intellect
...在於...	...zàiyú...	... lie in ... , ... rest with ... , ... be determined by ... , ... depend on ...
真理	zhēnlǐ	truth
世間	shìjiān	世界上

境的逼迫，受習慣的支配，受迷信與成見的拘束。只有眞理可以使你自由，使你強有力，使你聰明聖智；只有眞理可以使你打破你的環境裏的一切束縛，使你戡天，使你縮地，使你天不怕，地不怕，堂堂地做一個人。

求知是人類天生的一種精神上的最大要求。東方的舊文明對於這個要求，不但不想滿足他，並且常想裁制他，斷絕他。所以東方古聖人勸人要「無知」，要「絕聖棄智」，要「斷思惟」，要「不識不知，順帝之則。」這是畏難，這是懶惰。這種文明，還能自誇可以滿足心靈上的要求嗎？

東方的懶惰聖人說，「吾生也有涯，而知也無涯，以有涯逐無涯，殆已。」所以他們要人靜坐澄心，不思不慮，而物來順應。這是自欺欺人

逼迫	bīpò	to force, to compel, to coerce
支配	zhīpèi	to control, to dominate, to govern
迷信	míxìn	superstition, superstitious belief, blind faith; to have blind faith in
拘束	jūshù	restraint, restriction; to restrain, to restrict; constrained, awkward
聰明聖智	cōngmíngshèngzhì	intelligent, holy and wise

打破	dǎpò	to break, to smash
束縛	shùfú	restraint, restriction, bondage; to tie, to bind up, to fetter
戡天	kāntiān	戡: 刺, to pierce, to stab
縮地	suōdì	把地縮小 (to contract, to reduce)
堂堂	tángtáng	dignified, venerable
裁制	cáizhì	制裁, to sanction, to punish
斷絕	duànjué	to break off, to cut off, to sever
聖人	shèngrén	sage, wise man, saint
勸	quàn	to advise, to try to persuade
絕聖棄智	juéshèngqìzhì	to reject sageness and cast away wisdom
斷思惟 (維)	duànsīwéi	(lit.) to cease to think, to cease thinking
順帝之則	shùndìzhīzé	(lit.) to follow the ways of God (Heaven)
畏難	wèinán	怕困難
吾	wú	(lit.) 我
生也有涯	shēngyěyǒuyá	(lit.) 生命是有限的, life is limited 也: a particle indicating a pause
知也無涯	zhīyěwúyá	(lit.) 知識是無限的
以有涯逐無涯	yǐyǒuyázhúwúyá	用有限的生命去追求無限的知識 逐: 追, to pursue, to chase
殆已	dàiyǐ	(lit.) in grave danger, very dangerous indeed, nearly impossible, hopeless
靜坐澄心	jìngzuòchéngxīn	to sit still and calm one's mind 澄: to purify, to make clear or transparent and still
不思不慮	bùsībúlǜ	not to think and ponder 慮: to ponder or consider
物來順應	wùláishùnyìng	when something comes (happens), (man) accords with it

的誑語,這是人類的誇大狂。眞理是深藏在事物之中的;你不去尋求探討,他決不會露面。科學的文明教人訓練我們的官能智慧,一點一滴地去尋求眞理,一絲一毫不放過,一銖一兩地積起來。這是求眞理的唯一法門。自然(Nature) 是一個最狡滑的妖魔,只有敲打逼拶可以逼她吐露眞情。不思不慮的懶人只好永永作愚昧的人,永永走不進眞理之門。

誑語	kuángyǔ	lies 誑: to deceive, to delude
藏	cáng	to hide, to conceal
事物	shìwù	事情,東西
尋求	shúnqiú	to seek, to explore, to go in quest of 尋: 找, to seek, to strive for
探討	tàntǎo	to probe into, to inquire into 探: to try to find out, to explore; 討: 討論, to discuss, to study
露面	lùmiàn	to show one's face, to appear or reappear on public occasions 露: to appear, to emerge, to show
訓練	xùnliàn	to train, to drill; training
官能	guānnéng	(of human) physical faculty; (organic) function, sense
慧智	huìzhì	智慧, wisdom, intelligence
一點一滴	yìdiǎnyìdī	"a dot and a drop" — bit by bit, little by little
一絲一毫	yìsīyìháo	the slightest amount, an iota 絲: a threadlike thing; a unit of

		weight (0.0005 grams);
		毫: fine long hair; a unit of length (one third decimillimeter); a unit of weight (0.005 grams)
放過	fàngguò	to let off, to let slip
一銖一兩	yìzhūyìliǎng	bit by bit, little by little
		銖: an ancient unit of weight, one twenty-fourth *liang*(兩);
		兩: a unit of weight (50 grams)
積	jī	to accumulate, to build up
唯一	wéiyī	only, sole
法門	fǎmén	*dharmaparyaya*, the doctrine or wisdom of Buddha regarded as the door to enlightenment; the right way or method of learning something
狡滑	xiáhuá	slippery, cunning
妖魔	yāomó	demon, evil spirit
敲打逼拶	chiāodǎbīzǎn	敲: to pound, to tap;
		打: to hit, to strike;
		逼: to press, to compel;
		拶: to use the torture device "拶刑," consisting of five contractible wooden sticks in between which the fingers of a suspect are placed and pressed to extort a confession
吐露	tǔlù	to reveal, to tell
		吐: to spit, to pour out;
		露: to show, to emerge
真情	zhēnqíng	真實的情況
永永	yǒngyǒng	永遠, always, forever
愚昧	yúmèi	ignorant, benighted
		愚: foolish, stupid;
		昧: obscure, dark, ignorant (of)

東方的懶人又說:「眞理是無窮盡的,人的求知的欲望如何能滿足呢?」誠然,眞理是發現不完的。但科學決不因此而退縮。科學家明知眞理無窮,知識無窮,但他們仍然有他們的滿足:進一寸有一寸的愉快,進一尺有一尺的滿足。二千多年前,一個希臘哲人思索一個難題,想不出道理來;有一天,他跳進浴盆去洗澡,水漲起來,他忽然明白了,他高興極了,赤裸裸地跑出門去,在街上亂嚷道,「我尋着了!我尋着了!」(Eureka! Eureka!)這是科學家的滿足。Newton, Pasteur以至於Edison時時有這樣的愉快。一點一滴都是進步,一步一步都可以躊躇滿志。這種心靈上的快樂是東方的懶聖人所夢想不到的。

　　這裏正是東西文化的一個根本不同之點。一邊是自暴自棄的不思不慮,一邊是繼續不斷的尋求眞理。

無窮盡	wúqióngjìn	infinite, endless, boundless, inexhaustible
		窮: limit, end;
		盡: exhausted, finished
如何	rúhé	(lit.) 怎麼
誠然	chéngrán	true, indeed, to be sure
退縮	tuìsuō	to shrink back, to flinch, to cower
仍然	réngrán	still

寸	cùn	a measure of length (one tenth foot)
愉快	yúkuài	快樂
尺	chǐ	a unit in Chinese linear measurement slightly longer than a foot
希臘	Xīlà	Greece
思索	sīsuǒ	to think deeply, to ponder (over), to reflect on
難題	nántí	困難的問題
道理	dàolǐ	principle, truth, hows and whys, reason, rationality
浴盆	yùpén	bathtub
洗澡	xǐzǎo	to have (or take) a bath, to bathe
漲	zhǎng	(of water, prices) to rise or go up
赤裸裸	chìluǒluǒ	without a stitch of clothing, naked
亂嚷	luànrǎng	to clamor 亂: in disorder, confusion; 嚷: to shout, to yell, to make an uproar
道	dào	説
尋着	xúnzháo	找着, 找到
躊躇滿志	chóuchúmǎnzhì	enormously proud of one's success; complacent, confident, smug
正是	zhèngshì	precisely is, exactly is
自暴自棄	zìbàozìqì	to give oneself up as hopeless, to abandon oneself to a dissipated life, to have no ambition at all
繼續	jìxù	to continue
不斷	búduàn	unceasing, uninterrupted, constant 斷: to break off

朋友們，究竟是那一種文化能滿足你們的心靈上的要求呢？

其次，我們且看看人類的情感與想像力上的要求。

文藝，美術，我們可以不談，因爲東方的人，凡是能睜開眼睛看世界的，至少還都能承認西洋人並不曾輕蔑了這兩個重要的方面。

我們來談談道德與宗教罷。

近世文明在表面上還不曾和舊宗教脫離關係，所以近世文化還不曾明白建立他的新宗教新道德。但我們研究歷史的人不能不指出近世文明自有他的新宗教與新道德。科學的發達提高了人類的知識，使人們求知的方法更精密了，評判的能力也更進步了，所以舊宗教的迷信部分漸漸被淘汰到最低限度，漸漸地連那最低限度的信仰——上帝的存在與靈魂的不滅——也發生疑問了。所以這

究竟	jiūjìng	after all, in the end; the very truth, the very source, the very end
其次	qícì	next, second, then; secondary, less important
且	qiě	for the time being
情感	qínggǎn	emotion, feeling

想像力	xiǎngxiànglì	imaginative power, imagination 想像: to imagine
文藝	wényì	文學藝術
美術	měishù	fine arts, art
睜開	zhēngkāi	to open (the eyes)
至少	zhìshǎo	最少
道德	dàodé	morals, morality, ethics; moral
宗教	zōngjiào	religion
罷	ba	an interjection
脫離關係	tuōlíguānxì	to break off relations, to cut ties 脫離: to separate oneself from, to break away from, to be divorced from
明白	míngbái	清楚的
建立	jiànlì	to establish, to build, to found, to set up
發達	fādá	developed, flourishing
精密	jīngmì	minute or detailed, precise, accurate, careful, thorough
評判	píngpàn	to criticize and judge, to pass judgement on
淘汰	táotài	to eliminate through selection or competition, to die out, to fall into disuse 淘: to wash (rice, etc.) in a pan or basket, to clean out; 汰: to sift, to eliminate
信仰	xìnyǎng	(religious or political) belief, faith or conviction
上帝	Shàngdì	"Heavenly Emperor," God
存在	cúnzài	existence; to exist, to be
靈魂	línghún	soul, spirit
不滅	bùmiè	imperishable, indestructible 滅: to go out, to destroy, to exterminate, to extinguish, to wipe out
疑問	yíwèn	question, doubt, query

個新宗教的第一特色是他的理智化。近世文明仗着科學的武器，開闢了許多新世界，發現了無數新真理，征服了自然界的無數勢力，叫電氣趕車，叫「以太」送信，真個作出種種動地掀天的大事業來。人類的能力的發展使他漸漸增加對於自己的信仰心，漸漸把向來信天安命的心理變成信任人類自己的心理。所以這個新宗教的第二特色是他的人化。智識的發達不但抬高了人的能力，並且擴大了他的眼界，使他胸襟闊大，想像力高遠，同情心濃摯。同時，物質享受的增加使人有餘力可以顧到別人的需要與痛苦。擴大了的同情心加上擴大了的能力，遂產生了一個空前的社會化的新道德，所以這個新宗教的第三特色就是他的社會化的道德。

　　古代的人因為想求得感情上的安慰，不惜犧牲理智上的要求，專靠信心(Faith)，不問證據

化	huà	a suffix for "-ized"; to transform, to change
仗	zhàng	靠, to depend on, to rely on
武器	wǔqì	weapon, arms
開闢	kāipì	to open up, to start
征服	zhēngfú	to conquer, to subjugate
趕車	gǎnchē	to drive a cart or carriage; to

		catch a bus or train
以太	yǐtài	ether
真個	zhēnge	真的, really, truly, indeed
動地掀天	dòngdìxiāntiān	"to move the earth and lift the heavens" — earthshaking, worldshaking
事業	shìyè	undertaking, enterprise; career, pursuit
向來	xiànglái	hitherto, heretofore, all along
信任	xìnrèn	to trust, to have confidence in; trust
智識	zhìshì	智慧知識, wisdom and knowledge
抬高	táigāo	to raise, to lift up
擴大	kuòdà	to enlarge, to widen, expand or extend
眼界	yǎnjiè	field of vision or view, outlook
胸襟	xiōngjīn	mind, breadth of mind, mental outlook
闊大	kuòdà	wide, broad, vast
濃摯	nóngzhì	strong and sincere
顧到	gùdào	to attend to, to take into account, to give consideration to
遂	suì	(lit.) 就
產生	chǎnshēng	to produce, to engender; to emerge, to come into being
空前	kōngqián	unprecedented
不惜	bùxī	do not stint, do not spare, do not hesitate (to do something); do not scruple (to do something) 惜: to cherish, to value highly
犧牲	xīshēng	to sacrifice oneself, to sacrifice (something of value for the sake of something else); sacrifice (for deity)
證據	zhèngjù	evidence, proof, testimony

，於是信鬼，信神，信上帝，信天堂，信淨土，信地獄。近世科學便不能這樣專靠信心了。科學並不菲薄感情上的安慰；科學只要求一切信仰須要禁得起理智的評判，須要有充分的證據。凡沒有充分證據的，只可存疑，不足信仰。赫胥黎（Huxley）說的最好：

如果我對於解剖學上，或生理學上的一個小小困難，必須要嚴格的不信任一切沒有充分證據的東西，方才可望有成績，那麼，我對於人生的奇秘的解決，難道就可以不用這樣嚴格的條件嗎？

這正是十分尊重我們的精神上的要求。我們買一畝田，賣二間屋，尚且要一張契據；關於人生的最高希望的根據，豈可沒有證據就胡亂信仰嗎？

這種「拿證據來」的態度，可以稱為近世宗教的「理智化」。

從前人類受自然的支配，不能探討自然界的秘密，沒有能力抵抗自然的殘酷，所以對於自然常懷著畏懼之心。拜物，拜畜牲，怕鬼，敬神，

鬼	guǐ	ghost, spirit, apparition
天堂	tiāntáng	heaven, paradise
淨土	jìngtǔ	*sukhavat*, the land of the pure, land of Buddha
地獄	dìyù	hell, Hades
菲薄	fěibó	to belittle, to despise; humble,

		poor
禁得起	jīndeqǐ	to be able to stand (tests, trials, etc.); negative: 禁不起
存疑	cúnyí	to leave a question open, to leave a matter for future consideration
		疑: 疑問, doubt, query
解剖學	jiěpōuxué	anatomy
		解剖: to dissect
生理學	shēnglǐxué	physiology, physiological science
		生理: physiological functions and processes
嚴格	yángé	strict, rigid, rigorous, stringent
方才	fāngcái	才, only then, not until
望	wàng	希望
成績	chéngjī	result, achievement, success
那麼	nàmo	then, in that case, such being the case
奇秘	qímì	strange and mysterious
條件	tiáojiàn	requirement, qualification, prerequisite
尊重	zūnzhòng	to respect, to esteem
畝	mǔ	a unit of area (0.0667 hectares)
尚且 ... 豈可 ...	shàngqiě ... qǐkě ...	even ... how can ... ?
契據	qìjù	contract, receipt
胡亂	húluàn	隨便, carelessly, casually, at random
稱為	chēngwéi	叫做
抵抗	dǐkàng	to resist, to stand up to
殘酷	cánkù	cruelty; cruel, brutal, ruthless
懷	huái	to harbor, to hold, to embrace, to entertain
畏懼	wèijù	怕
拜	bài	to do obeisance, to worship
畜牲	chùsheng	animal, beast (a reviling term)

「小心翼翼，昭事上帝，」都是因為人類不信任自己的能力，不能不依靠一種超自然的勢力。現代的人便不同了。人的智力居然征服了自然界的無數質力，上可以飛行無礙，下可以潛行海底，遠可以窺算星辰，近可以觀察極微。這個兩隻手一個大腦的動物——人——已成了世界的主人翁，他不能不尊重自己了。一個少年的革命詩人曾這樣的歌唱：

　　我獨自奮鬥，勝敗我獨自承當，
　　我用不着誰來放我自由，
　　我用不着什麼耶穌基督
　　妄想他能替我贖罪替我死。

I fight alone and, win or sink,
　I need no one to make me free,
　I want no Jesus Christ to think
　　That he could ever die for me.

這是現代人化的宗教。信任天不如信任人，靠上帝不如靠自己。我們現在不妄想什麼天堂天國了，我們要在這個世界上建造「人的樂園」。我們

小心翼翼	xiǎoxīnyìyì	with great care, cautiously
昭事上帝	zhāoshì Shàngdì	(lit.) to serve God openly
倚靠	yǐkào	靠, to rely on, to depend on, to

		count on
超自然	chāozìrán	supernatural
		超: to exceed, to surpass, to go beyond, to transcend
飛行	fēixíng	to fly, as a plane; flying; flight
無礙	wúài	without obstacle; no harm, not in the way, do not matter
潛行	qiánxíng	to move under water; to move stealthily, to slink
窺	kuī	偷看, to peep (at), to spy (on)
星辰	xīngchén	star
極微	jíwéi	(lit.) 很小的東西
大腦	dànǎo	cerebrum; reference to mental capacity
動物	dòngwù	animal
主人翁	zhǔrénwēng	master; a leading figure in a novel, hero or heroine, protagonist
革命	gémìng	revolution
歌唱	gēchàng	to sing (in praise)
獨自	dúzì	alone, by oneself
奮鬥	fèndòu	to struggle, to strive, to fight
勝敗	shèngbài	to win or to lose; victory or defeat, success or failure
承當	chéngdāng	to take, bear or shoulder (a task, responsibility, etc.)
耶穌基督	Yēsū Jīdū	Jesus Christ
		耶蘇 now standardized as 耶穌
妄想	wàngxiǎng	to desire wildly, to daydream; daydreaming; a daydream, fancy, vain hope, wishful thinking
贖罪	shúzuì	to atone for crime or sin
A 不如 B	A bùrú B	A is not equal to (not as good as, inferior to) B
建造	jiànzào	to build, to construct, to make
樂園	lèyuán	paradise

不妄想做不死的神仙了，我們要在這個世界上做個活潑健全的人。我們不妄想什麼四禪定六神通了，我們要在這個世界上做個有聰明智慧可以戡天縮地的人。我們也許不輕易信仰上帝的萬能了，我們却信仰科學的方法是萬能的，人的將來是不可限量的。我們也許不信靈魂的不滅了，我們却信人格是神聖的，人權是神聖的。

這是近世宗教的「人化」。

但最重要的要算近世道德宗教的「社會化」。

古代的宗教大抵注重個人的拯救；古代的道德也大抵注重個人的修養。雖然也有自命普渡眾生的宗教，雖然也有自命兼濟天下的道德，然而

神仙	shénxiān	immortal, celestial being
活潑	huópō	lively, vivacious, vivid
健全	jiànquán	sound, perfect, in good order, in good condition; to make sound, perfect; to strengthen, to amplify
四禪定	sìchándìng	佛教修養的一種境界
六神通	liùshéntōng	佛教修養的一種境界
輕易	qīngyì	rashly, lightly, easily
萬能	wànnéng	甚麼都能, omnipotent, all-powerful, serving all purposes

不可限量	bùkěxiànliàng	cannot be limited and measured, beyond measure; very promising
人格	réngé	human dignity; personality, character, moral quality
神聖	shénshèng	sacred, holy
人權	rénquán	human rights, rights of man
大抵	dàdǐ	generally speaking, on the whole
注重	zhùzhòng	to lay stress on, to pay attention to, to attach importance to
個人	gèrén	individual (person) as contrasted with the group; oneself
拯救	zhěngjiù	to save, to rescue, to deliver
修養	xiūyǎng	self-cultivation; accomplishment, training or mastery in scholastic, artistic or ethical pursuits
自命	zìmìng	to consider oneself, to regard oneself as
普渡眾生	pǔdùzhòngshēng	(in Buddhism) to deliver or save all beings 普: universal, widespread, general, everywhere, all; 渡: to cross or sail across (a river or ocean); 眾生: (in Buddhism) all living creatures
兼濟天下	jiānjìtiānxià	to benefit all the peoples in the world 兼: to unite in one; double or twice, simultaneously or concurrently; 濟: to aid, to relieve; 天下: "(land) under heaven" — China or the world
然而	ránér	可是

終苦於無法下手,無力實行,只好仍舊回到個人的身心上用工夫,做那向內的修養。越向內做工夫,越看不見外面的現實世界;越在那不可捉摸的心性上玩把戲,越沒有能力應付外面的實際問題。即如中國八百年的理學工夫居然看不見二萬萬婦女纏足的慘無人道!明心見性,何補於人道的苦痛困窮!坐禪主敬,不過造成許多「四肢不動,五穀不分」的廢物!

終	zhōng	eventually, after all, in the end
苦於	kǔyú	to suffer from (a disadvantage)
下手	xiàshǒu	to put one's hand to, to start, to set about, to set to; assistant, helper; right-hand seat
實行	shíxíng	to put into practice (or effect), to carry out, to practice, to implement
仍舊	réngjiù	(now) as before, still, yet; to remain the same, to follow the beaten track
身心	shēnxīn	身體心理, body and mind
現實	xiànshí	real, actual; realistic, practical, pragmatic; reality, actuality
不可捉摸	bùkězhuōmō	to be unable to ascertain or fathom; cannot be ascertained or fathomed; unpredictable, elusive 捉摸: "to seize and feel or touch" — to ascertain or fathom

心性	xīnxìng	constitution of the mind, temperament, tempers
玩把戲	wánbǎxì	to play little tricks, to juggle 把戲: acrobatic performances such as juggling, etc.
實際	shíjì	real, actual, concrete; practical, realistic; reality, actual situation, actuality
即如	jírú	就如, 就像, just like
理學	lǐxué	a school of learning during the Song dynasty (907-1279) devoted to the study of the Confucian classics with a rational approach
居然	jūrán	unexpectedly, to one's surprise
婦女	fùnǚ	女人
纏足	chánzú	to bind the feet (as was done by women in old China)
慘無人道	cǎnwúréndào	inhuman, inhumane, brutal, cold-blooded 慘: cruel, savage, merciless; 人道: humanity, human sympathy
明心見性	míngxīnjiànxìng	to enlighten the mind and realize the Buddha-nature immanent in all beings
A何補於B	A hé bǔyú B	(lit.) A 對 B 有甚麼幫助呢? 補: to repair, to mend, to help
苦痛	kǔtòng	pain, suffering
困窮	kùnqióng	under great financial difficulty, in straitened circumstances, poverty-stricken
坐禪	zuòchán	(in Buddhism) to sit in meditation
主敬	zhǔjìng	to regard reverence as essential
廢物	fèiwù	沒有用的東西

近世文明不從宗教下手,而結果自成一個新宗教;不從道德入門,而結果自成一派新道德。十五十六世紀的歐洲國家簡直都是幾個海盜的國家,哥侖布(Columbus)馬汲倫(Magellan)都芮克(Drake)一班探險家都只是一些大海盜。他們的目的只是尋求黃金,白銀,香料,象牙,黑奴。然而這班海盜和海盜帶來的商人開闢了無數新地,開拓了人的眼界,抬高了人的想像力,同時又增加了歐洲的富力。工業革命接着起來,生產的方法根本改變了,生產的能力更發達了。二三百年間,物質上的享受逐漸增加,人類的同情心也逐漸擴大。這種擴大的同情心便是新宗教新道德的基礎。自己要爭自由,同時便想到別人的自由。所以不但自由須以不侵犯他人的自由為界限,並且還進一步要要求絕大多數人的自由。自己要享受幸福,同時便想到人的幸福,所以樂利主義(Utilitarianism)的哲學家便提出「最大多數的最大幸福」的標準來做人類社會的目的。這都是「社會化」的趨勢。

從...下手	cóng ... xiàshǒu	to start from, to set about (something or doing something) from 下手: to put one's hand to, to start
入門	rùmén	"to enter (a house) by crossing

		the threshold" — to learn or have the rudiments of a subject
派	pài	group, school, faction, clique
世紀	shìjì	century
海盜	hǎidào	"sea bandit or robber" — pirate
哥倫布	Gēlúnbù	Christopher Columbus (1451-1506), discoverer of the Americas
馬汲倫	Mǎjílún	Ferdinand Magellan (1480?-1521), first to circumnavigate the globe
都芮克	Dūruìkè	Francis Drake (1540?-1596), sailed around the world (1577-1580), commander at defeat of Spanish Armada (1588)
探險家	tànxiǎnjiā	explorer 探險: to explore, to venture into the unknown; 家: a specialist in a certain field
目的	mùdì	purpose, goal, objective
香料	xiāngliào	spice, balm, perfume
象牙	xiàngyá	elephant's tusk, ivory
黑奴	Hēinú	Negro slaves
開拓	kāituò	to open up
逐漸	zhújiàn	漸漸, gradually, by degrees, little by little
爭	zhēng	to contend, vie, strive, or fight (for)
以...為...	yǐ...wéi...	把...當作..., to take...as..., to regard...as...
侵犯	qīnfàn	to encroach on, to infringe upon, to violate
界限	jièxiàn	demarcation line, dividing line; limits, bounds
主義	zhǔyì	doctrine, -ism
哲學	zhéxué	philosophy
趨勢	qūshì	trend, tendency

十八世紀的新宗教信條是自由、平等、博愛。十九世紀中葉以後的新宗教信條是社會主義。這是西洋近代的精神文明，這是東方民族不曾有過的精神文明。

固然東方也曾有主張博愛的宗教，也曾有公田均產的思想。但這些不過是紙上的文章，不曾實地變成社會生活的重要部分，不曾變成範圍人生的勢力，不曾在東方文化上發生多大的影響。在西方便不然了。「自由、平等、博愛」成了十八世紀的革命口號。美國的革命，法國的革命，一八四八年全歐洲的革命運動，一八六二年的南北美戰爭，都是在這三大主義的旗幟之下的大革命。美國的憲法，法國的憲法，以至於南美洲諸國的憲法，都是受了這三大主義的絕大影響的。舊階級的打倒，專制政體的推翻，法律之下人人平等的觀念的普遍，「信仰、思想、言論、出版

信條	xìntiáo	article of creed (or faith), creed, precept, tenet, dogma
平等	píngděng	equality, equal
博愛	bó'ài	universal love, universal fraternity, brotherhood 博: vast, wide, abundant
中葉	zhōngyè	middle period
主張	zhǔzhāng	to advocate, to stand for, to maintain, to hold; view, position, proposition
公田	gōngtián	government or public farmland (or cropland, agricultural land, etc.)

均產	jūnchǎn	to allot the property (estate, possessions) equally
思想	sīxiǎng	thinking, thought, idea, ideology; to think, to ponder
實地	shídì	實際上, actually, in reality; on the spot
範圍	fànwéi	to circumscribe, to surround by a boundary; sphere, jurisdiction
不然	bùrán	不是這樣, not so; 要不然, or else, otherwise
口號	kǒuhào	slogan, watchword
運動	yùndòng	(political or social) movement, drive, campaign; movement, motion; sports, athletics, exercise
旗幟	qízhì	banner, flag; (figuratively) stand, colors
憲法	xiànfǎ	constitution, charter
諸	zhū	various, all
取	qǔ	to get, to take, to fetch
階級	jiējí	(social) class, rank, (official) position or grade
打倒	dǎdǎo	to knock down, to overthrow, (in slogans) "down with ..."
專制	zhuānzhì	autocratic, despotic, dictatorial
政體	zhèngtǐ	political system or form; system or form of government
推翻	tuīfān	to overthrow, to overturn, to topple, to cancel, reverse, or repudiate (an agreement, an original plan, etc.)
法律	fǎlǜ	law
普遍	pǔbiàn	universal, general, widespread, common
言論	yánlùn	speech, public speech, open discussion
出版	chūbǎn	to publish, to come off the press, to come out, to put out; publication

」幾大自由的保障的實行,普及教育的實施,婦女的解放,女權的運動,婦女參政的實現,⋯⋯都是這個新宗教新道德的實際的表現。這不僅僅是三五個哲學家書本子裏的空談;這都是西洋近代社會政治制度的重要部分,這都已成了範圍人生,影響實際生活的絕大勢力。

十九世紀以來,個人主義的趨勢的流弊漸漸暴白於世了,資本主義之下的苦痛也漸漸明瞭了。遠識的人知道自由競爭的經濟制度不能達到真正「自由、平等、博愛」的目的。向資本家手裏要求公道的待遇,等於「與虎謀皮」。救濟的方法只有兩條大路:一是國家利用其權力,實行裁制資本家,保障被壓迫的階級;一是被壓迫的階級團結起來,直接抵抗資本階級的壓迫與掠奪。于是各種社會主義的理論與運動不斷地發生。西洋近代文明本建築在個人求幸福的基礎之上,所以向來承認「財產」爲神聖的人權之一。但十九

保障	bǎozhàng	to protect, guarantee, ensure, or safeguard; protection, guarantee
普及教育	pǔjíjiàoyù	universal education 普及: universal, popular; to popularize, to spread, to disseminate
實施	shíshī	實行, to put into practice (or effect), to carry out, to implement

女權	nǚquán	women's rights
參政	cānzhèng	to participate in government and political affairs
實現	shíxiàn	to come true, to realize, to bring about, to achieve
空談	kōngtán	empty talk, idle talk, prattle; to indulge in empty talk
流弊	liúbì	long accumulated evil effect, corrupt practices, abuses
暴白於世	pù (bào) báiyúshì	to be exposed to the world
資本主義	zīběnzhǔyì	capitalism
明瞭	míngliǎo	clear and evident, 清楚; to understand, to get a clear idea of something, 明白
遠識	yuǎnshì	farsightedness (as a product of wisdom)
競爭	jìngzhēng	competition; to compete
達到	dádào	to reach, to achieve, to attain
公道	gōngdào	justice; reasonable (prices)
待遇	dàiyù	treatment, the manner of treating people; salary, pay, or remuneration
等於	děngyú	to amount to, to be tantamount to, to be equal to, to be equivalent to
與虎謀皮	yǔhǔmóupí	"to negotiate with tiger for its hide" — to request someone (usually an evil person) to act against his own interests 謀: to seek, to try to get
救濟	jiùjì	to aid, to relieve (the suffering, the poor, etc.)
其	qí	(lit.) its, his, her, their
團結	tuánjié	to unite
于是 (於是)	yúshì	thereupon, hence, consequently, as a result
理論	lǐlùn	theory
財產	cáichǎn	property

世紀中葉以後，這個觀念根本動搖了；有的人竟說「財產是賊贓」，有的人竟說「財產是掠奪」。現在私有財產制雖然還存在，然而國家可以徵收極重的所得稅和遺產稅，財產久已不許完全私有了。勞動是向來受賤視的；但資本集中的制度使勞工有大組織的可能，社會主義的宣傳與階級的自覺又使勞工覺悟團結的必要，于是幾十年之中有組織的勞動階級遂成了社會上最有勢力的分子。十年以來，工黨領袖可以執掌世界強國的政權，同盟總罷工可以屈伏最有勢力的政府，俄國的勞農階級竟做了全國的專政階級。這個社會主義的大運動現在還正在進行的時期。但他的成績

動搖	dòngyáo	to shake, to waver, to vacillate
竟	jìng	居然, unexpectedly, to one's surprise
賊贓	zéizāng	stolen goods or property, booty, loot, spoils
私有	sīyǒu	privately owned, private
制	zhì	制度, system
徵收	zhēngshōu	to levy and collect (taxes, duty, etc.)
極	jí	非常
所得稅	suǒdéshuì	income tax
遺產稅	yíchǎnshuì	inheritance tax, legacy tax, succession duty 遺產: property left behind by a deceased person, legacy; 遺: to leave behind intentionally or unintentionally;

		產: 財產, property
勞動	láodòng	to work, to labor; physical labor, manual labor
賤視	jiànshì	to slight, to look down on
集中	jízhōng	to concentrate, to centralize, to focus, to amass, to put together
勞工	láogōng	laborer, worker
組織	zǔzhī	organization, organized system; to organize, to form
宣傳	xuānchuán	propaganda, promotion (of a social or political cause, of sales, etc.); to propagate, to conduct propaganda, to disseminate, to give publicity to
自覺	zìjué	self-consciousness, self-realization; to feel, or think about something concerning oneself, aware, conscious
覺悟	juéwù	to come to understand, to become aware of, to become awakened to; consciousness, awareness, understanding
必要	bìyào	necessity, need
分子	fēnzǐ	member, element
領袖	lǐngxiù	leader, leading figure
執掌	zhízhǎng	to take full charge of, to superintend 執: to hold, to grasp; 掌: to hold in one's hand, to control
同盟	tóngméng	joint, allied; alliance, league
罷工	bàgōng	(of workers) strike, walk-out; to stage a strike, to go on a strike
專政	zhuānzhèng	dictatorship
進行	jìnxíng	to be in progress, to be underway, to go on; to conduct, to carry on, to carry out; to march, to advance

已很可觀了。各國的「社會立法」(Social Legislation)的發達,工廠的視察,工廠衛生的改良,兒童工作與婦女工作的救濟,紅利分配制度的推行,縮短工作時間的實行,工人的保險,合作制之推行,最低工資(Minimum Wage)的運動,失業的救濟,級進制的(Progressive)所得稅與遺產稅的實行,……這都是這個大運動已經做到的成績。這也不僅僅是紙上的文章,這也都已成了近代文明的重要部分。

這是「社會化」的新宗教與新道德。

東方的舊腦筋也許要說:「這是爭權奪利,算不得宗教與道德。」這裏又正是東西文化的一個根本不同之點。一邊是安分、安命、安貧、樂天、不爭、認吃虧;一邊是不安分、不安貧、不肯吃虧、努力奮鬥、繼續改善現成的境地。東方

可觀	kěguān	considerable, impressive, sizable; to be worth seeing
立法	lìfǎ	"to establish a law" — legislation
工廠	gōngchǎng	factory, plant, workshop
視察	shìchá	to inspect; inspection
兒童	értóng	children
紅利	hónglì	net profit, bonus, extra dividend
分配	fēnpèi	distribution, allocation; to distribute, to portion out, to

		allocate
推行	tuīxíng	to promote (a cause, movement, etc.), to implement (a policy)
縮短	suōduǎn	to shorten, to cut down, to reduce
保險	bǎoxiǎn	insurance; to insure, to guarantee; safe
合作	hézuò	cooperation; to cooperate, to work together, to collaborate
工資	gōngzī	wage, pay
失業	shīyè	to lose one's job, to be out of work, to be unemployed; unemployment
腦筋	nǎojīn	brains, mind, head, mental capacity; way of thinking, mentality
奪	duó	to take by force, to seize
利	lì	profit, benefit, advantage
算不得	suànbude	cannot be considered, cannot be regarded as, cannot be counted as 算: to consider, to regard as, to count as; positive: 算得
安分	ānfèn	not go beyond one's bounds, be law-abiding 分: what is within one's rights or duty
認	rèn	to accept as unavoidable, to resign oneself to
吃虧	chīkuī	to suffer losses, to be at a disadvantage, to be in an unfavorable situation
現成	xiànchéng	ready, at hand; ready-made
境地	jìngdì	情況, condition, situation, circumstances

人見人富貴，說他是「前世修來的」；自己貧，也說是「前世不曾修」，說是「命該如此」。西方人便不然；他說，「貧富的不平等，痛苦的待遇，都是制度的不良的結果，制度是可以改良的。」他們不是爭權奪利，他們是爭自由、爭平等、爭公道；他們爭的不僅僅是個人的私利，他們奮鬥的結果是人類絕大多數人的福利。最大多數人的最大幸福，不是袖手唸佛號可以得來的，是必須奮鬥力爭的。

朋友們，究竟是那一種文化能滿足你們的心靈上的要求呢？

我們現在可綜合評判西洋近代的文明了。這一系的文明建築在「求人生幸福」的基礎之上，確然替人類增進了不少的物質上的享受；然而他也確然很能滿足人類的精神上的要求。他在理智的方面，用精密的方法，繼續不斷地尋求真理，探索自然界無窮的秘密。他在宗教道德的方面，推翻了迷信的宗教，建立合理的信仰；打倒了神權，建立人化的宗教；拋棄了那不可知的天堂淨土，努力建設「人的樂園」「人世的天堂」；丟開了那自稱的個人靈魂的超拔，儘量用人的新想像力和新智力去推行那充分社會化了的新宗教與新道德，努力謀人類最大多數的最大幸福。

東方的文明的最大特色是知足。西洋的近代文明的最大特色是不知足。

前世	qiánshì	previous existence, previous life
修來	xiūlái	to attain or accomplish by practicing Buddhist or Taoist rules (often strict and ascetic in nature)
如此	rúcǐ	(lit.) 像這樣, like this, in this way, so, such
奮鬥	fèndòu	to strive, to struggle
福利	fúlì	material benefits, welfare, well-being
袖手	xiùshǒu	把手放在袖子 (sleeve) 裏 — with folded arms (giving no help)
念佛號	niànfóhào	to chant the name of Buddha
力爭	lìzhēng	to work hard for, to do all one can to; to argue strongly, to contend vigorously
綜合	zōnghé	to synthesize, to sum up
系	xì	system, series
確然	quèrán	really, truly, indeed
探索	tànsuǒ	to explore, to probe 探: to explore, to venture into the unknown
合理	hélǐ	reasonable, rational, equitable
神權	shénquán	divine right
拋棄	pāoqì	丟掉, 扔掉, to abandon, to forsake, to cast aside
自稱	zìchēng	to call oneself, to claim to be, to profess
超拔	chāobá	to transcend
儘量	jìnliàng	to the best of one's ability, to the fullest, as far as possible

知足的東方人自安於簡陋的生活，故不求物質享受的提高；自安於愚昧，自安於「不識不知」，故不注意真理的發見與技藝器械的發明；自安於現成的環境與命運，故不想征服自然，只求樂天安命，不想改革制度，只圖安分守己，不想革命，只做順民。

　　這樣受物質環境的拘束與支配，不能跳出來，不能運用人的心思智力來改造環境改良現狀的文明，是懶惰不長進的民族的文明，是真正唯物的文明。這種文明只可以遏抑而決不能滿足人類精神上的要求。

　　西方人大不然。他們說「不知足是神聖的」（Divine Discontent）。物質上的不知足產生了今日鋼鐵世界，汽機世界，電力世界。理智上的不知足產生了今日的科學世界。社會政治制度上的不知足產生了今日的民權世界，自由政體，男女平權的社會，勞工神聖的喊聲，社會主義的運動。神聖的不知足是一切革新一切進化的動力。

　　這樣充分運用人的聰明智慧來尋求真理以解放人的心靈，來制服天行以供人用，來改造物質的環境，來改革社會政治的制度，來謀人類最大多數的最大幸福，——這樣的文明應該能滿足人類精神上的要求；這樣的文明是精神的文明，是真正理想主義的（Idealistic）文明，決不是唯物的文明。

安於	ānyú	to be content with, to be satisfied with
簡陋	jiǎnlòu	simple and crude
發見	fāxiàn	same as 發現, to discover, to find; discovery
技藝	jìyì	skill, artistry, craft
器械	qìxiè	apparatus, appliance, instrument
命運	mìngyùn	destiny, fate, lot
改革	gǎigé	to reform; reform, reformation
圖	tú	to desire, to plan, to scheme
安分守己	ānfènshǒujǐ	to be content or happy to be what one is, to be law-abiding, to know one's place
順民	shùnmín	the people who surrendered to their lord, people who leave their fate to heaven
改造	gǎizào	to remake, to remold, to reform, to transform
現狀	xiànzhuàng	現在的情況, present (or current) situation, status quo, existing state of affairs
長進	zhǎngjìn	to make progress (especially in intellectual or scholastic pursuit, etc.); progress
揭抑	èyì	to check and restrain, to hold back and repress (or suppress), to keep within limits
鋼鐵	gāngtiě	steel and iron
民權	mínquán	people's rights, civil rights
平權	píngquán	equal rights
進化	jìnhuà	evolution; to evolve
動力	dònglì	driving force, motive force, impetus, motive power, power
制服	zhìfú	to bring under control, to subdue; uniform
供	gōng	for (the use or convenience of); to supply

固然，眞理是無窮的，物質上的享受是無窮的，新器械的發明是無窮的，社會制度的改善是無窮的。但格一物有一物的愉快，革新一器有一器的滿足，改良一種制度有一種制度的滿意。今日不能成功的，明日明年可以成功；前人失敗的，後人可以繼續助成。盡一分力便有一分的滿意；無窮的進境上，步步都可以給努力的人充分的愉快。所以大詩人鄧內孫（Tennyson）借古英雄 Ulysses 的口氣歌唱道：

然而人的閱歷就像一座穹門，
從那裏露出那不曾走過的世界，
越走越遠，永永望不到他的盡頭。
半路上不幹了，多麼沉悶呵！
明晃晃的快刀爲什麼甘心上銹！
難道留得一口氣就算得生活了？
……………………

朋友們，來罷！
去尋一個更新的世界是不會太晚的。
……………………

用掉的精力固然不回來了，剩下的還不少呢。
現在雖然不是從前那樣掀天動地的身手了，
然而我們畢竟還是我們，——

格	gé	to study thoroughly, to pursue to the very source
助成	zhùchéng	幫助完成, to help to succeed, to help to accomplish
盡	jìn	to put to the best use
分	fēn	one-tenth
鄧內孫	Dèngnèisūn	Alfred Tennyson (1809-1892), English poet, poet laureate (1850-1892)
口氣	kǒuqì	the way or manner of speaking, tone; meaning (usually hidden) of words said
閱歷	yuèlì	what one has seen, heard or done, experience
座	zuò	Numerary Adjunct for mountains or hills, bridges, city gates, etc.
穹門	qióngmén	arched door
盡頭	jìntóu	the extremity, the end
幹	gàn	作, to do, to work
沉悶	chénmèn	in low spirits, depressed; (said of personality or character) withdrawn, not outgoing, low-keyed; (said of weather, atmosphere, etc.) depressing, oppressive
呵	o	a particle used after a phrase for emphasis, expressing surprise
明晃晃	mínghuǎnghuǎng	shining, gleaming
快刀	kuàidāo	sharp knife
上鏽 (銹)	shàngxiù	to become rusty
一口氣	yìkǒuqì	one breath; in one breath, without a break, at one go, at a stretch
身手	shēnshǒu	skill, talent
畢竟	bìjìng	after all, in the final analysis

光陰與命運頹唐了幾分壯志！
終止不住那不老的雄心，
去努力，去探尋，去發見，
永不退讓，不屈服。

　　　　　　　一九二六，六，六。

光陰	guāngyīn	time
頹唐	tuítáng	to make dejected, to cause to be dispirited; dejected, dispirited
壯志	zhuàngzhì	great aspiration, lofty ideal
止不住	zhǐbúzhù	unable to stop
雄心	xióngxīn	"ambitious heart" — great ambition, lofty aspiration
退讓	tuìràng	"to move back and give way" — to make a concession, to give in, to yield

句型

1. 凡(是)... 都... — all those (any, whoever, whichever, whatever) ...

■ 凡一種文明的造成,(都)必有兩個因子...

　例 (1): 凡是去過紐約的人都知道紐約的交通很亂.

　例 (2): 凡是不到二十歲的人都不許喝酒.
　　　　(所有不到二十歲的人都不許喝酒).

2. A 不亞於 B — A is not worse than B

■ 其實一部摩托車所代表的人類的心思智慧決不亞於一首詩所代表的人類的心思智慧.

　例 (1): 美國製造的汽車在品質¹方面不亞於日本車.
　　　　(美國製造的汽車在品質方面不比日本車差).

　例 (2): 那個年輕人雖然剛畢業可是他做事的能力並不亞於在社會上做了好多年事的人.

　　　¹ 品質　　　　pǐnzhì　　　　quality

3. A 建築在 B(之)上 — A is built on B

■ 我們深信,精神的文明必須建築在物質的基礎之上.

　例 (1): 不要把自己的快樂建築在別人的痛苦上.

　例 (2): 這兩國的關係建築在什麼基礎上?

4. ... 在於 ... — ... lies in (resides in, rests on) ...

■ 科學的根本精神在於求真理.

　例 (1): 學生的責任在於把書讀好.

　例 (2): 將來是成功還是不成功全在於自己現在努力不努力.

5. (決) 不因此而 ...　－ not to do ... because of this

■ 誠然,真理是發現不完的,但科學決不因此而退縮.

　　例 (1): 雖然這一次我沒成功但是我決不因此而退縮.

　　例 (2): 雖然他讓我鬧了一個笑話,但是我並不因此而跟他吵架.

6. 先從 ... 的方面說起 ..., 其次 ..., 最後 ...　－ talk (about something) first from the aspect of ... ; next ... ; finally ...

■ 我們先從理智的方面說起 ..., 其次,我們且看看人類 ...

　　例: 我們先從美國的教育制度說起 ...;其次讓我們談談經濟制度 ...;最後讓我們討論一下美國的社會問題 ...

7. ... 便 (就) 不然了.　－ is not so

■ ... 在西方便不然了.

　　例 (1): 在中國舊社會裏父母比較喜歡男孩子,但是在新社會裏就不然了.
　　　　 (在舊社會裏父母比較喜歡男孩子,但是在新社會裏這種情形已經改變了.)

　　例 (2): 在紐約買中國東西很方便,但是在別的地方便不然了.
　　　　 (...在別的地方買中國東西不方便.)

8. ... 為 (是) N 之一　－ one of the

■ 「財產」為神聖的人權之一.

　　例 (1): 買東西方便是住在紐約的好處之一.

　　例 (2): 中文是最難學的外國話之一.

討論

1. 基本上,胡適認爲西方的文明是**積極**[1]的,**進取**[2]的,而東方的文明是消極[3]的,退讓的.你同意這樣的"二分法[4]"嗎?
2. 用"精神的"與"物質的"來分別東方與西方的文明有什麼缺點?
3. 胡適認爲"物質享受"在人的生活中應該佔什麼地位?
4. 什麼是近世宗教的"人化"?
5. 什麼是近世道德宗教的"社會化"?
6. 中國人讀了這篇文章以後會不會有什麼壞影響?
7. 一個傳統[5]衛道[6]的中國人在看了這篇文章以後,可能會有怎麼樣的批評[7]?

[1] 積極	jījí	positive; active
[2] 進取	jìnqǔ	to be eager to make progress; keep forging ahead
[3] 消極	xiāojí	passive; inactive
[4] 二分法	èrfēnfǎ	dichotomy
[5] 傳統	chuántǒng	tradition
[6] 衛道	wèidào	defend traditional moral principles
[7] 批評	pīpíng	criticism

Confidence and Self-Examination
信心與反省

Further Discussion on Confidence and Self-Examination
再論信心與反省

In Selections Three and Four Hu Shi again takes aim at the weaknesses he believes are inherent in traditional Chinese culture. He demands of the Chinese people that they reflect on themselves and their society, for it is only from such self-reflection that a firm, national self-confidence can be born. Chinese culture, Hu claimed, is far from "magnificent" and "rich," and is rather mediocre when compared to other societies. The Chinese people have little to take pride in, Hu believed. The Chinese must build their nation, Hu says, not by recalling or extolling the past but by a rigorous and realistic self-examination.

Selection Three was first published in *Independent Critic* (Dúlì pínglùn 獨立評論), 103:2-6 (June 3, 1934). Selection Four was first published in *Independent Critic*, 105:2-6 (June 17, 1934). Both were later included in *Collected Essays of Hu Shi* IV (Hú Shì wéncún, dì sì jí 胡適文存, 第四集; Taipei, 1953), iv., 458-64, 465-72.

信心與反省

這一期（獨立一○三期）裏有壽生先生的一篇文章，題為「我們要有信心」，在這文裏，他提出一個大問題：中華民族真不行嗎？他自己的答案是：我們是還有生存權的。

我很高興我們的青年在這種惡劣空氣裏還能保持他們對於國家民族前途的絕大信心。這種信心是一個民族生存的基礎，我們當然是完全同情的。

可是我們要補充一點：這種信心本身要建築在穩固的基礎之上，不可站在散沙之上。如果信仰的根據不穩固，一朝根基動搖了，信仰也就完了。

Confidence and Self-Examination

與	yǔ	跟, 和
反省	fǎnxǐng	self-examination, reflection; to make a soul-searching self-examination
期	qī	Numerary Adjunct for an issue of a periodical
獨立	Dúlì	the name of a magazine
壽生	Shòushēng	人名
題為	tíwéi	entitled as

中華民族	Zhōnghuá mínzú	a name for the ethnic group that constitutes the Chinese nation
		民族: a people, an ethnic group
答案	dá'àn	an answer (to exam question, puzzle)
生存權	shēngcúnquán	生存: survival, existence
		權: rights, privileges
惡劣	èliè	of very poor quality
空氣	kōngqì	air or atmosphere (here used figuratively)
保持	bǎochí	to maintain, to keep, to preserve
前途	qiántú	(used only figuratively) the future, the prospect
基礎	jīchǔ	basis or foundation (of a building, an argument, etc.)
補充	bǔchōng	to supplement, to make up for a deficiency, to complement, to replenish, to add; additional, complimentary
建築	jiànzhú	to build, to construct; a building or structure, architecture
穩固	wěngù	stable, steady, firm
之	zhī	(lit.) 的
散沙	sǎnshā	loose sand
		散: loose, loosened, scattered
信仰	xìnyǎng	religious or political belief; to believe in
根據	gēnjù	basis, root, source; according to, in accordance with, on the strength of
一朝	yìzhāo	once, in case; in a single day, in a very short time
		朝: morning, day
根基	gēnjī	根據, 基礎
動搖	dòngyáo	to move and shake, to waver

壽生先生不贊成那些舊人「拿什麼五千年的古國喲，精神文明喲，地大物博喲，來遮醜。」這是不錯的。然而他自己提出的民族信心的根據，依我看來，文字上雖然和他們不同，實質上還是和他們同樣的站在散沙之上，同樣的擋不住風吹雨打。例如他說：

　　我們今日之改進不如日本之速者，就是因為我們的固有文化太豐富了。富於創造性的人，個性必強，接受性就較緩。這種思想在實質上和那五千年古國精神文明的迷夢是同樣的無稽的誇大。第一，他的原則「富於創造性的人，個性必強，接受性就較緩，」這個大前提就是完全無稽之

遮醜	zhēchǒu	to hide one's shame 遮: to cover, to conceal; 醜: ugly, shameful, infamous
提出	tíchū	to put forth, to raise (a question)
依我看來	yīwǒkànlái	as I look at it, in my opinion 依: to depend on, to rely on, to comply with, to follow
實質上	shízhíshàng	essentially, in substance 實質: essence, substance
擋不住	dǎngbúzhù	incapable of blocking, resisting, hindering, impeding, etc.

		擋: to resist, to obstruct, to block, to stop, to impede, to ward off;
		住: Resultative Verb ending meaning "fixity, security"
速	sù	(lit.) 快
固有文化	gùyǒuwénhuà	traditional culture (of a nation)
富於	fùyú	rich in (creative ability, imagination)
創造	chuàngzào	to create
		創: to start (doing something), to achieve (something for the first time);
		造: to make, to do, to produce
性	xìng	a suffix meaning "nature, characteristic or essential quality"
個性	gèxìng	personality, individuality
必	bì	一定
較	jiào (jiǎo)	比較
緩	huǎn	慢
迷夢	mímèng	delusive dream, illusion, delusion
		迷: to bewitch, to enchant, to charm, to confuse, to stupefy, to delude
同樣的	tóngyàngde	一樣的
無稽的	wújīde	groundless, baseless, unfounded, wild (rumors, talk, etc.)
		稽: to investigate, to examine, to inspect
誇大	kuādà	exaggeration; to exaggerate, to boast
原則	yuánzé	a principle (in handling something)
前提	qiántí	a (logical) premise
無稽之談	wújīzhītán	無稽: (see explanation above);
		談: talk, utterances

談，就是懶惰的中國士大夫捏造出來替自己遮醜的胡說。事實上恰是相反的：凡富於創造性的人必敏於模倣，凡不善模倣的人決不能創造。創造是一個最誤人的名詞，其實創造只是模倣到十足時的一點點新花樣。古人說的最好：「太陽之下，沒有新的東西。」一切所謂創造都從模倣出來。我們不要被新名詞騙了。新名詞的模倣就是舊名詞的「學」字；「學之為言效也」是一句不磨的老話。例如學琴，必須先模倣琴師彈琴；學畫必須先模倣畫師作畫；就是畫自然界的景物，也是模倣。模倣熟了，就是學會了，工具用的熟了，方法練的密了，有天才的人自然會「熟能生巧」，這一點功夫到時的奇巧新花樣就叫做創造。凡不肯模倣，就是不肯學人的長處。不肯學如何

士大夫	shìdàifu	the intelligentsia, the scholarly community; a person with official rank, a person of learning, a scholar
捏造	niēzào	to fabricate, to make up (false evidence, etc.) 捏: to knead, to mold (mud, etc.)
恰	qià	by coincidence
相反	xiāngfǎn	contrary, opposed to each other
敏於	mǐnyú	quick, agile, clever (in doing or learning something)

模倣	mófǎng	to imitate, to copy
善	shàn	善於, good at, skilled in
誤人	wùrén	to mislead or harm others 誤: to mislead, to harm, to injure
名詞	míngcí	a term; a noun
十足	shízú	one hundred percent, perfect, complete; perfectly, completely, extremely
花樣	huāyàng	(usually varied or different) patterns, styles, designs
學之為言效也	xuézhīwéiyánxiàoyě	(lit.) "學" 的意思就是模倣
不磨的	bùmóde	不可磨滅, indelible 磨: to rub, to grind — to wear out, to obliterate
自然界	zìránjiè	the natural world
景物	jǐngwù	風景, scenes, landscape
工具	gōngjù	tools, implements, equipment
練	liàn	練習
細密	xìmì	fine and delicate 細: thin, tiny, fine, delicate; 密: dense, tight
熟能生巧	shú (shóu) néng shēngqiǎo	"Skill comes from long experience," "Dexterity is the product of long practice" 生: to give birth to, to give rise to; 巧: clever, ingenious, skillful, artful
工夫	gōngfu	skill, art, workmanship; time; efforts put into a piece of work
奇巧	qíqiǎo	rare and artful
長處	chángchù	good points, strength
如何	rúhé	an interrogative indicating a rhetorical question — how ... ?

能創造？葛理略（Galileo）聽說荷蘭有個磨鏡匠人做成了一座望遠鏡，他就依他聽說的造法，自己製造了一座望遠鏡。這就是模倣，也就是創造。從十七世紀初年到如今，望遠鏡和顯微鏡都年年有進步，可是這三百年的進步，步步是模倣，也步步是創造。一切進步都是如此：沒有一件創造不是先從模倣下手的。孔子說的好：

　　三人行，必有我師焉：擇其善者而從之，其不善者而改之。

　　這就是一個聖人的模倣。懶人不肯模倣，所以決不會創造。一個民族也和個人一樣，最肯學人的時代就是那個民族最偉大的時代；等到他不肯學人的時候，他的盛世已過去了，他已走上老僵化的時期了，我們中國民族最偉大的時代，正是我們最肯模倣四鄰的時代：從漢到唐宋，一切建築、繪畫、雕刻、音樂、宗教、思想、算學

葛理略	Gělǐlüè	Galileo Galilei (1564-1642), Italian astronomer and physicist
荷蘭	Hélán	Holland, the Netherlands
鏡	jìng	lens, glass; mirror
匠人	jiàngrén	a craftsman, an artisan
望遠鏡	wàngyuǎnjìng	telescope 望: to view, to watch
製造	zhìzào	造

如今	rújīn	現在, now, nowadays
顯微鏡	xiǎnwēijìng	microscope
		顯: to show, to manifest, to unveil;
		微: 細小
步步	bùbù	每一步
		步: a step (in the act of walking, running, etc.)
如此	rúcǐ	像這樣
下手	xiàshǒu	to put or set one's hand to, to start doing something; helper, assistant; right-hand seat
行	xíng	(lit.) 走路
焉	yān	(lit.) in there, among (them)
擇	zé	選, to select, to choose, to pick
從	cóng	跟隨, to follow
聖人	shèngrén	a sage, a saint
個人	gèrén	an individual (contrasted with a group)
盛世	shèngshì	a prosperous age or period, halcyon days
已	yǐ	已經
衰老	shuāilǎo	senile; senility, decrepitude
僵化	jiānghuà	to become rigid, to become set in a rigidly conventional pattern, to ossify; ossification
		僵: stiff, inactive, stagnant;
		化: a suffix combined with a noun or an adjective to form a verb that means "-ify" or "-ize"
四鄰	sìlín	neighbors on all four sides, all the neighbors, neighboring countries or neighboring households
繪畫	huìhuà	painting, drawing
雕刻	diāokè	sculpture
宗教	zōngjiào	religion
算學	suànxué	mathematics

、天文、工藝，那一件裏沒有模倣外國的重要成分？佛教和他帶來的美術建築，不用說了。從漢朝到今日，我們的曆法改革，無一次不是採用外國的新法；最近三百年的曆法是完全學西洋的，更不用說了。到了我們不肯學人家的好處的時候，我們的文化也就不進步了。我們到了民族中衰的時代，只有懶勁學印度人的吸食鴉片，卻沒有精力學滿州人的不纏脚，那就是我們自殺的法門了。

第二，我們不可輕視日本人的模倣。壽生先生也犯了一般人輕視日本的惡習慣，抹殺日本人善於模倣的絕大長處。日本的成功，正可以證明我在上文說的「一切創造都從模倣出來」的原則

天文	tiānwén	astronomy
工藝	gōngyì	technology, craft
成分	chéngfèn	a component, an ingredient or element
佛教	Fójiào	Buddhism
美術	měishù	fine arts
漢朝	Hàncháo	the Han dynasty, 206 B.C. – 220 A.D.
曆法	lìfǎ	calendar (as a system)
改革	gǎigé	a reformation; to reform 革: to get rid of, to eliminate, to change, to reform, to renovate

CONFIDENCE AND SELF-EXAMINATION

無	wú	沒有
採用	cǎiyòng	to adopt (a suggestion, an idea, a new method, a new technique, etc.)
西洋	Xīyáng	the West, European or American nations
好處	hǎochù	長處
中衰	zhōngshuāi	to decline midway
時代	shídài	an era, a period, an age, an epoch
勁	jìn	vigor, energy, strength, interest, enthusiasm
印度	Yìndù	India
吸食	xīshí	to smoke (opium) 吸: to smoke, to absorb, to inhale, to suck in
鴉片	yāpiàn	opium
滿洲	Mǎnzhōu	Manchuria
纏	chán	to wind around, to bind
法門	fǎmén	*dharmaparyāya* (the doctrine or wisdom of Buddha regarded as the gateway to enlightenment) — the way or method of doing or learning something
輕視	qīngshì	看輕, 看不起
犯	fàn	to commit (crimes, mistakes, etc.)
惡	è	壞
抹殺	mǒshā	to fail to mention (one's merits, achievements, etc.) purposely, to withhold recognition for, to give no credit to 抹: to wipe, to mop, to obliterate, to blot out
絕大	juédà	最大 絕: without match, peerless, the utmost
上文	shàngwén	the above text

○壽生說:

　　從唐以至日本明治維新，千數百年間，日本有一件事足爲中國取鏡者嗎？中國的學術思想在她手裏去發展改進過嗎？我們實無法說有。

　　這又是無稽的誣告了。三百年前，朱舜水到日本，他居留久了，能了解那個島國民族的優點，所以他寫信給中國的朋友說，日本的政治雖不能上比唐虞，可以說比得上三代盛世。這一個中國大學者在長期寄居之後下的考語，是值得我們注意的。日本民族的長處全在他們肯一心一意的學別人的好處。他們學了中國的無數好處，但始終不曾學我們的小腳，八股文，鴉片煙。這不夠「爲中國取鏡」嗎？他們學別國的文化，無論在

唐	Táng	the Tang dynasty (618-907)
以至	yǐzhì	一直到
明治維新	Míngzhì wéixīn	the Meiji restoration, which marked the beginning of Japan's modernization 明治: the reign of Emperor Mutsuhito of Japan (1867-1912)
足	zú	足以, sufficient to, enough to
取鏡	qǔjìng	"to take as a mirror" — to learn from another's experience, to pattern after another person
學術	xuéshù	learning
思想	sīxiǎng	thinking, thought
實	shí	實在,真的
誣告	wūgào	a false charge (or accusation); to bring a false charge against

誣: to accuse falsely;
告: to sue (someone), to accuse or charge (someone) in a written or verbal report to the authorities

朱舜水	Zhū Shùnshuǐ	朱之瑜 (1600-1682), scholar of the late Ming (1368-1644) period
居留	jūliú	to dwell, to reside, to inhabit
優點	yōudiǎn	長處, 好處
唐虞	TángYú	the reigns of Emperors Yao 堯 and Shun 舜, two sage kings of over 4,000 years ago
比得上	bǐdeshàng	able to be compared with, to be a peer for
三代	Sāndài	the three ancient Chinese dynasties: Xia 夏 (21ˢᵗ - 18ᵗʰ centuries B.C.), Shang 商 (18ᵗʰ century - *ca.* 1100 B.C.), and Zhou 周 (*ca.* 1100 - 221 B.C.)
學者	xuézhě	a scholar or learned person
寄居	jìjū	to reside temporarily (at a place, with a family, etc.)
考語	kǎoyǔ	remarks or comments made as the result of an inspection or examination
一心一意	yìxīnyíyì	of one heart and mind, wholehearted, single-minded, bent on (doing something)
無數	wúshù	countless, innumerable
始終	shǐzhōng	from the beginning to the end, throughout
小腳	xiǎojiǎo	the small feet deformed by the practice of footbinding
八股文	bāgǔwén	the "eight-legged essay" (a rigid style of literary writing during the era of the Imperial Examination)

那一方面,凡是學到家的,都能有創造的貢獻。這是必然的道理。淺見的人都說日本的山水人物畫是模倣中國的;其實日本畫自有他的特點,在人物方面的成績遠勝過中國畫,在山水方面也沒有走上四王的笨路。在文學方面,他們也有很大的創造。近年已有人賞識日本的小詩了。我且舉一個大家不甚留意的例子。文學史家往往說日本的源氏物語等作品是模倣中國唐人的小說遊仙窟等書的。現今遊仙窟已從日本翻印回中國來了,源氏物語也有了英國人衛來先生(Arthur Waley)的五巨冊的譯本。我們若比較這兩部書,就不能不驚歎日本人創造力的偉大。如果「源氏」真是從模倣遊仙窟出來的,那真是徒弟勝過師傅千萬倍了!壽生先生原文裏批評日本的工商業,也是中

貢獻	gòngxiàn	contribution; to offer or contribute
必然	bìrán	一定(會)這樣, inevitable
道理	dàolǐ	rationale, reason, principle, hows and whys
淺見	qiǎnjiàn	a superficial or shallow view, a short-sighted view
特點	tèdiǎn	special features, peculiarities
勝過	shèngguò	to excel, to surpass, to prevail over
四王	sì Wáng	four Wangs of the early Qing

		(1644-1911) period who were skilled in landscape painting: Wang Shimin 王時敏 (1592-1680); Wang Jian 王鑑 (1598-1677); Wang Hui 王翬 (1632-1717); Wang Yuanqi 王原祁 (1642-1715)
賞識	shǎngshì	to appreciate and recognize the virtues or worth of a person or thing
且	qiě	暫且, for the time being, for the moment
甚	shèn	(lit.) 很
留意	liúyì	留心注意, to pay attention to, to take heed
源氏物語	Yuánshì wùyǔ	Genji Monogatari, 日本小説名, 作者是紫氏部 (Murasaki Shikibu, b. 978?)
等	děng	等等, and so forth, et cetera
作品	zuòpǐn	the work done by a writer or an artist, a literary or artistic work
遊仙窟	Yóuxiānkū	唐朝小説名, 作者是張鷟 (Zhang Zu, ca. 660 - ca. 741)
翻印	fānyìn	to reprint (a book with or without proper permission)
巨	jù	大
冊	cè	volume, book
譯本	yìběn	a translated version
部	bù	a volume, a complete work of writing
徒弟	túdì	an apprentice, a disciple, a pupil
師傅	shīfu	a teacher, a master (to an apprentice), a tutor
原文	yuánwén	the original text
批評	pīpíng	to criticize; criticism

了成見的毒。日本今日工商業的長腳發展，雖然也受了生活程度比人低和貨幣低落的恩惠，但他的根基實在是全靠科學與工商業的進步。今日大阪與蘭肯歇的競爭，骨子裏還是新式工業與舊式工業的競爭。日本今日自造的紡織器是世界各國公認為最新最良的。今日英國紡織業也不能不購買日本的新機器了。這是從模倣到創造的最好的例子。不然，我們工人的工資比日本更低，貨幣平常也比日本錢更賤，為什麼我們不能「與他國資本家搶商場」呢？我們到了今日，若還要抹煞事實，笑人模倣，而自居於「富於創造性者」的不屑模倣，那真是盲目的誇大狂了。

中毒	zhòngdú	to be poisoned 中: to hit (a target), to attain (a goal); (note pronunciation) 毒: poison
成見	chéngjiàn	a preconception, a prejudice, a bias 成: completed, accomplished, settled, fixed, finished; 見: a view
長腳發展	chángjiǎo fāzhǎn	a rapid development 長腳: (to make) great strides forward, (to advance) by leaps and bounds
生活程度	shēnghuó chéngdù	the standard of living 程度: degree, state or condition
貨幣	huòbì	currency, money
恩惠	ēnhuì	favor, benevolence, benignity

根基	gēnjī	根本, 基礎, basis, foundation
大阪	Dàbǎn	日本地名 (Osaka)
蘭肯歇	Lánkěnxiē	英國地名 (Lancashire)
競爭	jìngzhēng	competition; to compete, to vie
骨子裏	gǔzili	in one's bones, in one's innermost nature, in substance, quintessentially
自造	zìzào	自己做
紡織	fǎngzhī	to spin and weave; spinning and weaving
機	jī	機器, a machine, machinery
公認	gōngrèn	to recognize or acknowledge generally; generally recognized or acknowledged
為	wéi	是, to be
良	liáng	好
購買	gòumǎi	買 購: 買
工資	gōngzī	wages
賤	jiàn	cheap, inferior, of little worth
資本家	zīběnjiā	capitalist
商場	shāngchǎng	a market place
若	ruò	要是, 如果
抹煞	mǒshā	抹殺, to give no credit to
事實	shìshí	fact, truth, reality
自居於	zìjūyú	to situate oneself in, to consider oneself (a genius, famous figure) 居: 住, to dwell, reside or inhabit
不屑	bùxiè	not to condescend to do something (due to one's dignity or pride), to feel it beneath one's dignity to do something
盲目	mángmù	blind (fig.), lacking insight, perception
誇大狂	kuādàkuáng	megalomania; megalomaniac 狂: crazy, mad, mentally deranged

第三，再看看「我們的固有文化」是不是真的「太豐富了」。壽生和其誇大本國固有文化的人們，如果真肯平心想想，必然也會明白這句話也是無根的亂談。這個問題太大，不是這篇短文裏所能詳細討論的，我只能指出這個比較重要之點，使人明白我們的固有文化實在是很貧乏的，談不到「太豐富」的夢話。近代的科學文化，工業文化，我們可以撇開不談，因為在那些方面，我們的貧乏未免太丟人了。我們且談談老遠的過去時代罷。我們的周秦時代當然可以和希臘羅馬相提比論，然而我們如果平心研究希臘羅馬的文學，雕刻，科學，政治，單是這四項就不能不使我們感覺我們的文化的貧乏了，尤其是造形美術與算學的兩方面，我們真不能不低頭愧汗。我們試想想，「幾何原本」的作者歐幾里得（Euclid）正和孟子先後同時；在那麼早的時代，在二千多年前，我們在科學上早已太落後了！（少年愛國的

平心	píngxīn	to be calm and fair (in resolving a dispute), to do something with equanimity
詳細	xiángxì	in every detail and particular 詳: complete, detailed; details
指出	zhǐchū	to point out
點	diǎn	a point, an item

貧乏	pínfá	wanting, destitute, insufficient, deficient 貧: poor, impoverished; 乏: without, in want of
談不到	tánbudào	out of the question
夢話	mènghuà	dream talk, wishful thinking
撇開	piēkāi	to set aside, to dismiss or exclude (from discussion or consideration)
未免	wèimiǎn	unavoidably
丟人	diūrén	丟臉, to lose face
老遠	lǎoyuǎn	很遠
秦	Qín	the Qin dynasty (221-207 B.C.)
希臘	Xīlà	Greece, Greek
羅馬	Luómǎ	Rome
相提比論	xiāngtíbǐlùn	mentioned, compared and discussed together; to mention in the same breath
研究	yánjiū	to study and research, to examine
單是	dānshì	只是
項	xiàng	an item; Numerary Adjunct for items
尤其是	yóuqíshì	特別是
造形美術	zàoxíngměishù	plastic arts 形: form, shape, appearance
愧汗	kuìhàn	to perspire because of shame 愧: ashamed, shameful
作者	zuòzhě	著作的人, an author, the writer of a book, article, etc.
歐幾里得	Oūjīlǐdé	Euclid, Greek mathematician of the third century B.C.; author of *Elements*, which forms the basis for modern geometry
孟子	Mèngzǐ	Mencius, Chinese philosopher of the fourth century B.C.

人何不試拿墨子經上篇裏的三五條幾何學界說來比較「幾何原本」？）從此以後，我們所有的，歐洲也都有；我們所沒有的，人家所獨有的，人家都比我們強。試舉一個例子：歐洲有三個一千年的大學，有許多個五百年以上的大學，至今繼續存在，繼續發展：我們有沒有？至於我們所獨有的寶貝，駢文，律詩，八股，小脚，太監，姨太太，五世同居的大家庭，貞節牌坊，地獄活現的監獄，廷杖

何不	hébù	why not?
墨子經	Mòzǐjīng	a classic book named after Mozi or Mocius, a Chinese philosopher of the fifth century B.C. 經: a classic book, a book of value
上篇	shàngpiān	篇: Numerary Adjunct for articles, compositions, poems, etc.; a chapter, section, part
條	tiáo	Numerary Adjunct for the articles, sections, items, clauses of an agreement, statement, pact, law; an item, article, section, clause
界說	jièshuō	definition, delimination 界: to define, to demarcate, to limit; domain, territory
此	cǐ	這(個時候, etc.)
獨	dú	alone
繼續	jìxù	to continue
存在	cúnzài	to exist, to be present
寶貝	bǎobèi	a cherished thing or person, treasure

駢文	piánwén	an euphemistically antithetic style of writing prevalent in the sixth and seventh centuries A.D.
律詩	lǜshī	a poem of eight lines with five or seven characters each and with certain rules about rhymes, tones and antitheses 律: to control or restrain by rules, regulations, law, etc.; a law, rule
太監	tàijiàn	eunuch
姨太太	yítàitai	concubine
五世同居	wǔshìtóngjū	five generations under the same roof
貞節牌坊	zhēnjié páifāng	a stone arch erected by the government in traditional China in honor of a chaste woman widowed at a young age 貞節: (of woman) chastity, purity, virtue; (of man) tenacity to hold on to one's virtuous way or integrity; 牌坊: an honorific arch or portal
地獄	dìyù	hell, Hades 獄: a prison
活現	huóxiàn	vivid, as if it were taking place here and now
監獄	jiānyù	prison, jail 監: to supervise, to oversee, to confine, to keep in custody, to imprison
廷杖	tíngzhàng	punitive beating with a cane administered at court in the presence of other courtiers 廷: the imperial court;

，板子夾棍的法庭，……雖然「豐富」，雖然「在這世界無不足以單獨成一系統」，究竟都是使我們抬不起頭來的文物制度。即如壽生先生指出的「那更光輝萬丈」的宋明理學，說起來也眞正可憐！講了七八百年的理學，沒有一個理學聖賢起來指出裹小脚是不人道的野蠻行爲，只見大家崇信「餓死事極小，失節事極大」的吃人禮教：請問那萬丈光輝究竟照耀到那裏去了？

以上說的，都只是略略指出壽生先生代表的民族信心是建築在散沙上面，禁不起風吹草動，就會倒塌下來的。信心是我們需要的，但無根據的信心是沒有力量的。

可靠的民族信心，必須建築在一個堅固的基礎之上，祖宗的光榮自是祖宗之光榮，不能救我

		杖: a stick, cane, club; to punish by caning
板子	bǎnzi	a flat bamboo, a rod for beating criminals in old China or for disciplining children
夾棍	jiāgùn	rods or sticks for pressing something or holding things together 夾: to clamp, to place in between; 棍: a rod, a stick
法庭	fǎtíng	a law court
系統	xìtǒng	a system
究竟	jiūjìng	到底, after all, in the end
文物	wénwù	cultural artifacts

制度	zhìdù	a system of regulations
即如	jírú	就像, 就比方說
光輝萬丈	guānghuīwànzhàng	光輝: radiance, brightness; 萬丈: 100,000 feet — very long; 丈: a unit in Chinese lineal measurement slightly longer than ten feet
宋	Sòng	the Song dynasty (960-1279)
明	Míng	the Ming dynasty (1368-1644)
理學	lǐxué	a school of learning devoted to the study of Confucian classics with a rational approach
聖賢	shèngxián	聖人: a saint, a sage; 賢人: a person of virtue and talent
裹	guǒ	to wrap, to bind
人道	réndào	humanitarian; humanitarianism
野蠻	yěmán	barbarous, savage, uncivilized, brutal
行為	xíngwéi	conduct, behavior
崇信	chóngxìn	崇拜: to worship; 相信: to believe in
失節	shījié	(of woman) 失貞節, to lose chastity
禮教	lǐjiào	ethical education 禮: propriety, decorum, courtesy
照耀	zhàoyào	to radiate, to light up, to illuminate
略略	lüèlüè	slightly
禁不起	jīnbuqǐ	unable to endure, unable to withstand
倒塌	dǎotā	to collapse (said of a building)
堅固	jiāngù	durable, solid, firm, stable
祖宗	zǔzōng	ancestors, forefathers, forebears
光榮	guāngróng	glory, honor; glorious

們的痛苦羞辱。何況祖宗所建的基業不全是光榮呢？我們要指出：我們的民族信心必須站在「反省」的唯一基礎之上。反省就是要閉門思過，要誠心誠意的想，我們祖宗的罪孽深重，我們自己的罪孽深重；要認清了罪孽所在，然後我們可以用全副精力去消災滅罪。壽生先生引了一句「中國不亡是無天理」的悲歎詞句，他也許不知道這句傷心的話是我十三四年前在中央公園後面柏樹下對孫伏園先生說的，第二天被他記在晨報上，就流傳至今。我說出那句話的目的，不是要人消極，是要人反省：不是要人灰心，是要人起信心，發下大弘誓來懺悔，來替祖宗懺悔，替我們自

痛苦	tòngkǔ	suffering, pain, anguish; painful
羞辱	xiūrǔ	shame, dishonor, humiliation; to humiliate, to put to shame 羞: shame, disgrace; to feel ashamed; 辱: disgrace, humiliation; to bring disgrace or humiliation to, to insult
何況	hékuàng	not to mention
建	jiàn	建立, to establish, to build, to set up
基業	jīyè	the initial achievements (of an empire, household, etc.)
唯一	wéiyī	the only one, the only kind, sole
閉門思過	bìménsīguò	to reflect on one's faults or misdeeds in private

誠心誠意	chéngxīnchéngyì	earnestly and sincerely, in all sincerity
罪孽深重	zuìnièshēnzhòng	the sin is great 罪孽: sin, evil
認清	rènqīng	認識清楚
所在	suǒzài	在的地方
全副精力	quánfùjīnglì	all the mental and phsical strength, vitality, stamina
消災滅罪	xiāozāimièzuì	消, 滅: to disperse, to eliminate, to remove, to extinguish, to quench; 災: calamity, disaster, catastrophe; 罪: sin, crime, vice, evil, guilt
引	yǐn	to quote
天理	tiānlǐ	the law of Heaven (which always punishes the guilty and rewards the innocent)
悲歎	bēitàn	to lament, to deplore, to sigh over
詞句	cíjù	phrase, expression
柏	bái	the cypress, the cedar
孫伏園	Sūn Fúyúan	人名
晨報	Chénbào	*Morning Gazette*, Peking
流傳	liúchuán	to transmit or be transmitted from person to person or generation to generation, to spread
目的	mùdì	purpose, objective, aim
消極	xiāojí	pessimistic, negative
發誓	fāshì	to vow, to swear, to take an oath 誓: a vow, an oath
弘	hóng	great, immense
懺悔	chànhuǐ	to repent one's sins 懺: to confess one's sins, to repent; 悔: to regret, to repent

己懺悔；要發願造新因來替代舊日種下的惡因。

今日的大患在於全國人不知恥。所以不知恥者，只是因為不曾反省。一個國家兵力不如人，被人打敗了，被人搶奪了一大塊土地去，這不算是最大的恥辱。一個國家在今日還容許整個的省分遍種鴉片煙，一個政府在今日還要依靠鴉片烟的稅收—公賣稅，吸戶稅，烟苗稅，過境稅—來做政府的收入的一部分，這是最大的恥辱。一個現代民族在今日還容許他們的最高官吏公然提倡什麼「時輪金剛法會」，「息災利民法會」，這是最大的恥辱。一個國家有五千年的歷史，而沒有一個四十年的大學，甚至於沒有一個真正完備的大學，這是最大的恥辱。一個國家能養三百萬

發願	fāyuàn	to vow to achieve an objective
因	yīn	the reason, cause (of some future development)
替代	tìdài	to replace, to substitute
患	huàn	trouble, peril, disaster, adversity
在於	zàiyú	在, to lie in, to be in
知恥 (耻)	zhīchǐ	to have a sense of shame 恥: disgrace, shame
搶奪	qiǎngduó	to take by force, to rob, to loot, to plunder

恥辱	chǐrǔ	disgrace, shame, humiliation
容許	róngxǔ	to allow, to permit, to tolerate
省分	shěngfèn	a province
遍	piàn	all over, everywhere, throughout
依靠	yīkào	靠, to depend on, to rely on
稅收	shuìshōu	tax revenue
吸戶	xīhù	吸鴉片煙的人家
煙苗	yānmiáo	poppy-plants for opium
過境	guòjìng	to pass through a territory in transit 境: a territory, a boundary
官吏	guānlì	a government official
公然	gōngrán	openly, in public
提倡	tíchàng	to promote (a cause), to advocate
輪	lún	(in religion) *cakra*: wheel, disc, rotation; to revolve; the "three wheels" are illusion, *karma* and suffering, and are constantly rotating; the "five wheels" are earth, water, fire, wind and space, with earth resting on the other four
金剛	jīn gāng	*vajra*, the thunderbolt of the deity Indra, often called the diamond club, though recent research considers it a sun symbol; the diamond, synonym of hardness, indestructibility, power
法會	fǎhuì	an assembly for worship or preaching
息災	xīzāi	to stop, to end or to terminate calamities
利民	lìmín	to benefit people
完備	wánbèi	complete, having no deficiency 備: completeness, perfection

不能捍衛國家的兵,而至今不肯計劃任何區域的國民義務教育,這是最大的恥辱。

　　真誠的反省自然發生與真誠的愧恥。孟子說的好:「不恥不若人,何若人有?」真誠的愧恥自然引起向上的努力,要發弘願努力學人家的好處,剗除自家的罪惡。經過這種反省與懺悔之後,然後可以起新的信心:要信仰我們自己正是撥亂反正的人,這個擔子必須我們自己來挑起。三四十年的天足運動已經差不多完全剗除了小腳的風氣:從前大腳的女人要裝小腳,現在小腳的女人要裝大腳了。風氣轉移的這樣快,這不夠堅定我們的自信心嗎?

　　歷史的反省自然使我們明瞭今日的失敗都因為過去的不努力,同時也可以使我們格外明瞭「

捍衛	hànwèi	to defend (a nation's territory, etc.) 捍: to defend, to guard against, to ward off; 衛: to defend, to guard, to protect
任何	rènhé	隨便哪一個,不論哪一個, any, whatever
區域	qūyù	a district, an area, a region, a zone
義務教育	yìwù jiàoyù	obligatory, compulsory, mandatory education 義務: duty, obligation
不恥不若人	bùchǐbúruòrén	(lit.) (要是一個人)不認為不像別人(那麼好)是

CONFIDENCE AND SELF-EXAMINATION

		一種恥辱
		若: 像, to be like
何若人有	héruòrényǒu	(lit.) (這個人) 怎麼能像別人 (那麼好) 呢?
引起	yǐnqǐ	to give rise to, to cause, to trigger
向上	xiàngshàng	to strive upward, to try to improve oneself; turned upward
剗 (剷) 除	chǎnchú	to root out, to eradicate
		剗: to level, to tear down;
		除: to remove, to rid of, to wipe out
自家	zìjiā	自己
罪惡	zuìè	罪
撥亂反正	bōluàn fǎnzhèng	to put down rebellion and restore order
		撥: to dispel, to remove, to set aside;
		反: to return (to), to turn back
擔子	dànzi	a load or burden upon the shoulder
挑起	tiāoqǐ	挑: to carry (load) with a pole on one's shoulder, to shoulder
天足	tiānzú	(women's) natural feet (as distinguished from feet deformed by the practice of foot binding in old China)
風氣	fēngqì	custom, common practice, fashion, fad
裝	zhuāng	to pretend, to feign
轉移	zhuǎnyí	to change in direction or position, to shift, to turn
堅定	jiāndìng	to strengthen; determined, firm of purpose, objective
		堅: strong and durable
自信心	zìxìnxīn	self-confidence
明瞭	míngliǎo (-liáo)	明白, 了解
格外	géwài	特別的

種瓜得瓜,種豆得豆」的因果鐵律。剗除過去的罪孽只是割斷已往種下的果。我們要收新果。必須努力造新因。祖宗生在過去的時代,他們沒有我們今日的新工具,也居然能給我們留下了不少的遺產。我們今日有了祖宗不曾夢見的種種新工具,當然應該有比祖宗高明千百倍的成績,纔對得起這個新鮮的世界。日本一個小島國,那麼貧瘠的土地,那麼少的人民,只因為伊籐博文,大久保利通,西鄉隆盛等幾十個人的努力,只因為他們肯拼命的學人家,肯拼命的用這個世界的新工具,居然在半個世紀之內一躍而為世界三五大強國之一。這不夠鼓舞我們的信心嗎?

反省的結果應該使我們明白那五千年的精神文明,那「光輝萬丈」的宋明理學,那並不太豐富的固有文化,都是無濟於事的銀樣蠟鎗頭。我們的前途在我們自己的手裏。我們的信心應該望

種瓜得瓜	zhòngguā dēguā	what one sows, so shall he reap
種豆得豆	zhòngdòu dédòu	瓜: melons, gourds, cucumbers, etc.;
		豆: beans and peas collectively
因果律	yīnguǒlǜ	law of causality
		果: fruit of a plant; effect, result, consequence
鐵	tiě	iron; definite, not subject to change
割斷	gēduàn	to cut off

已往	yǐwǎng	從前
收	shōu	to harvest
遺產	yíchǎn	property left behind by a deceased person, bequest, legacy 遺: to leave behind either intentionally or unintentionally
高明	gāomíng	superior; an expert, a master
纔	cái	才, only then, not until
新鮮	xīnxiān	novel, new and unusual; fresh
島國	dǎoguó	an island nation
貧瘠	pínjí	(of land) poor and barren, wanting in natural resources
伊藤博文	Yīténg Bówén	Itô Hirobumi (1841-1909), 日本政治家
大久保利通	Dàjiǔbǎo Lìtōng	Ôkubo Toshimichi (1830-1878), 日本政治家
西鄉隆勝	Xīxiāng Lóngshèng	Saigô Takamori (1827-1877), 日本政治家
拼命	pīnmìng	to risk one's life; exerting the utmost strength, desperately
在...之內	zài ... (time period) ... zhīnèi	在 (time period) 裏
世紀	shìjì	century
躍	yuè	跳, to jump, to leap
爲...之一	wéi ... zhīyī	to be one of ...
鼓舞	gǔwǔ	"to drum and dance" — to rouse, to stir up, to excite, to spur on
精神文明	jīngshén wénmíng	spiritual civilization
無濟於事	wújìyúshì	對事情沒有幫助
銀樣蠟槍頭	yínyànglàqiāngtóu	a pewter spearhead that looks like silver — an impressive-looking but useless thing or person 蠟 should be 鑞, pewter

在我們的將來。我們的將來全靠我們下什麼種，出多少力。「播了種一定會有收穫，用了力決不至於白費；」這是翁文灝先生要我們有的信心。

二十三，五，二十八。

下種	xiàzhǒng	to sow seed
出力	chūlì	to put forth strength, to exert efforts
播	bō	to sow, to broadcast seed
收穫	shōuhuò	harvest — fruit of efforts
決	jué	絕對，一定
至於	zhìyú	to go so far as, to reach the extent of; as for ...
白費	báifèi	白: in vain, for nothing; 費: to spend, to cast, to expend
翁文灝	Wēng Wénhào	人名

句型

1. A 遠勝過 B —   A far surpasses B

■日本畫在人物方面的成績遠勝過中國畫．

　例 (1): 我用中文聽,說的能力遠勝過讀,寫的能力．
　　　　(我用中文聽,說的能力比讀,寫的能力好的多．
　　　　我用中文讀,寫的能力遠不如聽,說的能力．)

2. 未免太 Adj. 了 — it must be ... ; rather

- 在那些方面,我們的貧乏未免太丟人了.

    例 (1): 才十幾歲的孩子就抽煙,喝酒未免太不像話了.

    例 (2): 這麼小的房間要那麼多房錢,未免太貴了.

    例 (3): 你未免太天真 (naïve) 了,你以為他那麼容易就會上你的當嗎?

3. A 和 (跟) B 相提並論 — A and B are mentioned (discussed) together

- 我們的周秦時代當然可以和希臘羅馬相提並論.

    例 (1): 有人把蘇格拉底 (Socrates) 跟孔子相提並論.

    例 (2): 他是生意人,我是讀書人,你怎麼能把我們兩個人相提並論?

討論

1. 就胡適的看法而論,模倣與創造有什麼相互[1]的關係?
2. 一般[2]中國人對日本的看法如何?胡適的看法又如何?
3. 在胡適眼裏,所謂中國的"固有文化"是什麼?
4. 胡適把"五世同居的大家庭"與太監,小腳等不人道的制度並提,為什麼?
5. 討論"中國不亡是無天理"這句話.
6. 胡適所說的"信心"是什麼?

[1] 相互　　　xiānghù　　　mutual, reciprocal
[2] 一般　　　yìbān　　　general, ordinary

再論信心與反省

在獨立第一〇三期，我寫了一篇信心與反省，指出我們對國家民族的信心不能建築在歌頌過去上，只可以建築在「反省」的唯一基礎之上。在那篇討論裏，我曾指出我們的固有文化是很貧乏的，決不能說是「太豐富了」的。我們的文化，比起歐洲一系的文化來，「我們所有的，人家也都有；我們所沒有的，人家所獨有的，人家都比我們強。至於我們所獨有的寶貝，駢文，律詩，八股，小腳，⋯⋯又都是使我們抬不起頭來的文物制度。」所以我們應該反省：認清了我們的祖宗和我們自己的罪孽深重，然後肯用全力去消災

Further Discussion on Confidence and Self-Examination

論	lùn	討論, to discuss
信心	xìnxīn	confidence, faith
與	yǔ	跟, 和
反省	fǎnxǐng	reflection, self-examination; to make a soul-searching self-examination
篇	piān	Numerary Adjunct for compositions, poems
指出	zhǐchū	to point out

A 對 B 的信心	A duì B de xìnxīn	the confidence or faith that A has in B
民族	mínzú	a people, an ethnic group
建築在 ... 上	jiànzhúzài ... shàng	to build on (the foundation of) ... 建築: to build, to construct; a building or structure
歌頌	gēsòng	to sing praises
過去	guòqu	the past; in the past, formerly; to go over
唯(惟)一	wéiyī	the only (one, kind, etc.), sole
基礎	jīchǔ	foundation (used either literally or figuratively)
曾	céng	once, ever; to have had the experience of, to have already
固有文化	gùyǒuwénhuà	the traditional culture (of a nation, a people) 固: solid, secure, sure, certain; 固有: inherent, intrinsic, innate
貧乏	pínfá	wanting, destitute, deficient, insufficient
決	jué	(when followed by a negative) definitely, certainly, under any circumstances
豐富	fēngfù	abundant, copious or plentiful, rich; to enrich
A 比起 B 來	A bǐqǐ B lái	A in comparison with B
認清	rènqīng	認識清楚
祖宗	zǔzōng	ancestors, forefathers, forebears
罪孽	zuìniè	sin
罪孽深重	zuìniè shēnzhòng	the sin is great
全力	quánlì	所有的力量
消	xiāo	to eliminate, to remove, to extinguish, to quench
災	zāi	disaster, calamity, catastrophe

滅罪；認清了自己百事不如人，然後肯死心塌地的去學人家的長處。

我知道這種論調在今日是很不合時宜的，是觸犯忌諱的，是至少要引起嚴厲的抗議的。可是我心裏要說的話，不能因為人不愛聽就不說了。正因為人不愛聽，所以我更覺得有不能不說的責任。

果然，那篇文章引起了一位讀者子固先生的悲憤，害他終夜不能睡眠，害他半夜起來寫他的抗議，直寫到天明。他的文章，「怎樣纔能建立起民族的信心」是一篇很誠懇的，很沉痛的反省。我很尊敬他的悲憤，所以我很願意討論他提出的論點，很誠懇的指出他那「一半不同」正是全部不同。

滅	miè	消滅, to extinguish, to exterminate, to wipe out, to put out
百事	bǎishì	所有的事,每一件事
死心塌地	sǐxīntādì	dead set, unreservedly, whole-heartedly
長處	chángchù	good qualities, strong points, advantages
論調	lùndiào	(often used in a derogatory sense) view, argumentation
今日	jīnrì	今天,現在
不合時宜	bùhéshíyí	not in keeping with the times, incompatible with present needs

觸犯	chùfàn	to violate or infringe regulations, law, to offend, to incur the displeasure of
忌諱	jìhuì	taboo; to avoid as taboo or harmful, to abstain from
至少	zhìshǎo	最少
引起	yǐnqǐ	to give rise to, to bring about, to cause, to trigger
嚴厲	yánlì	stern, severe
抗議	kàngyì	a protest, an objection; to protest, to object
讀者	dúzhě	the reader (as opposed to the writer)
子固	Zǐgù	人名
悲憤	bēifèn	grief and indignation
害	hài	to do harm to, to cause trouble to
終夜	zhōngyè	整個晚上 終: the end, to come to the end; whole, entire, all
睡眠	shuìmián	睡覺
直	zhí	一直, continuously, all along, all the way; (to go) straight ahead
天明	tiānmíng	天亮 (的時候)
纔	cái	才, only then, not until
建立	jiànlì	to establish, set up, build or found 建立起來: to succeed in establishing
誠懇	chéngkěn	sincere, true-hearted, cordial
沉(沈)痛	chéntòng	heavy or painful at heart
尊敬	zūnjìng	to respect
提出	tíchū	to put forward, advance, pose, or raise
論點	lùndiǎn	point of discussion, point at issue

子固先生的主要論點是：
「我們民族這七八十年以來，與歐美文化接觸，許多新奇的現象炫盲了我們的眼睛，在這炫盲當中，我們一方面沒出息地丟了我們固有的維繫並且引導我們向上的文化，另一方面我們又沒有能夠抓住外來文化之中那種能夠幫助我們民族更為強盛的一部份。結果我們走入迷途，墮落下去！

忠孝仁愛信義和平是維繫並且引導我們民族向上的固有文化，科學是外來文化中能夠幫助我們民族更為強盛的一部分。」

子固先生的論調，其實還是三四十年前的老輩的

以來	yǐlái	for (a given period of time), since (a given point of time in the past)
歐美	ŌuMěi	Europe and America — Western; the West
接觸	jiēchù	to come in contact with, to make contact with, (military) to encounter (the enemy), to contact
新奇	xīnqí	novel, new
現象	xiànxiàng	phenomenon
炫盲	xuànmáng	(often used in a figurative sense) to dazzle one's eyes and make them blind
在…當中	zài…dāngzhōng	在…裏(頭), in the midst of
一方面…另一方面…	yìfāngmiàn…lìng yìfāngmiàn…	on the one hand … on the other hand … 方面: aspect, respect, side, field

出息	chūxí	promise, prospects, future
維繫	wéixì	to bind together, to make secure, to keep, to maintain 維: to tie, to hold fast; 繫: to tie, to fasten
引導	yǐndǎo	to lead, to guide
向上	xiàngshàng	to strive forward, to try to improve oneself, (to move) upward; turned upward
能夠	nénggòu	能
抓住	zhuāzhù	to grasp, grip, clutch, hold, or keep from going away
外來	wàilái	從別的地方來(的)
...之中	... zhīzhōng	...的裏頭, in the midst of ... , within ...
強盛	qiángshèng	(of a nation, dynasty, etc.,) strong and prosperous
結果	jiéguǒ	in the end, finally, consequently, as a result; consequence, result, outcome; (of plants) to bear fruit
走入	zǒurù	走進
迷途	mítú	wrong path; to go astray, to get lost 迷: to bewitch, to confuse, to delude; 途: 路
墮落	duòluò	to sink in moral standard, to degenerate 落: to fall, sink, or indulge in evil ways
忠孝	zhōngxiào	loyalty and filial piety
仁愛	rénài	benevolence and love
信義	xìnyì	honesty and righteousness
和平	hépíng	harmony and peace
科學	kēxué	science
老輩	lǎobèi	older generation, one's seniors

論調。他們認得了富強的需要,所以不反對西方的科學工業;但他們心裏很堅決的相信一切倫紀道德是我們所固有而不須外求的。老輩之中,一位最偉大的孫中山先生,在他的通俗講演裏,也不免要敷衍一般誇大狂的中國人,說:「中國先前的忠孝仁愛信義種種的舊道德」都是「駕乎外國人」之上。中山先生這種議論在今日往往被一般人利用來做復古運動的典故,所以有些人就說「中國本來是一個由美德築成的黃金世界」了!

認得	rènde	認識
富強	fùqiáng	(of a nation) rich and strong
西方	Xīfāng	the West
工業	gōngyè	industry
但	dàn	但是,可是
堅決	jiānjué	firm, determined, resolute
相信	xiāngxìn	to believe
一切	yíqiè	所有的
倫紀	lúnjì	rules or regulations which govern relationships among people 倫: normal relationships among people; 紀: institutions, laws and regulations; to arrange, to put in order
道德	dàodé	morality, moral, ethics
外求	wàiqiú	to seek from outside
偉大	wěidà	great, lofty
孫中山	Sūn Zhōngshān	or Sun Yat-sen 孫逸仙, or Sun Wen 孫文 (1867-1925),

		founder of the Republic of China
通俗	tōngsú	capable of being understood or appreciated by the less well-educated; popular, common
講演	jiǎngyǎn	lecture, speech; to give a lecture, to deliver a speech; (also 演講)
不免	bùmiǎn	cannot avoid, have to, must; unavoidable, invariably
敷衍	fūyǎn	to act in a perfunctory manner, to deal insincerely with another person
一般	yìbān	common, general; commonly, generally, as a rule
誇大狂	kuādàkuáng	megalomania; megalomaniac 誇大: to exaggerate; exaggeration; 狂: crazy, mad, mentally deranged
先前	xiānqián	以前, 從前
A 駕乎 B 之上	A jiàhū B zhīshàng	A excels over B, A surpasses B 駕: to ride, to drive, to control, to excel, to surpass
議論	yìlùn	argument, comment, discussion; to discuss
一般人	yìbānrén	ordinary people, people in general
復古運動	fùgǔ yùndòng	the movement of "back to the ancients" 復古: to restore ancient ways, to return to the ancients; 運動: a social movement, a campaign, a drive
典故	diǎngù	an allusion (to history, the classics), origin (of a proverb or aphorism)
黃金	huángjīn	gold

(這是民國十八年葉楚傖先生的名言：)

　　子固先生也特別提出孫中山先生的偉大，特別頌揚他能「在當時一班知識階級盲目崇拜歐美文化的狂流中，巍然不動地指示我們救國必須恢復我們固有文化，同時學習歐美科學。」但他如果留心細讀中山先生的講演，就可以看出他當時說那話時是很費力的，很不容易自圓其說的。例如講「修身」，中山先生很明白的說：但是從修身一方面來看，我們中國人對於這些功夫是很

民國	Mínguó	i.e. 中華民國, Republic of China
葉楚傖	Yè Chǔcāng	人名
名言	míngyán	有名的話
頌揚	sòngyáng	to praise, to acclaim, to eulogize
當時	dāngshí	at that time, then, in those days
一班	yìbān	a small body of people (working together), a squad (of soldiers), a class (of students)
知識階級	zhīshijiējí	the intellectual class, intelligentsia 知識: knowledge, learning, information; 階級: a class (of people), a rank

盲目	mángmù	(fig.) blind, lacking insight or understanding, reckless, aimless
崇拜	chóngbài	to worship, to idolize
狂流	kuángliú	violent stream of water, violent or raging waves, violent disturbances
巍然不動	wēiránbúdòng	巍然: lofty, towering, majestic; 不動: "motionless" — immutable
指示	zhǐshì	to instruct, to show, to indicate; instruction 指: the finger; to point, to direct; 示: to show, to demonstrate, to indicate
恢復	huīfù	to restore, to regain, to recover
留心	liúxīn	to pay attention, to take heed, to be careful, to exercise caution
細讀	xìdú	to read carefully
看出	kànchū	to make out, to see, to perceive
費力	fèilì	to expend significant effort, to put in a lot of work
自圓其說	zìyuánqíshuō	to make one's statement consistent, to make one's story sound plausible, to explain oneself away
例如	lìrú	for example, for instance
修身	xiūshēn	to cultivate oneself, to practice moral culture
從 A 一方面來看	cóng A yìfāngmiàn láikàn	to view or consider from the perspective of A
功夫	gōngfū	effort (devoted to a task), time (to do something)

缺乏的。中國人一舉一動都欠檢點,只要和中國人來往過一次,便看得很清楚。〔三民主義六〕

他還對我們說:

所以今天講到修身,諸位新青年,便應該學外國人的新文化。〔三民主義六〕

可是他一會兒又回過去頌揚固有的舊道德了。本來有保守性的讀者只記得中山先生頌揚舊道德的話,卻不曾細想他所頌揚的舊道德都只是幾個人類共有的理想,並不是我們這個民族實行最力的道德。例如他說的「忠孝仁愛信義和平」,那一件不是東西哲人共同提倡的理想?除了割股治病

缺乏	quēfá	to lack, to be short of, to be deficient in
一舉一動	yìjǔyídòng	every movement and action, behavior 舉: to lift, to raise
欠	qiàn	deficient, lacking
檢點	jiǎndiǎn	to be cautious (about what one says or does), to behave with circumspection 檢: to inspect, to examine; 點: to check one by one
只要 ... 便 ...	zhǐyào ... biàn ...	as long as ... then ...
A 和 B 來往	A hé B láiwǎng	A has contacts or dealings with B 來往: come and go, coming and going — dealings, contact, intercourse

三民主義	Sānmínzhǔyì	*The Three Principles of the People* — Nationalism (民族), Democracy (民權) and Livelihood (民生) — formulated by Dr. Sun Yat-sen, founding father of the Republic of China
諸位	zhūwèi	(an honorific) all of you; "Ladies and Gentlemen" 諸: all, various
保守性	bǎoshǒuxìng	保守: conservative; 性: nature, natural property, disposition, temper
細想	xìxiǎng	to think over or consider carefully, to give careful thought to, to ponder
人類	rénlèi	mankind, the human race
共有	gòngyǒu	to possess in common, to be possessed by all
理想	lǐxiǎng	ideal, dream
實行	shíxíng	to carry out (a principle), to put into practice
東西	DōngXī	the East and the West
哲人	zhérén	wise men, sagacious men
共同	gòngtóng	shared by all, common; to co-operate in (an undertaking, etc.)
提倡	tíchàng	to promote (a cause, etc.)
割股	gēgǔ	to cut a slice of flesh from one's own thigh (and mix it with medicine to cure the illness of one's parent) — the epitome of filial devotion 割: to cut, to sever, to divide; 股: the thigh, the haunches, the hips
治病	zhìbìng	to treat a disease or ailment

，臥冰求鯉，一類不近人情的行動之外，那一件不是世界文明人類公有的理想？孫中山先生也曾說過：

照這樣實行一方面講起來，仁愛的好道德，中國人現在似乎遠不如外國。……但是仁愛還是中國的舊道德。我們要學外國，只要學他們那樣實行，把仁愛恢復起來，再去發揚光大，便是中國固有的精神。（同上書）

在這短短一段話裏，我們可以看出中山先生未嘗不明白在仁愛的「實行」上，我們實在遠不如人。所謂「仁愛還是中國的舊道德」者，只是那個道德的名稱罷了。中山先生很明白的教人：修身應該學外國人的新文化，仁愛也「要學外國」。但這些話中的話都是一般人不注意的。

在這些方面，吳稚暉先生比孫中山先生澈底多了。吳先生在他的一個新信仰的宇宙觀及人生

臥冰	wòbīng	to lie on ice (in order to melt it and catch fish to feed one's parent) — the epitome of filial devotion
鯉	lǐ	carp
一類	yílèi	of the same class, category, or species 類: a species, kind, class, race or group
不近人情	bùjìnrénqíng	not amenable to reason, disre-

		garding others' feelings
行動	xíngdòng	conduct, movement, acts, behavior; to act, to move
文明	wénmíng	civilization; civilized
公有	gōngyǒu	to be publicly owned
似乎	sìhū	好像
恢復	huīfù	to restore, to regain, to recover
發揚光大	fāyángguāngdà	to enhance and glorify
同上書	tóngshàngshū	same as the book (mentioned) above
未嘗	wèicháng	(used before a negative expression to form a positive statement) not necessarily
在...上	zài ... (abstract noun) shàng	as far as ... is concerned
所謂	suǒwèi	what is called, so-called
者	zhě	a particle indicating that a certain explanation is expected; used after an adjective, a verb or a verbal phrase, with which it forms a noun phrase to indicate or substitute for a certain person, place, or thing
名稱	míngchēng	name or designation (of a thing)
罷了	bàle	(as sentence-final phrase) merely, only, that's all; that's enough, let's have no more of it, be done with it
吳稚暉	Wú Zhìhuī	人名
澈底	chèdǐ	thorough, complete, thoroughgoing 澈: clear water
信仰	xìnyǎng	(religious or political) belief; to believe in
宇宙	yǔzhòu	the universe
觀	guān	看法
人生	rénshēng	human life, life

觀裏，很大膽的説中國民族的「總和道德是低淺的；」同時他又指出西洋民族什麼仁義道德，孝弟忠信，吃飯睡覺，無一不較上三族（亞剌伯，印度，中國）的人較有作法，較有熱心。⋯⋯講他們的總和道德叫做高明。

這是很公允的評判。忠孝信義仁愛和平，都是有文化的民族共有的理想；在文字理論上，猶太人，印度人，亞剌伯人，希臘人，以至近世各文明民族，都講的頭頭是道。所不同者，全在吳先生説的「有作法，有熱心」兩點。若沒有切實的辦法，沒有眞摯的熱心，雖然有整千萬冊的理學書，終無救於道德的低淺。宋明的理學聖賢，談性談心，談居敬，談致良知，終因爲沒有作法，只

大膽	dàdǎn	bold, daring, audacious 膽: the gall — courage, bravery, audacity
總和	zǒnghé	sum total, grand total, total 總: to gather, to collect, to assemble; all, total, complete; 和: sum or aggregate
低淺	dīqiǎn	low and superficial
西洋	Xīyáng	the West
孝弟	xiàotì	孝: of or having to do with filial piety or devotion; 弟: 悌, to show brotherly love (note pronunciation)
無一	wúyī	沒有一個
A不較B	A bújiào (bùjiào) B	A 不如 B, A is not as ... as B

三族	sānzú	三個民族
亞剌伯	Yǎlàbó	Arab
印度	Yìndù	India
作法	zuòfǎ	作事的法子
叫做	jiàozuò	叫
高明	gāomíng	clever, wise, superior
公允	gōngyǔn	fair and proper
評判	píngpàn	criticism and judgement, comment
文字	wénzì	written language
理論	lǐlùn	theory
猶太	Yútài	Jews or Hebrews; Jewish
希臘	Xīlà	Greece; Greek
以至	yǐzhì	down to, up to, to the point of
近世	jìnshì	the present era, modern times
各	gè	each, every
頭頭是道	tóutóushìdào	clear and logical, closely reasoned and well argued
在	zài	to lie in
點	diǎn	a point (of discussion)
若	ruò	要是, 如果
切實	qièshí	feasible, practical, realistic
真摯	zhēnzhì	sincere, faithful, true
整	zhěng	whole, complete, entire
冊	cè	volume, book
理學	lǐxué	a school of learning in the Song Dynasty (960-1279) devoted to the study of the classics with a rational approach
終	zhōng	finally, at last, in the end, after all, in the long run
A無救於B	A wújiùyú B	A cannot be of help to B
宋	Sòng	the Song Dynasty (960-1279)
明	Míng	the Ming Dynasty (1368-1644)
聖賢	shèngxián	sages and virtuous men
性	xìng	nature, character, disposition
居敬	jūjìng	to be respectful
致良知	zhì liángzhī	to bring about (result in, occasion) an innate knowledge

能走上「終日端坐，如泥塑人」的死路上去。

　　我所以要特別提出子固先生的論點，只因為他的悲憤是可敬的，而他的解決方案還是無補於他的悲憤。他的方案，一面學科學，一面恢復我們固有的文化，還只是張之洞一輩人說的「中學為體，西學為用」的方案。老實說，這條路是走不通的。如果過去的文化是值得恢復的，我們今天不至糟到這步田地了。況且沒有那科學工業的現代文化基礎，是無法發揚什麼文化的「偉大精神」的。忠孝仁愛信義和平是永遠存在書本子裏的；但是因為我們的祖宗只會把這些好聽的名詞

終日	zhōngrì	整天，一天到晚
端坐	duānzuò	to sit straight, to sit properly 端: correct, proper, upright, righteous
如	rú	像，好像
泥塑人	nísùrén	a clay statue — a person without motion of any kind, as wooden as a dummy
所以 A ... 　因為 B	suǒyǐ A ... yīnwèi B	因為 B, 所以 A
可敬	kějìng	worthy of respect 可: 值得 (see below); 敬: to respect

解決方案	jiějué fāng'àn	a plan or program designed to resolve a problem
A無補於B	A wúbǔyú B	A is of no avail or use to B 補: to repair, to patch, to mend, to make up, to help
一面A... 一面B	yīmiàn A ... yīmiàn B	on the one hand A, on the other hand B
張之洞	Zhāng Zhīdòng	(1837-1909) noted for his advocacy of modernization of China during the late 19th century
輩	bèi	people of a certain kind, the like
中學為體,西學為用	Zhōngxuéwéitǐ, Xīxuéwéiyòng	Chinese learning as the substance (or as a base), Western learning for practical application.
老實	lǎoshí	honest, truthful, frank
值得	zhíde	to be worth it, be worthy of, or deserve
不至(於)	búzhì (yú)	cannot go so far as ... , be unlikely that ... 至於: to reach the extent of
糟	zāo	to become a mess, to be in bad shape
步	bù	Numerary Adjunct for condition, situation, or state
田地	tiándì	(always carrying a negative connotation) situation, plight
況且	kuàngqiě	moreover, besides, furthermore
基礎	jīchǔ	(used literally and figuratively) basis, foundation
無法	wúfǎ	沒有法子
永遠	yǒngyuǎn	forever, eternally, perpetually
存在	cúnzài	to exist, to be present
書本子	shūběnzi	書
名詞	míngcí	a term, a noun

都寫作八股文章,畫作太極圖,編作理學語錄,所以那些好聽的名詞都不能變成有作法有熱心的事實。西洋人跳出了經院時代之後,努力做征服自然的事業,征服了海洋,征服了大地,征服了空氣電氣,征服了不少的原質,征服了不少的微生物,——這都不是什麼「保存國粹」「發揚固有文化」的口號所能包括的工作,然而科學與工業發達的自然結果是提高了人民的生活,提高了人類的幸福,提高了各個參加國家的文化。結果就是吳稚暉先生說的「總和道德叫做高明」。

　　世間講「仁愛」的書,莫過於華嚴經的淨行

寫作	xiězuò	寫成
八股(文)	bāgǔ (wén)	the eight-legged essay (originally, a rigid style of literary writing during the era of the Imperial Examination; hence, a writing that reeks of pedantry or triteness)
畫作	huàzuò	畫成
太極圖	Tàijítú	diagram representing the *Yin* and *Yang* elements
編作	biānzuò	編成
		編: to compile, to edit

語錄	yǔlù	recorded utterance
事實	shìshí	fact, truth, reality
經院時代	jīngyuàn shídài	"Period of Scholasticism," here referring to the European Middle Ages
征服	zhēngfú	conquer; conquest
事業	shìyè	enterprise, undertaking, career, pursuit
電氣	diànqì	electric
原質	yuánzhí	elements
微生物	wēishēngwù	microbes, micro-organism 微:小; 物:東西
保存	bǎocún	to maintain, to preserve
國粹	guócuì	unique cultural features of a nation, national essence 粹: pure, unadulterated; essence, the best
口號	kǒuhào	slogan, watchword
包括	bāokuò (bāoguā)	to include, to comprise
然而	ránér	但是, 可是
發達	fādá	developed, flourishing
提高	tígāo	to raise (prices, living standards, etc.), to lift (morale, etc.), to heighten (vigilance, etc.), to elevate
人民	rénmín	the people (as opposed to the ruler or the government)
幸福	xìngfú	happiness and well-being, bliss; happy and blissful
參加	cānjiā	to participate in, to join
世間	shìjiān	世界上
莫過(於)	mòguò (yú)	nothing (no one) is more ... than ...
華嚴經	*Huáyánjīng*	the Avatamsaka Sutra (a Buddhist scripture)

品,那一篇妙文教人時時刻刻不可忘了人類的痛苦與缺陷,甚至於大便小便時都要發願不忘眾生:

左右便利,當願眾生,蠲除污穢,無淫怒癡。
已而就水,當願眾生,向無上道,得出世法。
以水滌穢,當願眾生,具足淨忍,畢竟無垢。
以水盥掌,當願眾生,得上妙手,受持佛法。……

但是一個和尚的弘願,究竟能做到多少實際的「仁愛?」回頭看看那一心想征服自然的科學救世者

妙文	miàowén	excellent article, a masterpiece
時時刻刻	shíshíkèkè	每一時,每一刻;每一個時候
痛苦	tòngkǔ	suffering, pain, anguish, agony; painful
缺陷	quēxiàn	flaw, shortcoming, defect
甚至於	shènzhìyú	even, even to the extent that, to go as far as
大便	dàbiàn	to have a bowel movement, to empty the bowels; human excrement
小便	xiǎobiàn	to empty one's bladder, to urinate; urine
發願	fāyuàn	to vow to achieve an objective
眾生	zhòngshēng	(in Buddhism) all living creatures
便利	biànlì	大小便
當	dāng	應當
願	yuàn	希望
蠲除	juānchú	去除
污穢	wūhuì	filth, gross moral corruption
無	wú	沒有

淫	yín	licentious, lewd, lascivious, dissolute; things related to improper sexual desire and behavior
怒	nù	angry, furious; anger, rage, fury
癡	chī	idiotic, silly, foolish, stupid, senseless, crazy, insane
已而	yǐér	然後,後來,過了一會兒
就水	jiùshuǐ	to approach water
無上道	wúshàngdào	(Buddhism) 最高的教義
出世法	chūshìfǎ	(Buddhism) the way or method of achieving nirvana
以	yǐ	用
滌	dí	洗
具足	jùzú	to possess, to be provided with
畢竟	bìjìng	eventually, in the end
垢	gòu	dirt, filth, stains
盥掌	guànzhǎng	洗手掌, to wash palms (of the hands)
受持	shòuchí	to receive and keep or maintain forever
佛法	fófǎ	Buddha dharma, the Buddhist doctrines, the power of Buddha
和尚	héshàng	a Buddhist monk
弘願	hóngyuàn	偉大的願望
究竟	jiūjìng	到底, after all, in the end, finally, at last
做到	zuòdào	to succeed in doing (something), to complete (a job)
實際	shíjì	real, actual, concrete, practical, realistic; reality, actual situation
回頭	huítóu	to go back, return, turn the head around, or turn back after a short while
一心	yìxīn	of one heart — wholeheartedly
救世者	jiùshìzhě	救世界(上的人)的人

，他們發現了一種病菌，製成了一種血清，可以救活無量數的人類，其為「仁愛」豈不是千萬倍的偉大？

以上的討論，好像全不曾顧到「民族的信心」的一個原來問題。這是因為子固先生的來論，剔除了一些動了感情的話，實在只說了一個「中學為體，西學為用」的老方案，所以我要指出這個方案的「一半」是行不通的：忠孝仁愛信義和平等等並不是「維繫並且引導我們民族向上的固有文化」，他們不過是人類共有的幾個理想，如果沒有作法，沒有熱力，只是一些空名詞而已。這些好名詞的存在並不曾挽救或阻止「八股，小腳，太監姨太太，貞節牌坊，地獄的監牢，夾棍板子的法庭」的存在。這些八股，小腳，……等

病菌	bìngjùn	germ, bacteria, virus
製成	zhìchéng	作成, to have produced or manufactured (something)
血清	xiěqīng	serum
救活	jiùhuó	to bring (someone) back to life
無量數	wúliàngshù	countless, immeasurable, innumerable
		量: quantity, capacity;
		數: number
其	qí	a particle corresponding to "noun or pronoun + 的" (its antecedent can be a person, a thing, or an event)
豈	qǐ	interrogative particle implying a

		conflicting or dissenting view or response — how, what
倍	bèi	(joined to a numeral) times, -fold
以上	yǐshàng	above (a point or line)
顧到	gùdào	to care about, to take something into consideration, to be in consideration of
		顧: to mind, to care for, to concern oneself about
原來	yuánlái	original, former; originally, as it turns out
來論	láilùn	incoming discussion or argument
剝除	bōchú	剝: to strip, peel, or make bare;
		除: to remove, to rid of, to eliminate
動感情	dònggǎnqíng	to be carried away by emotion
		動: to move, to stir, to arouse, to touch (one's heart);
		感情: feeling, emotion, devotion or affection (between friends, relatives)
行不通	xíngbùtōng	blocked, unable to go through — not feasible, impractical, won't do; to get nowhere
熱力	rèlì	heat energy, heating power, thermal energy — fervor, enthusiasm
空	kōng	(used in a literal or figurative sense) empty, hollow
而已	éryǐ	(as sentence-final phrase) 罷了, merely, only, that's all
挽救	wǎnjiù	to save, to remedy, to rescue
		挽: to draw, to pull — to restore
阻止	zǔzhǐ	to stop or prevent, to prohibit or proscribe

等「固有文化」的崩潰,也全不是程顥,朱熹,顧亭林,戴東原……等等聖賢的功績,乃是「與歐美文化接觸」之後,那科學工業造成的新文化叫我們相形之下太難堪了,這些東方文明的罪孽方纔逐漸崩潰的。我要指出:我們民族這七八十年來與歐美文化接觸的結果,雖然還不曾學到那個整個的科學工業的文明,(可憐丁文江,翁文灝,顏任光諸位先生都還是四十多歲的少年,他們的工作剛開始哩!)究竟已替我們的祖宗消除了無數的罪孽,打倒了「小腳,八股,太監,五世同居的大家庭,貞節牌坊,地獄活現的監獄,夾棍板子的法庭」的一大部分或一小部分。這都是我們的「數不清的聖賢天才」從來不曾指摘譏彈的;這都是「忠

崩潰	bēngkuì	to collapse, to disintegrate, to fall into pieces, to break down; a collapse, a breakdown
程顥	Chéng Hào	(1032-1085) a great Confucian scholar of the Song Dynasty
朱熹	Zhū Xī	(1130-1200) a Confucian scholar of the Song Dynasty, known for his commentary on the Confucian classics which was considered the standard exposition through the Qing Dynasty
顧亭林	Gù Tínglín	i.e. Gu Yanwu 顧炎武 (1613-1682), a great scholar of the Ming Dynasty
戴東原	Dài Dōngyuán	i.e. Dai Zhen 戴震 (1723-1777), a great scholar of the Qing Dynasty

功績	gōngjī	meritorious record, meritorious deeds, achievements
不是...乃是	búshì...nǎishì	is not ... but (rather) is ...
相形之下	xiāngxíngzhīxià	by comparison, in contrast, when compared 相: each other, one another, mutually, reciprocal; 形: to compare, to contrast
難堪	nánkān	hard to stand or bear — embarrassed, intolerable, unbearable
方纔	fāngcái	才, only then, not ... until ...
逐漸	zhújiàn	漸漸, little by little, gradually, by degrees
學到	xuédào	to succeed in learning, to learn as far as
可憐	kělián	it is a pity that ... ; pitiable, pitiful, poor; to have pity on, to pity
丁文江	Dīng Wénjiāng	人名
翁文灝	Wēng Wénhào	人名
顏任光	Yán Rènguāng	人名
打倒	dǎdǎo	to knock down, to overthrow; (in slogans) "Down with ..."
數不清	shǔbuqīng	unable to count, too many to count, innumerable, countless 數: to count
天才	tiāncái	a genius; talent, (intellectual or artistic) endowment
從來	cónglái	heretofore, in the past (usually co-occurs with a negative verb)
指摘	zhǐzhāi (zhǐzhé)	to point out faults of others and to criticize, to blame, to censure 指: to point at, to point to; 摘: to pick, to pluck, to unveil
譏彈	jītán	to ridicule and impeach 譏: to ridicule, to mock, to satirize, to sneer; 彈: to impeach, to put down

孝仁愛信義和平」的固有文化從來不曾「引導向上」的。這些祖宗罪孽的崩潰,固然大部分是歐美文明的恩賜,同時也可以表示我們在這七八十年中至少也還做到了這些消極的進步。子固先生說我們在這七八十年中「走入迷途,墮落下去,」這真是無稽的誣告!中國民族在這七八十年中何嘗「墮落」?在幾十年之中,廢除了三千年的太監,一千年的小腳,六百年的八股,五千年的酷刑,這是「向上」,不是墮落!

不過我們的「向上」還不夠,努力還不夠。八股廢止至今不過三十年,八股的訓練還存在大多數老而不死的人的心靈裏,還間接直接的傳授到我們的無數的青年人的腦筋裏。今日還是一個大家做八股的中國,雖然題目換了。小腳逐漸絕

固然	gùrán	indeed, no doubt, it is true (used in a statement to acknowledge the existence, truth, or fact of something)
恩賜	ēncì	a favor or gift of grace (from Heaven, an emperor); to bestow (favors, charity) 恩: favor, grace, charity, mercy, benevolence; 賜: favor, gift; to grant or

		bestow
表示	biǎoshì	to express, to show, to indicate; expression, reaction
至少	zhìshǎo	最少
消極	xiāojí	negative, passive, inactive
進步	jìnbù	progress, improvement; to progress, to improve
無稽	wújī	groundless, unfounded, wild (talk, rumors, etc.) 稽: to investigate, to examine, to inspect
誣告	wūgào	a false charge; to bring a false charge, to accuse falsely
何嘗	hécháng	"how could it have been the case?" (used in rhetorical question, meaning "have not," "did not," "never," etc.)
廢除	fèichú	to abolish, to cancel, to annul, to abrogate, to rescind, to discontinue
酷刑	kùxíng	cruel punishment — torture 酷: cruel, relentless, ruthless, brutal; 刑: punishment, penalty
廢止	fèizhǐ	廢除停止, to abolish and terminate
至今	zhìjīn	到現在
訓練	xùnliàn	training; to train
心靈	xīnlíng	mind, spirit
間接	jiànjiē	indirectly; indirect
直接	zhíjiē	directly; direct
傳授	chuánshòu	to pass on (knowledge, skill, etc.), to teach, to impart 傳: to pass on (to); 授: to give or hand over (to)
腦筋	nǎojīn	腦子, brains, mental capacity
換	huàn	to change

跡了，夾棍板子，砍頭碎剮廢止了，但裹小腳的殘酷心理，上夾棍打屁股的野蠻心理，都還存在無數老少人們的心靈裏，今日還是一個殘忍野蠻的中國，所以始終還不曾走上法治的路，更談不到仁愛和平了。

　　所以我十分誠摯的對全國人說：我們今日還要反省，還要閉門思過，還要認清祖宗和我們自己的罪孽深重，決不是這樣淺薄的「與歐美文化接觸」就可以脫胎換骨的。我們要認清那個容忍擁戴「小腳，八股，太監，姨太太，駢文，律詩，五世同居的大家庭，貞節牌坊，地獄的監牢，夾棍板子的法庭」到幾千幾百年之久的固有文化，是不足迷戀的，是不能引我們向上的。那裏面

絕跡 (迹)	juéjī	to vanish completely, to be completely wiped out, to be extinct
砍頭	kǎntóu	to behead, to decapitate 砍: to chop, to cut, to hack, to fell (trees, etc.)
碎剮	suìguā	to cut to pieces (a form of capital punishment in ancient times)
裹	guǒ	to wrap or bind
殘酷	cánkù	cruel, brutal, ruthless
心理	xīnlǐ	mentality, psychology, thought and ideas
上	shàng	to put on, to fasten onto
屁股	pìgǔ	the buttocks
野蠻	yěmán	barbarous, savage, uncivilized, unreasonable, brutal, rude

殘忍	cánrěn	殘酷
始終	shǐzhōng	從開始到最後, from beginning to end — throughout
法治	fǎzhì	to rule by law 法: law, regulations; 治: to rule, to govern, to administer
談不到	tánbúdào	談不上, cannot (begin to) talk about — out of the question
十分	shífēn	very, fully, utterly, extremely, one hundred percent
誠摯	chéngzhì	sincere, true-hearted, cordial
閉門思過	bìménsīguò	to close the door and ponder on one's faults or misdeeds — to reflect on one's faults or misdeeds in private 閉: 關; 思: 想; 過: 錯
淺薄	qiǎnbó	shallow and thin — shallow, superficial
脫胎換骨	tuōtāihuàngǔ	to be reborn, to cast off one's old self, to remold oneself thoroughly 脫: to take off, to cast off; 胎: fetus, embryo
容忍	róngrěn	to tolerate, to put up with
擁戴	yōngdài	to support (somebody as a leader)
到...之久	dào ... zhījiǔ	到(or 有)...那麼久
不足	bùzú	不值得, not to deserve, not to be worthy of
迷戀	míliàn	to be blindly in love with, to be infatuated with 迷: to bewitch, to enchant, to confuse; enchanted, spellbound, deluded, charmed

浮沉着的幾個聖賢豪傑,其中當然有值得我們崇敬的人,但那幾十顆星兒終究照不亮那滿天的黑暗。我們的光榮的文化不在過去,是在將來,是在那掃清了祖宗的罪孽之後重新改造出來的文化。替祖國消除罪孽,替子孫建立文明,這是我們人人的責任。古代哲人曾參說的最好:「士不可以不弘毅:任重而道遠。」先明白了「任重而道遠」的艱難,自然不輕易灰心失望了。凡是輕易灰心失望的人,都只是不曾認清他挑的是一個百斤的重擔,走的是一條萬里的長路。今天挑不動

浮沉 (沈)	fúchén	to rise and fall 浮: to float, to waft; 沉: to sink, to submerge
其中	qízhōng	among those (persons, things, etc.)
崇敬	chóngjìng	to honor, revere, or regard with esteem
顆	kē	Numerary Adjunct (for stars, bombs, bullets, etc.)
星	xīng	stars, any heavenly body that shines
終究	zhōngjiù	finally, after all, in the end, in the long run
照不亮	zhàobúliàng	cannot light up or illuminate 照: to shine upon, to light, to illuminate
滿天	mǎntiān	to have the sky filled (with)
黑暗	hēiàn	darkness, dark (usually used figuratively)
光榮	guāngróng	glorious; glory, honor

掃清	sǎoqīng	to sweep clean — to wipe out, to mop up, to exterminate
重新	chóngxīn	anew, afresh
改造	gǎizào	to remold, rebuild, convert, or reconstruct
		改: to change, correct, alter, or transform;
		造: 作
祖國	zǔguó	motherland, one's native country
子孫	zǐsūn	descendants, posterity
古代	gǔdài	古時候
士	shì	讀書人, 知識份子
弘毅	hóngyì	having a broad and resolute mind
		弘: great, magnanimous, capacious;
		毅: firm, resolute, determined
任	rèn	責任, duty, responsibility
重	zhòng	heavy, weighty
道	dào	路, 道路
艱難	jiānnán	difficulty, hardship
輕易	qīngyì	easily, lightly, rashly
灰心	huīxīn	disappointed, discouraged, disheartened
失望	shīwàng	disappointed
凡是…都	fánshì … dōu …	all …
挑	tiāo	to carry things with a pole on one's shoulder, to shoulder, to pick, to select, to choose
斤	jīn	a Chinese unit of weight (half a kilogram)
擔	dàn	a load or burden upon the shoulder
里	lǐ	a Chinese unit of distance (half a kilometer or about one third of a mile)
挑不動	tiāobúdòng	to be too heavy to carry

，努力磨鍊了總有挑得起的一天。今天走不完，走得一里前途就縮短了一里。「播了種一定會有收穫，用了力決不至於白費，」這是我們最可靠的信心。

二十三，六，十一夜。

磨鍊	mólìan	to put oneself through the mill, to temper, steel, strain, harden or discipline oneself
		磨: a mill; to rub, to grind;
		鍊: to refine, forge, or temper
前途	qiántú	前面的路; (usually used figuratively) the future, the prospect
縮短	suōduǎn	to shorten, to cut down, to curtail
		縮: to contract, to shrink
可靠	kěkào	reliable
		靠: to lean on, to depend on, to rely on

句型

1. A 比起 B 來 … — A compared with B …

- 我們的文化比起歐洲一系的文化來 …

    例 (1): 我的中文水平比起你的來簡直差多了.

    例 (2): 坐飛機比起坐火車來不但快而且舒服.

2. 只要 … 便 (or 就) … — As long as (provided) … then …

- 中國人一舉一動都欠檢點,只要和中國人來往過一次,便看得很清楚.

    例 (1): 只要有信心便能成功.

    例 (2): 東西貴不貴不要緊,只要你喜歡就買吧.

3. 未嘗不 (or 沒) V — (used before another negative expression to form a positive statement)

- 我們可以看出中山先生未嘗不明白在仁愛的「實行」上我們實在遠不如人.

    例 (1): "你抽煙抽那麼多,難道你不知道抽煙對身體不好嗎?" "我未嘗不知道抽煙對身體不好,但是我已經習慣了,不抽不行."
    (…"我何嘗不知道抽煙 …"
    …"我怎麼不知道抽煙 …"
    …"我哪裡不知道抽煙 …")

    例 (2): "放假了.你怎麼不去旅行呢?" "我未嘗不想去,可是我還有很多功課得做."

4. 若(要是)沒有 … 雖然有 … 還是無法(沒有法子) …

- 若沒有切實的辦法,沒有真摯的熱心,雖然有整千萬冊的理學書,終無救於道德的低淺.

    例: 若沒有良好的技術¹配合,²雖然有最進步的機器,³還是無法使國家現代化.

(...就算有最進步的機器,如果沒有良好的技術還是無法使國家現代化.)

[1] 技術	jìshù	technology
[2] 配合	pèihé	coordinate with
[3] 機器	jīqì	machine

5. ...莫過於... — nothing is more than ...

■ 世間講「仁愛」的書,<u>莫過於</u>華嚴經的淨行品.

例 (1): 人生最快樂的事<u>莫過於</u>和所愛的人在一起.
(和所愛的人在一起是人生最快樂的事.
人生再也沒有比和所愛的人在一起更快樂的事了.)

例 (2): 人生最痛苦的事<u>莫過於</u>和所愛的人分離.

6. 何嘗 V 過 — How could it have been the case?

■ 中國民族在這七,八十年中<u>何嘗</u>「墮落」(<u>過</u>)?

例 (1): 過去幾十年來,中國<u>何嘗</u>有<u>過</u>真的民主.

例 (2): 你生病的時候我為了照顧[1]你,<u>何嘗</u>好好睡<u>過</u>覺,吃<u>過</u>飯.

| [1] 照顧 | zhàogù | take care of |

7. 總有...的一天 — there will eventually be a day when ...

■ 今天挑不動,努力磨鍊了,<u>總有</u>挑得起<u>的一天</u>.

例 (1): 你做壞事<u>總有</u>被人發現<u>的一天</u>.
(你做壞事遲早會被人發現.
你做壞事早晚會被人發現.)

例 (2): 要是你努力,<u>總有</u>成功<u>的一天</u>.

討論

1. 就這篇文章所論,孫中山對中國固有文化的看法是什麼?
2. 討論什麼是"忠孝仁愛信義和平."這些德行[1]是中國人所獨有,還是其他文明所共有?
3. 什麼是"中學為體,西學為用?"胡適對這個方案[2]有什麼意見?
4. 胡適認為[3]中西文化接觸以後,對中國文化有什麼影響?
5. 胡適用"殘忍野蠻"來形容[4]中國,以你個人的經驗[5]就這一點發表[6]意見.

[1] 德行	déxing	moral conduct
[2] 方案	fāngàn	scheme, plan, programme
[3] 認為	rènwéi	think, consider
[4] 形容	xíngróng	describe
[5] 經驗	jīngyàn	experience
[6] 發表	fābiǎo	express

Problems and -Isms
問題與主義

Selection Five presents Hu Shi's views regarding the overall problems of China and how they relate to the various solutions (or "-isms") which were then being hotly debated in China. Hu, with his usual realism and practicality, felt that China's problems were so complicated and varied that no single solution would work. He put little faith in "-isms" such as socialism, then quite in vogue in China. He would rather that China tackle its problems one by one and urged the intellectuals to "study problems more and talk less of -isms." As usual, his views sparked intense conflict and debate. Later, in the fifties, his views again came under attack, this time by the Communist Party.

Originally entitled "Study More Problems, Talk Less of -Isms" (Duō yánjiū xiē wèntí, shǎo tán xiē zhǔyì 多研究些問題, 少談些主義), this essay was first published in *Weekly Critic*, 31 (July 20, 1919). It was later included in *Collected Essays of Hu Shi*, I, 342-46.

問題與主義

多研究些問題，少談些「主義」！

本報（每週評論）第二十八號裏，我曾說過：「現在輿論界大危險，就是偏向紙上的學說，不去實地考察中國今日的社會需要究竟是什麼東西。那些提倡尊孔祀天的人，固然是不懂得現時社會的需要。那些迷信軍國民主義或無政府主義的人，就可算是懂得現時社會的需要麼？」「要知道輿論家的第一天職，就是細心考察社會的實在情形。一切學理，一切『主義』，都是這種考察的工具。有了學理作參考材料，便可使我們容易懂得所考察的情形，容易明白某種情形有什麼意義

Problems and -Isms

主義	zhǔyì	doctrine, -ism
研究	yánjiū	to study and research
本	běn	our, this, present, current
每週評論	Měizhōu pínglùn	name of a magazine
輿論界	yúlùnjiè	the media, press circles 輿論: public opinion; 界: circles

偏向	piānxiàng	to lean or be inclined toward
學說	xuéshuō	theory
實地	shídì	on the spot
考察	kǎochá	to investigate, examine, or inspect; investigation, inspection
究竟	jiūjìng	到底, after all, in the end, finally
提倡	tíchàng	to promote (a cause, etc.)
尊孔祀天	zūnKǒng sìtiān	to respect Confucius and worship (or offer sacrifices to) Heaven
固然	gùrán	no doubt, it is true, indeed, admittedly
迷信	míxìn	to believe blindly, to have blind faith in; superstition, blind worship
無政府主義	wúzhèngfǔzhǔyì	anarchism
算是	suànshì	to be counted, considered, or regarded as
天職	tiānzhí	a duty from heaven, a bounden duty
細心	xìxīn	with care; careful, cautious
一切	yíqiè	所有的
學理	xuélǐ	a (scientific) theory
工具	gōngjù	tools, implements, equipment
參考材料	cānkǎo cáiliào	reference material 參考: to consult, to refer to, to compare and examine; 材料: raw material, ingredients; material such as data, figures, or statistics; material for all building purposes
便	biàn	就
使	shǐ	(a causative verb) to make, to cause, to enable
某	mǒu	a certain person or thing
意義	yìyì	meaning, significance

，應該用什麼救濟的方法。」

　　我這種議論，有許多人一定不願意聽。但是前幾天北京公信報、新民國報、新民報，（皆安福部的報）和日本的新支那報，都極力恭維安福部首領王揖唐主張民生主義的演說，並且恭維安福部設立「民生主義的研究會」的辦法。有許多人自然嘲笑這種假充時髦的行為。但是我看了這種消息，發生一種感想。這種感想是：「安福部也來高談民生主義了，這不夠給我們這班新輿論家一個教訓嗎？」什麼教訓呢？這可分三層說：第一，空談好聽的「主義」，是極容易的事，是阿貓阿狗都能做的事，是鸚鵡和留聲機器都能做的事。

救濟	jiùjì	to save and aid, to relieve (the suffering, the poor, etc.)
議論	yìlùn	argument, discussion, comments; to comment or discuss
但是	dànshì	可是
公言報	Gōngyánbào	報紙名
新民國報	Xīnmínguóbào	報紙名
新民報	Xīnmínbào	報紙名
皆	jiē	(lit.) 都
極力	jílì	to make the utmost effort, to make every effort
恭維	gōngwéi	to pay compliments, to flatter
安福部	Ānfúbù	Anfu Clique, 當時的一個政治組織

新支那報	Xīn Zhīnà bào	*Shin Shina hô*, 報紙名
首領	shǒulǐng	chief, leader
王揖唐	Wáng Yītáng	安福部首領
主張	zhǔzhāng	to advocate, to hold the view of; an opinion or idea
民生主義	Mínshēngzhǔyì	The Principle of the People's Livelihood, one of the Three Principles of the People
演説	yǎnshuō	a speech, a talk; to deliver a speech, to make an address
并且	bìngqiě	並且, 而且
設立	shèlì	to establish, to set up, to install or inaugurate
嘲笑	cháoxiào	to laugh at, to ridicule, to deride
假充	jiǎchōng	to pretend to be, to pose as, to feign
時髦	shímáo	fashionable, modern
消息	xiāoxi	news, tidings, information
感想	gǎnxiǎng	mental reaction, what one thinks or feels about something; one's impression or opinion
高談	gāotán	to talk freely or in a lively manner, to talk volubly; to indulge in loud and empty talk, to harangue
教訓	jiàoxùn	a moral, a lesson (learned the hard way), a teaching, an admonition; to admonish (someone), to teach (someone a lesson)
層	céng	a part in a sequence
空談	kōngtán	to indulge in empty talk, to prattle
鸚鵡	yīngwǔ	a parrot
留聲機器	liúshēng jīqì	a phonograph

第二，空談外來進口的「主義」，是沒有什麼用處的。一切主義都是某時某地的有心人，對於那時那地的社會需要的救濟方法。我們不去實地研究我們現在的社會需要，單會高談某某主義，好比醫生單記得許多湯頭歌訣，不去研究病人的症候，如何能有用呢？

第三，偏向紙上的「主義」，是很危險的。這種口頭禪很容易被無恥政客利用來做種種害人的事。歐洲政客和資本家利用國家主義的流毒，都是人所共知的。現在中國的政客，又要利用某種某種主義來欺人了。羅蘭夫人說，「自由自由，天下多少罪惡，都是借你的名做出的！」一切好聽的主義，都有這種危險。

這三條合起來看，可以看出「主義」的性質。凡「主義」都是應時勢而起的。某種社會，到了某時代，受了某種的影響，呈現某種不滿意的

外來	wàilái	從外國來的
進口	jìnkǒu	to import; importation
用處	yòngchù	utility
有心人	yǒuxīnrén	an observant and conscientious person; a person who sets his mind on doing something useful; a person with high aspirations and determination
單	dān	只, 就
某某	mǒumǒu	so-and-so, a certain (person or

		thing)
好比	hǎobǐ	to be like, to be just like
湯頭歌訣	tāngtóu gējué	(said of traditional Chinese medicine) prescriptions in rhyme, medical recipes in jingles
		湯: liquid preparation for medicinal herbs;
		湯頭: a prescription for a medical decoction
口頭禪	kǒutóuchán	a pet phrase, an expression which one uses repetitiously
無恥	wúchǐ	without a sense of shame, shameless
政客	zhèngkè	a politician who places personal gain above public interest
資本家	zīběnjiā	capitalist
國家主義	guójiāzhǔyì	nationalism
流毒	liúdú	pernicious or baneful influence, detrimental effect
人所共知	rénsuǒgòngzhī	大家都知道
欺人	qīrén	to cheat or deceive others
羅蘭夫人	Luólán fūrén	Mme. Jean-Marie de la Platière (1754-1793)
自由	zìyóu	freedom, liberty; free, at one's free will; at ease, (to feel) at home
罪惡	zuìè	sin, crime, guilt, evil, vice
合起來	héqǐlái	to put together, to combine
看出	kànchū	看得出 (來), able to perceive, discern, detect, foresee
性質	xìngzhí	characteristics, nature, property
凡...都	fán ... dōu ...	all those (any one) ...
應	yìng	to respond to, to react to, to answer (note pronunciation)
時勢	shíshì	the time and circumstances
呈現	chéngxiàn	to appear, to show, to manifest, to display, to exhibit
滿意	mǎnyì	satisfactory; satisfied, content

現狀。於是有一些有心人，觀察這種現象，想出某種救濟的法子。這是「主義」的原起。主義初起時，大都是一種救時的具體主張。後來這種主張傳播出去，傳播的人要圖簡便，便用一兩個字來代表這種具體的主張，所以叫他做「某某主義」。主張成了主義，便由具體的計劃，變成一個抽象的名詞。「主義」的弱點和危險，就在這裏。因為世間沒有一個抽象名詞能把某人某派的具體主張都包括在裏面。比如「社會主義」一個名詞，馬克思的社會主義，和王揖唐的社會主義不同；你的社會主義，和我的社會主義不同：決不是這一個抽象名詞所能包括。你談你的社會主義，我談我的社會主義，王揖唐又談他的社會主義，同用一個名詞，中間也許隔開七八個世紀，也許隔開兩三萬里路，然而你和我和王揖唐都可自稱社會主義家，都可用這一個抽象名詞來騙人。這不是「主義」的大缺點和大危險嗎？

現狀	xiànzhuàng	things as they are, the status quo
於是	yúshì	then, so, thus, thereupon
觀察	guānchá	to observe, to inspect; observation
現象	xiànxiàng	phenomenon
原起	yuánqǐ	that which causes something to arise, cause, reason, origin
初起	chūqǐ	(something) just beginning to

		arise or come into existence
大都	dàdōu	in most cases, for the most part
救時	jiùshí	to save the age (from degeneration)
具體	jùtǐ	concrete, specific, particular, tangible
		opposite: 抽象
傳播	chuánbō	to disseminate (news, information), to spread
圖	tú	to desire, to intend to seek
簡便	jiǎnbiàn	簡單方便
代表	dàibiǎo	to represent, to stand for; representative, delegate, proxy
A 叫 B 做 C	A jiào B zuò C	A calls B 'C'
成	chéng	to become, to constitute
由	yóu	從
計劃	jìhuà	plan, program, device; to plan
抽象	chōuxiàng	abstract
		opposite: 具體
名詞	míngcí	term, (in grammar) noun
弱點	ruòdiǎn	weak point, weakness, vulnerability
世間	shìjiān	世界上
派	pài	faction; school (of thought)
包括	bāokuò	to include, to comprise
比如	bǐrú	such as, like, for example
馬克思	Mǎkèsī	Karl (Heinrich) Marx (1818-1883), German economist, philosopher, socialist
同用	tóngyòng	to use the same or identical (term)
隔開	gékāi	to separate, to set apart, to partition
世紀	shìjì	century
然而	ránér	可是
自稱	zìchēng	自己叫自己做 ...
缺點	quēdiǎn	defect, shortcoming, flaw

我再舉現在人人嘴裏掛着的「過激主義」做一個例：現在中國有幾個人知道這一個名詞做何意義？但是大家都痛恨痛罵「過激主義」，內務部下令嚴防「過激主義」，曹錕也行文嚴禁「過激主義」，盧永祥也出示查禁「過激主義」。前兩個月，北京有幾個老官僚在酒席上歎氣，說，「不好了，過激派到了中國了。」前兩天有一個小官僚，看見我寫的一把扇子，大詫異道，「這不是過激黨胡適嗎？」哈哈，這就是「主義」的用處！

　　我因為深覺得高談主義的危險，所以，我現在奉勸新輿論界的同志道：「請你們多提出一些問題，少談一些紙上的主義。」

　　更進一步說：「請你們多多研究這個問題如何解決，那個問題如何解決，不要高談這種主義

舉	jǔ	to cite (an example, etc.)
嘴裏掛着	zuǐliguàzhe	嘴上掛着－常常談着，老(是)說着
過激	guòjī	too radical, violent, or outspoken, extremist, dangerously extreme
例	lì	例子, example, instance
何	hé	(an interrogative) 甚麼
痛罵	tòngmà	to revile, to berate, to vituperate
內務部	Nèiwùbù	Ministry of Internal Affairs, Ministry of the Interior
下令	xiàlìng	to issue orders, to give orders

嚴防	yánfáng	to strictly guard against, to take strict precautions against
曹錕	Cáo Kūn	(1862-1938), a warlord; fraudulently elected President of the Republic of China, a post he held from October 1923 to November 1924
行文	xíngwén	(of a government office) to send an official communication to other organizations
嚴禁	yánjìn	to prohibit strictly, to forbid
盧永祥	Lú Yǒngxiáng	(1867-1933), a warlord
出示	chūshì	to issue an official notice; to show (something to somebody)
查禁	chájìn	to investigate and prohibit or ban (said of pornographic books, immoral shows, gambling, dangerous views or thoughts)
官僚	guānliáo	bureaucrat; bureaucratic
酒席	jiǔxí	a banquet, feast
歎氣	tànqì	to sigh
大詫異	dàchàyì	to be greatly surprised
道	dào	説
黨	dǎng	(political) party, clique, faction; member of a party
奉勸	fèngquàn	to advise (somebody to do something) with respect, "May I venture to advise you to ..." 奉: to offer respectfully
同志	tóngzhì	comrade 志: desire, ambition, interest
提出	tíchū	to bring forth, to put forth, to raise (questions)
進一步	jìnyíbù	to take a step further, to move further ahead, to progress
如何	rúhé	(an interrogative) 怎麼樣, how?

如何新奇，那種主義如何奧妙。」

現在中國應該趕緊解決的問題，真多得很。從人力車夫的生計問題，到大總統的權限問題；從賣淫問題到賣官賣國問題；從解散安福部問題到加入國際聯盟問題；從女子解放問題到男子解放問題：……那一個不是火燒眉毛緊急問題？

我們不去研究人力車夫的生計，却去高談社會主義；不去研究女子如何解放，家庭制度如何救正，却去高談公妻主義和自由戀愛；不去研究安福部如何解散，不去研究南北問題如何解決，却去高談無政府主義；我們還要得意揚揚誇口道

新奇	xīnqí	novel, new
奧妙	àomiào	profound, mysterious, abstruse, hard to understand; the secret of doing something
趕緊	gǎnjǐn	趕快, hurriedly, in haste, with no loss of time
人力車夫	rénlìchēfū	rickshaw man 車夫: driver, chauffeur, cabman
生計	shēngjì	livelihood, living
大總統	Dàzǒngtǒng	the President, the chief of state in a republic
權限	quánxiàn	limitation of power or authority, jurisdiction within certain limits
賣淫	màiyín	to earn a living as a prostitute 淫: licentious, lewd, lascivious, obscene, pornographic

解散	jiěsàn	to dissolve (a parliament), to disband (an organization), to dismiss (a meeting)
加入	jiārù	to join (a group, organization), to accede to; to add, to mix, to put in
國際聯盟	Guójì liánméng	the League of Nations, 1920-1946 國際: between or among nations, international; 聯: to unite, to make alliance with; allied, joint; 盟: covenant, oath, vow; alliance, league; 聯盟: an alliance, a league; to form an alliance
解放	jiěfàng	to untie or set free, to liberate; liberation
火燒眉毛	huǒshāoméimáo	(fig.) like fire burning eyebrows, very urgent or imminent
緊急	jǐnjí	urgent, pressing, critical
卻	què	(contrary to expectation) but, yet, however
制度	zhìdù	system, institution
救正	jiùzhèng	to rectify, to correct
公妻主義	gōngqī zhǔyì	妻子(太太)與他人共享的主義
自由戀愛	zìyóu liànài	free love (between a man and a woman, as distinct from the old-fashioned idea of marriage by arrangement); freedom to choose one's spouse
得意揚揚	déyìyángyáng	with an air or appearance of extreme satisfaction, to be immensely proud, to look triumphantly
誇口	kuākǒu	to boast, to brag

，我們所談的是根本「解決」。老實說罷，這是自欺欺人的夢話，這是中國思想界破產的鐵證，這是中國社會改良的死刑宣告！

　　為什麼談主義的人那麼多，為什麼研究問題的人那麼少呢？這都由於一個懶字。懶的定義是避難就易。研究問題是極困難的事，高談主義是極容易的事。比如研究安福部如何解散，研究南北和議如何解決，這都是要費工夫，挖心血，收集材料，徵求意見，考察情形，還要冒險吃苦，方才可以得一種解決的意見。又沒有成例可援，又沒有黃梨洲柏拉圖的話可引，又沒有大英百科

根本	gēnběn	basic, fundamental; root, base, foundation, basis
老實	lǎoshí	honest, truthful, frank, candid; (euphemistically) simple-minded, naïve
罷	ba	an interjection of exasperating disappointment
自欺欺人	zìqīqīrén	自己騙自己，也騙別人
夢話	mènghuà	dream talk, wishful thinking
破產	pòchǎn	bankruptcy, insolvency; bankrupt, insolvent
鐵證	tiězhèng	ironclad proof, irrefutable evidence
改良	gǎiliáng	to reform, to improve, to better
死刑	sǐxíng	death penalty, death sentence, capital punishment

宣告	xuāngào	announcement, declaration; to announce, to declare, to pronounce
由於	yóuyú	因為
定義	dìngyì	definition
避難就易	bìnán jiùyì	to avoid the difficult and approach the easy, to take the easier way out, to choose the easier alternative
和議	héyì	a peace accord or agreement between two nations
費工夫	fèigōngfu	to take or need a lot of time; time-consuming
挖心血	wāxīnxiě (xuè)	to strain in mental effort, to make or use mental exertion 挖: dig, excavate, scoop; 心血: heart's blood — painstaking care or effort
收集	shōují	to draw together, to gather, to collect
徵求	zhēngqiú	to seek, solicit or ask for (others' opinions); to recruit or canvass for (members, employees, etc.)
冒險	màoxiǎn	to take risks, to brave dangers
方才	fāngcái	才, only then, not until
得	dé	得到, to obtain, to get, acquire, or attain
成例	chénglì	an established precedent
援	yuán	to cite (a precedent); aid, support
黃梨洲	Huáng Lízhōu	黃宗羲 (Huang Zongxi, 1610-1695), a late Ming philosopher
柏拉圖	Bólātú	Plato
引	yǐn	to cite (an example, etc.)

全書可查，全憑研究考察的工夫：這豈不是難事嗎？高談「無政府主義」便不同了。買一兩本實社自由錄，看一兩本西文無政府主義的小冊子，再翻一翻大英百科全書，便可以高談無忌了：這豈不是極容易的事嗎？

高談主義，不研究問題的人，只是畏難求易，只是懶。

凡是有價值的思想，都是從這個那個具體的問題下手的。先研究了問題的種種方面的種種的事實，看看究竟病在何處，這是思想的第一步工夫。然後根據於一生經驗學問，提出種種解決的方法，提出種種醫病的丹方，這是思想的第二步工夫。然後用一生的經驗學問，加上想像的能力，推想每一種假定的解決法，該有甚麼樣的效果

大英百科全書	Dàyīng bǎikē quánshū	*Encyclopedia Britannica*
憑	píng	靠, to lean on, to rely on, to count on, to depend on
工夫	gōngfu	efforts put into a piece of work; skill; time, leisure
豈	qǐ	an interrogative particle constituting a rhetorical question to imply a dissenting or conflicting view or response — "How?"
實社	Shíshè	Society for Reality, an organization promoting anarchism

自由錄	Zìyóu lù	*Liberal Record*, a publication of Society for Reality
西文	xīwén	Western languages
冊子	cèzi	booklet, pamphlet
翻	fān	turn over (or up); (of books, newspapers, magazines) look over, glance over, browse
高談無忌	gāotánwújì	to talk freely without fear, dread or scruple
畏難求易	wèinán qiúyì	to fear the difficult and seek the easy
有價值	yǒujiàzhí	valuable
方面	fāngmiàn	respect, aspect, side, field, direction, quarter, sphere
事實	shìshí	fact, truth, reality
何處	héchù	(lit.) 甚麼地方
根據於	gēnjù (yú)	based on, on the strength of, according to, in accordance with, in compliance with, in light of, in line with
經驗	jīngyàn	experience; to experience
醫病	yībìng	to cure a disease
丹方	dānfāng	(in traditional Chinese medicine) a prescription 丹: a pellet or powder, sophisticated decoction; 方: a method, plan, prescription, recipe
加上	jiāshàng	add, plus
想像	xiǎngxiàng	to imagine, to visualize
能力	nénglì	ability, capability, power (as the power of the Almighty)
推想	tuīxiǎng	to infer, to deduce
假定	jiǎdìng	supposition, hypothesis, assumption; if, supposing, assuming
效果	xiàoguǒ	effect, efficacy

，推想這種效果是否眞能解決眼前這個困難問題。推想的結果，揀定一種假定的解決，認爲我的主張，這是思想的第三步工夫。凡是有價値的主張，都是先經過這三步工夫來的。不如此，不算輿論家，只可算是鈔書手。

讀者不要誤會我的意思。我並不是勸人不研究一切學說和一切「主義」。學理是我們研究問題的一種工具。沒有學理做工具，就如同王陽明對着竹子癡坐，妄想「格物」，那是做不到的事。種種學說和主義，我們都應該研究。有了許多學理做材料，見了具體的問題，方才能尋出一個解決的方法。但是我希望中國的輿論家，把一切「主義」擺在腦背後，做參考資料，不要掛在嘴上做招牌，不要叫一知半解的人拾了這些半生不

是否	shìfǒu	是不是
眼前	yǎnqián	right before one's eyes; now, at present, at this moment
結果	jiéguǒ	bear fruit (of plants); result, outcome, consequence; in the end, finally
揀定	jiǎndìng	挑定, 選定, to select, to decide on 定: a Resultative Verb ending which means "fixity," "security"
認爲	rènwéi	to take (something) for … , to regard (something) as …
如此	rúcǐ	像這樣
鈔書手	chāoshūshǒu	one who copies or transcribes written works by hand

		鈔 (抄): to copy, to transcribe
讀者	dúzhě	the reader (as opposed to the writer)
誤會	wùhuì	to misunderstand; misunderstanding
勸	quàn	to advise, exhort or urge (someone) to do or not do (something)
如同	rútóng	如, like, as
王陽明	Wáng Yángmíng	王守仁 (Wang Shouren, 1472-1528), a Confucian scholar of the Ming Dynasty
對著	duìzhe	face to face, opposing
竹子	zhúzi	bamboo
癡坐	chīzuò	呆坐 癡: silly, idiotic
妄想	wàngxiǎng	to desire wildly; wishful thinking, preposterous hopes 妄: absurd, wild, reckless
格物	géwù	to pursue to the very source of a thing, to study a thing thoroughly
尋出	xúnchū	尋, to find
擺	bǎi	to place, to put, to arrange; to wave, to swing, to wag, to oscillate
腦背後	nǎobèihòu	behind one's head; a secondary or less significant position
資料	zīliào	data, material
招牌	zhāopái	the signboard of a store or any other business concern; reputation of a large business firm or a quality product
叫	jiào	讓, to cause, to permit, to allow
一知半解	yìzhībànjiě	to have half-baked knowledge, to have a smack or smattering of knowledge, to have incomplete comprehension

熟的主義去做口頭禪。

　　「主義」的大危險，就是能使人心滿意足，自以為尋着包醫百病的「根本解決」，從此用不着費心力去研究這個那個具體問題的解決法了。

　　　　　　　　　　　　民國八年七月。

拾	shí	to pick up, to collect
半生不熟	bànshēngbùshú (shóu)	"half raw and not well cooked" — not fully versed in something
心滿意足	xīnmǎnyìzú	"heart fulfilled and feeling (or desire) (made) sufficient" — perfectly content
自以為	zìyǐwéi	to consider oneself ... , to regard oneself as ... , (in total disregard of others' or public opinion)
尋着	xúnzháo	找著
包	bāo	to assure, to guarantee
從此	cóngcǐ	從這個時候起
民國	Mínguó	abbreviation for 中華民國 (the Republic of China)

句型

1. 好比 — is like (may be likened to)

- 我們不去實地研究我們現在的社會需要,單會高談某某主義,<u>好比</u>醫生單記得 ...

    例 (1): 做菜就<u>好比</u>做實驗,¹ 放多少糖, 放多少鹽² 都是一定的, 不能太多, 也不能太少.

    例 (2): 求學³ <u>好比</u>逆水行舟,⁴ 不進則退.
    (求學就如同逆水行舟, 不進則退.)

¹ 實驗	shíyàn	experiment
² 鹽	yán	salt
³ 求學	qiúxué	study
⁴ 逆水行舟	nìshuǐxíngzhōu	to sail a boat against the current

2. 可 V (有 N 可 V) ... — be worth (doing)

- 又沒有成例<u>可</u>援, 又沒有黃梨洲, 柏拉圖的話<u>可</u>引, 又沒有大英百科全書<u>可</u>查.

    例 (1): 吃東西: 家裏有沒有東西<u>可</u>吃?

    例 (2): 住房子: 很多人沒有房子<u>可</u>住.

3. A 就如同 B — A is just (precisely, exactly) like B

- 沒有學理做工具,<u>就如同</u>王陽明對著竹子癡坐, 妄想「格物」, 那是做不到的事.

    例 (1): 我的女朋友的脾氣<u>就如同</u>天氣一樣, 一會兒好, 一會兒壞.

    例 (2): 我現在住的房間<u>就如同</u>一個鳥籠¹ 一樣大.

| ¹ 鳥籠 | niǎolóng | bird cage |

討論

1. 胡適在這篇文章中說,所有的主義都是空洞[1]的,談主義解決不了實際的[2]社會問題,你同意這個看法嗎?

2. 如果主義都是空洞的,為什麼政府常怕知識分子[3]談與現行[4]政治不同的主義?

3. 談人力車夫的生計問題跟談社會主義有什麼基本的[5]不同?

4. 你覺得胡適這篇文章有沒有缺點?最大的缺點是什麼?

[1] 空洞	kōngdòng	empty, hollow, devoid of content
[2] 實際的	shíjide	real, actual, concrete
[3] 知識分子	zhīshifenzǐ	intellectual, the intelligentsia
[4] 現行	xiànxíng	currently in effect
[5] 基本的	jīběnde	basic, fundamental

The Patriotic Movement and Scholarly Pursuits
愛國運動與求學

Selection Six enables us to appreciate some of the conflicts between personal interests and professional responsibilities that troubled intellectuals during Hu's time. What is the proper role of the scholar or the student when the nation is imperiled? Hu Shi, himself, had a keen sense of personal mission and an intense concern for the continuity of the nation. But, at the same time, he opposed student interference in politics, especially if it resulted in campus disruption. He urged the students to forgo demonstrations and concentrate on transforming themselves so that they could better serve society. This view came under sharp attack, especially from the Communist Party.

This essay was first published in *Modern Critic*, 2.39:5-9 (September 5, 1925). It was later included in *Collected Essays of Hu Shi* III, ix, 1145-54.

愛國運動與求學

　　當五月七日北京學生包圍章士釗宅，警察拘捕學生的事件發生以後，北京各學校的學生團體即有罷課的提議。有些學校的學生因為北大學生會不曾參加五七的事，竟在北大第一院前辱罵北大學生不愛國。北大學生也有很憤激的，有些人竟貼出布告攻擊北大代理校長蔣夢麟媚章媚外。然而幾日之內，北大學生會舉行總投票表決罷課

The Patriotic Movement and Scholarly Pursuits

運動	yùndòng	a social movement, a campaign, a drive; physical exercise, sports
與	yǔ	跟, 和
求學	qiúxué	追求學問, to receive education; to pursue, seek, or go after education
當...以後	dāng...yǐhòu	在...以後
包圍	bāowéi	to surround, to besiege, to encircle
章士釗	Zhāng Shìzhāo	人名 (1881-1973), 一個復古主義者; 1924-1926 參加段祺瑞 (Duan Qirui, a warlord) 政治團體
宅	zhái	a dwelling, a residence, a house

警察	jǐngchá	police
拘捕	jūbǔ	to detain or arrest (a suspect)
團體	tuántǐ	a group, an organization
即	jí	就
罷課	bàkè	(of students) to stage a strike, to boycott classes 罷: to stop or cease
提議	tíyì	a proposal or motion; to propose, recommend, or raise a point
北大	Běidà	北京大學
學生會	xuéshēnghuì	a student government
參加	cānjiā	to participate in, to join
五七	wǔqī	五月七日
竟	jìng	居然
辱罵	rǔmà	to abuse and insult, to revile 辱: to insult, to disgrace
憤激	fènjī	vehement, furious
貼	tiē	to paste
布告	bùgào	a bulletin 布: 佈
攻擊	gōngjī	to attack, to assault
代理校長	dàilǐ xiàozhǎng	acting head (of a school) 代理: agent, deputy; to serve as the agent of, to act as the deputy for, to stand proxy for
蔣夢麟	Jiǎng Mènglín	人名 (1886-1964), 曾當北京大學代理校長
媚	mèi	to fawn on, to flatter, to please
外	wài	外國, 外國人
然而	ránér	可是
...之內	... zhīnèi	within ... (time period)
舉行	jǔxíng	to hold (examinations, rallies, parties)
總	zǒng	general, overall, complete
投票	tóupiào	to ballot, to cast ballots
表決	biǎojué	to put to a vote

問題，共投一千一百多票，反對罷課者八百餘票，這件事真使一班留心教育問題的人心裏歡喜。可喜的不在罷課案的被否決，而在①投票之多，②手續的有秩序，③學生態度的鎮靜。我的朋友高夢旦在上海讀了這段新聞，寫了一封長信給我，討論此事，說，這樣做去，便是在求學的範圍以內做救國的事業，可算是在近年學生運動史上開一個新紀元。——只可惜我還沒有回高先生的信，上海五卅的事件已發生了，前二十天的秩序與鎮靜都無法維持了。於是六月三日以後，全國學校遂都罷課了。

這也是很自然的。在這個時候，國事糟到這步田地，外間的刺激這麼強：上海的事件未了，

共	gòng	一共
者	zhě	(lit.) those who
餘	yú	多
使	shǐ	causative verb meaning "to cause," "to enable"
一班	yìbān	一般, common, general; commonly, generally
留心	liúxīn	to pay attention to, to take heed
歡喜	huānxǐ	高興
不在…而在	búzài…érzài	not in … but in
案	àn	a legal case
否決	fǒujué	to veto; a veto 否: a negative expressing denial, rejection, refusal
手續	shǒuxù	procedures
秩序	zhìxù	order (in the sense of a condi-

		tion in which everything or everyone is in its right place or functioning properly)
鎮靜	zhènjìng	composure, self-possession, calmness, coolness; calm, cool, self-composed
高夢旦	Gāo Mèngdàn	人名
段	duàn	Numerary Adjunct for sections, paragraphs or other parts of a text; a section, a part, a division
新聞	xīnwén	news
此	cǐ	這
在...範圍以內	zài...fànwéiyǐnèi	to be within the scope of 範圍: range, scope, sphere, extent
事業	shìyè	enterprise, undertaking; career
開紀元	kāijìyuán	to make (or mark) an epoch 紀元: the beginning of a new era
五卅的事件	Wǔsàde shìjiàn	1925年五月三十日上海公共租界發生外國人槍殺中國人的事件
維持	wéichí	to maintain, to preserve
遂	suì	然後就
糟	zāo	to become a mess, or to be in bad shape 糟: the sediment or dregs of wine
到這步田地	dào zhèbù tiándì	(usually with negative connotations) to this extent 田地: a state of affairs, a condition; agricultural land
外間	wàijiān	外頭
刺激	cìjī	stimulation, stimulus; to stimulate, to provoke
未	wèi	還沒有
了	liǎo	完, 結束

漢口的事件又來了，接着廣州、南京的事件又來了：在這個時候，許多中年以上的人尚且忍耐不住，許多六十老翁尚且要出來慷慨激昂地主張宣戰，何況這無數的少年男女學生呢？

我們觀察這七年來的「學潮」，不能不算民國八年的五四事件與今年的五卅事件為最有價值。這兩次都不是有什麼作用，事前預備好了然後發動的；這兩次都只是一般青年學生的愛國血誠，遇着國家的大恥辱，自然爆發；純然是爛縵的天眞，不顧利害地幹將去，這種「無所為而為」的表示是眞實的，可愛敬的。許多學生都是不願意犧牲求學的時間的；只因為臨時發生的問題太大了，刺激太強烈了，愛國的感情一時迸發，所

尚且...	shàngqiě...	(a rhetorical question) even ... much
何況...(呢)?	hékuàng ... (ne)?	less (or not to mention) ...
忍耐不住	rěnnàibúzhù	忍不住, cannot bear 忍: to endure, to bear, to tolerate
老翁	lǎowēng	an old man
慷慨激昂	kāngkǎi jīáng	(of speech or conduct) impassioned, rousing, ardent
主張	zhǔzhāng	to advocate (an opinion or idea)
宣戰	xuānzhàn	to declare war 宣: to announce, to declare
無數的	wúshùde	countless, innumerable

觀察	guānchá	to observe, to inspect; observation
學潮	xuécháo	student strike, campus upheaval 潮: tide
五四事件	Wǔsìshìjiàn	the May Fourth Incident (1919)
價值	jiàzhí	value
作用	zuòyòng	purpose, objective, function, use, usefulness
發動	fādòng	to start, to launch
恥辱	chǐrǔ	shame, disgrace, humiliation
爆發	bàofā	to explode, to blow up, to break out, to erupt, to flare up
純然	chúnrán	purely, entirely, completely
爛縵	lànmàn	爛漫, naïve, simple-minded; transliteration of "romantic"
天真	tiānzhēn	naïveté; naïve
不顧利害	búgùlìhài	disregard (careless of) profit or loss 不顧: not to care for, to neglect; 利害: interest and disinterest, good and harm, advantages and disadvantages
幹將去	gànjiāngqù	幹去, 作去
無所爲而爲	wúsuǒwèi érwéi	(lit.) 作一件事情不是爲了達到一個特別的目的 爲: for the sake of, for the good of; 爲: to do (note pronunciation)
表示	biǎoshì	expression, indication; to express, to show, to indicate
真實	zhēnshí	actual, true, real
可	kě	值得
敬	jìng	to respect
犧牲	xīshēng	to sacrifice (something of value for the sake of something else)
強烈	qiángliè	strong, intense
迸發	bìngfā	to explode, to erupt

以什麼都顧不得了：功課也不顧了，秩序也不顧了，辛苦也不顧了。所以北大學生總投票表決不罷課之後，不到二十天，也就不能不罷課了。二十日前不罷課的表決可以表示學生不願意犧牲功課的誠意；二十日後毫無勉強地罷課參加救國運動可以證明此次學生運動的犧牲的精神。這並非前後矛盾：有了前回的不願犧牲，方才更顯出後來的犧牲之難能而可貴。豈但北大一校如此？國中無數學校都有這樣的情形。

　　但羣衆的運動總是不能持久的。這並非中國人的「虎頭蛇尾」，「五分鐘的熱度」。這是世界人類的通病。所謂「民氣」，所謂「羣衆運動」，都只是一時的大問題刺激起來的一種感情上的反應。感情的衝動是沒有持久性的；無組織又無領袖的羣衆行動是最容易鬆散的。我們不看見

顧不得	gùbude	cannot look after (care for, take into account, attend to)
辛苦	xīnkǔ	hard, laborious, toilsome, in great pains; to work hard, to go to great trouble, to go through hardships
誠意	chéngyì	sincerity
毫無勉強	háowú miǎnqiǎng	毫無, 一點也沒有, not at all, not in the least 勉強: without spontaneity, in a forced manner, involuntarily, reluctantly; to force someone to

		do something
矛盾	máodùn	inconsistent, contradictory
顯出	xiǎnchū	to show (in contrast)
難能而可貴	nánnéng ér kěguì	難能: hard to get, rare; 可貴: 值得寶貴, worth treasuring, valuable
豈但	qǐdàn	(a rhetorical question) not only 豈: interrogative particle implying a conflicting or dissenting view or response; 但: 只
如此	rúcǐ	像這樣 (的情形)
羣眾	qúnzhòng	a crowd, a mob, the masses
持久	chíjiǔ	維持的很久, to last for a long time; lasting, durable
虎頭蛇尾	hǔtóushéwěi	"tiger-head snake-tail" — to start doing something with vigor but fail to see it through, a fine start but a poor finish
熱度	rèdù	heat
人類	rénlèi	mankind, the human race 類: kind, type, class, category
通病	tōngbìng	a common failing, deficiency, fault or ill
民氣	mínqì	morale or spirit of the people
反應	fǎnyìng	response
衝動	chōngdòng	an impulse, a sudden urge
性	xìng	nature, characteristic or intrinsic quality
領袖	lǐngxiù	a leader 領: collar; 袖: sleeve
行動	xíngdòng	action, movement; to act, to move
鬆散	sōngsǎn	(to become) loose and scattered 鬆: loose, lax, slack; 散: loose, loosened, scattered

北京大街的牆上大書著「打倒英、日」「不要五分鐘的熱度」嗎?其實寫那些大字的人,寫成之後,自己看著很滿意,他的「熱度」早已消除大半了;他回到家裏,坐也坐得下了,睡也睡得著了。所謂「民氣」,無論在中國在歐、美,都是這樣:突然而來,悠然而去。幾天一次的公民大會,幾天一次的示威遊行,雖然可以勉強多維持一會兒,然而那回天安門打架之後,國民大會也就不容易召集了。

我們要知道,凡關於外交的問題,民氣可以督促政府,政府可以利用民氣:民氣與政府相為聲援方才可以收效。沒有一個像樣的政府,雖有民氣,終不能單獨成功。因為外國政府決不能直接和我們的羣眾辦交涉;民眾運動的影響(無論是一時的示威或是較有組織的經濟抵制)終是間接的。一個

書	shū	寫
消除	xiāochú	to eliminate, to get rid of 消: to vanish, eliminate, or remove; 除: to rid of, to wipe out
突然	tūrán	忽然
悠然	yōurán	unhurriedly, in a leisurely manner
公民大會	gōngmín dàhuì	公民: citizens; 大會: a rally, a plenary meeting
示威	shìwēi	demonstration (by parade or mass meeting); to demonstrate,

		to make a show of force
		示: to demonstrate, to show;
		威: impressive strength, might, power, dignity, majesty, authority
遊行	yóuxíng	a parade; to parade
天安門	Tiānānmén	"The Gate of Heavenly Peace," in Beijing
打架	dǎjià	to have a brawl, a row, a fight
國民大會	guómín dàhuì	a national congress
		國民: citizen, the people
召集	zhàojí	to convene (a meeting)
		召: to summon, to call up;
		集: to assemble, to gather together
外交	wàijiāo	diplomacy, foreign affairs
督促	dūcù	to supervise and urge (someone to complete a task in time)
		督: to superintend and direct;
		促: to urge, to press
利用	lìyòng	to make use of, to take advantage of, to avail oneself of
相爲聲援	xiāngwèishēngyuán	互相幫助, A 幫助 B, B 也幫助 A, to give moral support
		援: 幫助
收效	shōuxiào	收到效果
像樣	xiàngyàng	to look respectable
終	zhōng	after all, in the long run, finally, eventually
單獨	dāndú	alone, singly, individually
直接	zhíjiē	direct; directly
		opposite: 間接
辦	bàn	to manage, to handle, to take care of (some business)
交涉	jiāoshè	negotiation; to negotiate
抵制	dǐzhì	resistence; to resist, boycott
間接	jiànjiē	indirect; indirectly
		opposite: 直接

健全的政府可以利用民氣作後盾,在外交上可以多得勝利,至少也可以少吃點虧。若沒有一個能運用民氣的政府,我們可以斷定民眾運動的犧牲的大部分是白白地糟蹋了的。

倘使外交部於六月二十四日同時送出滬案及修改條約兩照會之後即行負責交涉,那時民氣最盛,海員罷工的聲勢正大,滬案的交涉至少可以得一個比較滿人意的結果。但這個政府太不像樣了:外交部不敢自當交涉之衝,卻要三個委員來代掮末梢;三個委員都是很聰明的人,也就樂得三揖三讓,延擱下去。他們不但不能運用民氣,

健全	jiànquán	in good condition, in good order, flawless (usually referring to a system, institution, etc.) 健: healthy, strong
後盾	hòudùn	a prop to lean back on, backing, support; supporter 盾: a shield
勝利	shènglì	victory; to win, to triumph
吃虧	chīkuī	to be at a disadvantage
若	ruò	要是,如果
運用	yùnyòng	to employ, to make use of
斷定	duàndìng	to conclude, to determine
白白的	báibáide	in vain, to be of no avail, to no purpose
糟蹋	zāotā	to waste, to ruin
倘使	tǎngshǐ	要是,如果
外交部	wàijiāobù	Ministry of Foreign Affairs 部: a cabinet ministry
於	yú	在

滬案	Hùàn	指五卅事件 滬: 上海的簡稱; 案: a case at law
修改	xiūgǎi	to correct, to change, to amend 修: to repair, to mend, to overhaul
條約	tiáoyuē	a treaty (between nations)
照會	zhàohuì	diplomatic notes or memoranda
即行	jíxíng	馬上, 立刻
盛	shèng	rich, abundant, exuberant
海員	hǎiyuán	a sailor, a seaman, a mariner
罷工	bàgōng	(of workers) to stage a strike, to strike; a strike, a walkout
聲勢	shēngshì	power, strength, impetus, momentum
滿人意	mǎnrényì	使人(覺得)滿意
自	zì	oneself, itself
委員	wěiyuán	a member of a committee, board, commission, etc.
代掮末梢	dàiqiánmòshāo	代: to take the place of, to stand proxy for; 掮: to bear load on the shoulder; 末梢: tip, end
樂得	lède	to do something willingly (because of a sure reward for doing it), glad to do something
三揖三讓	sānyīsānràng	to abdicate (to give up a position for a better man) time and again 揖讓: a courtesy (between host and guests, etc.); 揖: to bow with hands folded in front; 讓: to give way, to make a concession, to back down, to yield
延擱	yángē	to put off, to defer, to postpone

反懼怕民氣了！況且某方面的官僚想借這風潮延長現政府的壽命；某方面的政客也想借這問題展緩東北勢力的侵逼。他們不運用民氣來對付外人，只會利用民氣來便利他們自己的私圖！於是一誤，再誤，至於今日，滬案及其他關連之各案絲毫不曾解決，而民氣却早已成了彊弩之末了！

　　上海的罷工本是對英、日的，現在却是對郵政當局、商務印書館、中華書局了。北京的學生運動一變而為對付楊蔭榆，又變而為對付章士釗了。廣州對英的事件全未了結，而廣州城却早已成為共產與反共產的血戰場了。三個月的「愛國運動」的變相竟致如此！

懼怕	jùpà	怕, to fear, to dread
況且	kuàngqiě	moreover, furthermore
某	mǒu	a certain (person or thing)
官僚	guānliáo	bureaucrats; bureaucratic
風潮	fēngcháo	direction of wind and tide — disturbance, upheaval, unrest
延長	yáncháng	to lengthen, to prolong, to extend
壽命	shòumìng	the life span
政客	zhèngkè	a politician who places personal gain above public interest
展緩	zhǎnhuǎn	to postpone or put off, to extend the deadline or time limit
侵逼	qīnbī	侵: to raid, to encroach upon, to use force stealthily; 逼: to press, to pressure, to compel, to coerce, to force

對付	duìfu	to deal with, to cope with
便利	biànlì	方便, to facilitate; convenient, expedient
誤	wù	to err, to mismanage, to cause an undue delay in
關連	guānlián	related, connected, involved; connection, involvement
絲毫不	sīháobù	一點也不, 一點也沒
彊弩之末	qiángnǔzhīmò	"at the end of an arrow's flight" — weakened, exhausted, powerless 彊: 強; 弩: a bow, a crossbow; 末: end
郵政	yóuzhèng	the postal administration
當局	dāngjú	the authorities 局: an office, a bureau
商務印書館	Shāngwù Yìnshūguǎn	The Commercial Press 印: to print
中華書局	Zhōnghuá shūjú	書局名
為	wéi	to be
楊蔭榆	Yáng Yīnyú	人名 (?-1938), 曾留學美國, 1924年當北京女子師範大學校長
了結	liǎojié	to bring to conclusion, to settle, to get through with
成為	chéngwéi	to become, to end in, to come to (be)
共產	gòngchǎn	Communism 共: to share; 產: properties
反	fǎn	prefix meaning "anti-"
變相	biànxiàng	(in) disguised form, convert 相: appearance, look, facial features, countenance
致	zhì	to bring about, to occasion or result in, to achieve, to attain

這時候有一件差強人意的事,就是全國學生總會議決秋季開學後各地學生應一律到校上課,上課後應努力於鞏固學生會的組織,為民眾運動的中心。北京學聯會也決議北京各校同學於開學前務必到校,一面上課,一面仍繼續進行。

　　這是很可喜的消息。全國學生總會的通告裏並且有「五卅運動並非短時間所可解決」的話。我們要為全國學生下一轉語:救國事業更非短時間所能解決;帝國主義不是赤手空拳打得倒的;「英、日強盜」也不是幾千萬人的喊聲咒得死的。救國是一件頂大的事業:排隊遊街,高喊着「打倒英、日強盜」,算不得救國事業;甚至於砍下手指寫血書,甚至於蹈海投江,殺身殉國,都

差強人意	chāqiángrényì	barely satisfactory, barely passable
總會	zǒnghuì	the central committee or administrative body (of an association, etc.)
議決	yìjué	to decide or resolve at a meeting
應	yīng	應當, 應該
一律	yīlǜ	uniformly, without exception or discrimination
於	yú	在
鞏固	gǒnggù	to consolidate (a position, strength)
學聯會	Xuéliánhuì	學生聯合會
決議	juéyì	議決, a resolution (reached at a meeting)
務必	wùbì	一定得

一面…一面…	yīmiàn … yīmiàn …	一邊兒 … 一邊兒 … ; on the one hand …, on the other …
仍	réng	仍然, still
繼續	jìxù	to continue
進行	jìnxíng	to proceed (with one's plan, business)
可喜	kěxǐ	值得歡喜, 值得高興 可: 值得
通告	tōnggào	an announcement, a public notice; to notify (a group of people)
非	fēi	不是
下	xià	to put down, to lay
轉語	zhuǎnyǔ	改變原來的話的意思, 另外作成一句話
帝國主義	dìguózhǔyì	imperialism
赤手空拳	chìshǒukōngquán	bare-handed 赤: bare, naked; 拳: a fist
強盜	qiángdào	a robber, a bandit
喊	hǎn	大聲地叫, to call aloud, to shout, to scream
咒	zhòu	to curse, to swear
頂	dǐng	the top of anything — topmost, extremely
排隊	páiduì	to line up, to form a queue 排: to arrange, to put in order; a row, a line; 隊: a group, a team
游街	yóujiē	to parade in the streets
砍	kǎn	to cut, to chop, to hack
蹈海投江	dàohǎi tóujiāng	to commit suicide by throwing oneself into the sea or a river 蹈: to tread, to stamp the feet; 投: to throw, to toss, to fling
殉	xùn	to die for a cause, faith, etc., e.g. 殉道, 殉教, 殉名, 殉情

算不得救國的事業。救國的事業須要有各色各樣的人才；真正的救國的預備在於把自己造成一個有用的人才。

易卜生說的好：「真正的個人主義在於把你自己這塊材料鑄造成個東西。」他又說：「有時候我覺得這個世界就好像大海上翻了船，最要緊的是救出我自己。」在這個高唱國家主義的時期，我們要很誠懇的指出：易卜生說的「真正的個人主義」正是到國家主義的唯一大路。救國須從救出你自己下手！

學校固然不是造人才的唯一地方，但在學生時代的青年却應該充分地利用學校的環境與設備來把自己鑄造成個東西。我們須要明白了解：

救國千萬事，
何一不當為？
而吾性所適，
僅有一二宜。

認清了你「性之所近，而力之所能勉」的方向，

各色各樣	gèsègèyàng	all sorts, kinds, or varieties of, various
人才	réncái	a man of talent, a man of ability
真正的	zhēnzhèngde	real, actual, genuine
造(成)	zào (chéng)	to make (into)
易卜生	Yìbǔshēng	Henrik Ibsen (1828-1906), a Norwegian playwright and poet
個人主義	gèrén zhǔyì	individualism, egoism

		個人: the individual (as contrasted with the group)
材料	cáiliào	raw material, material for all building purposes; material such as data, statistics, figures, information, for teaching or for writing an article, story, novel, or for other purposes; ingredients of a preparation (food, medicine, etc.)
鑄造（成）	zhùzào (chéng)	to make into 鑄: to melt or cast metal
翻	fān	to turn, to overturn, to upset, (of a boat) to capsize
高唱	gāochàng	to sing in a very high pitch or with great intensity, meaning "to be very much talked about," "on everyone's lips"
國家主義	guójiā zhǔyì	nationalism
誠懇	chéngkěn	sincere, cordial
唯一	wéiyī	the only one, the only kind, etc.
固然 ... 但 ...	gùrán ... dàn ...	surely (certainly, indeed) ... but nevertheless ...
充分	chōngfèn	sufficient, sufficiently
環境	huánjìng	surroundings, environment
設備	shèbèi	equipment, facilities
何	hé	(lit.) 哪
為	wéi	(lit.) 作
吾	wú	(lit.) 我, 我的
性	xìng	性情, disposition, personality
適	shì	適合
僅	jǐn	只
宜	yí	合適
認清	rènqīng	認識清楚
力	lì	(mental or physical) strength, power
勉	miǎn	to make effort
方向	fāngxiàng	a direction

努力求發展,這便是你對國家應盡的責任,這便是你的救國事業的預備工夫。國家的紛擾,外間的刺激,只應該增加你求學的熱心與興趣,而不應該引誘你跟着大家去吶喊。吶喊救不了國家。即使吶喊也算是救國運動的一部分,你也不可忘記你的事業有比吶喊重要十倍百倍的。你的事業是要把你自己造成一個有眼光有能力的人才。

你忍不住嗎?你受不住外面的刺激嗎?你的同學都出去吶喊了,你受不了他們的引誘與譏笑嗎?你獨坐在圖書館裏覺得難為情嗎?你心裏不安嗎?——這也是人情之常,我們不怪你;我們都有忍不住的時候。但我們可以告訴你一兩個故事,也許可以給你一點鼓舞:——

德國大文豪葛德(Goethe)在他的年譜裏(英譯本頁一八九)曾說,他每遇着國家政治上有大紛擾的時候,他便用心去研究一種絕不關係時局的

發展	fāzhǎn	development, to develop
紛擾	fēnrǎo	confusion and disturbance; to confuse, to disturb
增加	zēngjiā	to increase, to add to
興趣	xìngqù	interest, enthusiasm
引誘	yǐnyòu	to allure, to entice, to tempt; allurement, temptation
		引: to draw; to lead, to guide; to lure, to attract;
		誘: to guide, to induce; to seduce, to entice
吶喊	nàhǎn	to shout in battle; battlecry

救不了	jiùbuliǎo	cannot save, cannot rescue
即使 ... 也 ...	jíshǐ ... yě ...	就是 ... 也 (or 還, 都) ... , even if ... still ...
眼光	yǎnguāng	discerning ability, power of judgement
能力	nénglì	ability, capacity
受不住	shòubúzhù	cannot bear, cannot stand 受: to take, to stand, to endure
譏笑	jīxiào	derision, jeer, sneer, ridicule; to laugh at, to make fun of
難爲情	nánwéiqíng	to feel ashamed, uneasy or embarassed, to be bashful
人情之常	rénqíngzhīcháng	(said of human feelings or human relationships) natural and normal, what is natural and normal
鼓舞	gǔwǔ	to rouse, to stir up, to excite, to spur on 鼓: to drum; 舞: to dance
大文豪	dàwénháo	大文學家 豪: a person of outstanding talent, intelligence, or courage
葛德	Gědé	Johann Wolfgang von Goethe (1749-1832), German poet and dramatist
年譜	niánpǔ	a biography arranged chronologically 譜: a register, a record, a table, e.g. 年譜, 家譜, 食譜
譯本	yìběn	translated version
遇	yù	to meet, to encounter, to come across, to run into
研究	yánjiū	to study and research, to examine
時局	shíjú	the national situation, the state of national affairs, world situation

學問，使他的心思不致受外界的擾亂。所以拿破崙的兵威逼迫德國最厲害的時期裏，葛德天天用功研究中國的文物。又當利俾瑟之戰的那一天，葛德正關着門，做他的名著 Essex 的「尾聲」。

德國大哲學家費希特(Fichte) 是近代國家主義的一個創始者。然而他當普魯士被拿破崙踐破之後的第二年（一八○七）回到柏林，便着手計劃一個新的大學——即今日之柏林大學。那時候，柏林還在敵國駐兵的掌握裏。費希特在柏林繼續講學，在很危險的環境裏發表他的「告德意志

擾亂	rǎoluàn	紛擾
拿破崙	Nápòlún	Napoleon Bonaparte (1769-1821)
兵威	bīngwēi	military strength, military force
逼迫	bīpò	to press, pressure, force, or coerce
文物	wénwù	the products of a culture, cultural artifacts
利俾瑟	Lìbǐsè	德國地名 (Leipzig)
名著	míngzhù	a great book, a literary masterpiece
尾聲	wěishēng	the final or closing stage (of a story, activity or event)
哲學家	zhéxuéjiā	philosopher 哲學: philosophy; 家: a specialist in art or science
費希特	Fèixītè	Johann Gottlieb Fichte (1762-1814), German philosopher
創始者	chuàngshǐzhě	a founder, originator or initia-

		tor
		創: to start (doing something), to achieve (something for the first time);
		始: to begin, to start, to commence
普魯士	Pǔlǔshì	Prussia
踐破	jiànpò	to smash by trampling
		踐: to tread on, to trample
柏林	Bólín	Berlin
著手	zhuóshǒu	to put or set one's hand to, to start doing something
		著: to touch, to come into contact with
計劃	jìhuà	to plan, to devise; a plan, a program
即	jí	就是, namely, that is to say
駐兵	zhùbīng	troops stationed (at a place), garrison, troops, occupation force
		駐: to station (troops at a place for defensive purposes), to be stationed
掌握	zhǎngwò	to have charge of, to control, to grasp
		在...的掌握裏, to be in one's grasp, within one's power;
		掌: the palm of the hand; to have in hand; to have charge of, to control;
		握: to hold fast, to grasp, to grip
講學	jiǎngxué	to lecture (on academic subjects)
發表	fābiǎo	to make public, to make known, to publish (an article)
德意志	Déyìzhì	Deutschland, Germany

民族」(Reden an die deutsche nation)。往往在他講學的堂上聽得見敵人駐兵操演回來的笳聲。他一套講演—「告德意志民族」—忠告德國人不要灰心喪志,不要驚惶失措;他說,德意志民族是不會亡國的;這個民族有一種天付的使命,就是要在世間建立一個精神的文明,——德意志的文明:他說,這個民族的國家是不會亡的。

後來費希特計劃的柏林大學變成了世界的一個最有名的學府;他那部「告德意志民族」不但變成了德意志帝國建國的一個動力,並且成了十九世紀全世界的國家主義的一種經典。

上邊的兩段故事是我願意介紹給全國的青年男女學生的。我們不期望人人都做葛德與費希特。我們只希望大家知道:在一個擾攘紛亂的時期裏跟著人家亂跑亂喊,不能就算是盡了愛國的責任,此外還有更難更可貴的任務:在紛亂的喊聲裏,能立定腳跟,打定主意,救出你自己,努力把你這塊材料鑄造成個有用的東西!

十四,八,卅一夜,在天津脫稿。

民族	mínzú	a people, an ethnic group
堂	táng	a hall
操演	cāoyǎn	(of military training) to exercise, to drill
笳聲	jiāshēng	笳 (a reed whistle) 的聲音
講演	jiǎngyǎn	演講, a speech (before an audience); to give a speech

忠告	zhōnggào	to offer advice with sincerity and honesty; honest and sincere advice
灰心喪志	huīxīn sàngzhì	灰心: disappointed, discouraged, disheartened; 喪: to lose, to be deprived of; 志: will, aspiration, determination, ambition
驚皇失措	jīnghuángshīcuò	to lose one's head from fear, to be seized with panic, to be frightened out of one's wits 皇: apprehensive, frightened; 措: to place, to arrange, to manage, to handle
亡國	wángguó	to lose (one's) nation
天付	tiānfù	Heaven-conferred
使命	shǐmìng	a mission
文明	wénmíng	civilization
學府	xuéfǔ	seat of learning, eminent institute of higher learning
部	bù	a volume, a complete work of writing
動力	dònglì	a motive power, a driving force, impetus
經典	jīngdiǎn	classics, scriptures; classical
期望	qīwàng	to expect, to hope; expectation
擾攘紛亂	rǎorǎng fēnluàn	confused, disorderly
此外	cǐwài	除了這個以外
任務	rènwù	a duty, responsibility, mission
立定腳跟	lìdìngjiǎogēn	to stand firmly 腳跟: the heel of the foot
天津	Tiānjīn	Tientsin (port city)
脫稿	tuōgǎo	to complete a piece of writing 脫: to take off, to strip; 稿: a manuscript, a rough draft or copy

句型

1. 不在 ... 而在 ... — not in ... but in ...

- 可喜的<u>不在</u>罷課案的被否決,<u>而在</u>投票之多 ...

    例 (1): 教育的目的<u>不在</u>讓每個人成為大學問家,<u>而在</u>改變人的氣質.[1]
    or 讓每個人成為大學問家不是教育的目的;改變人的氣質才是教育的目的.

    例 (2): 我這次演講的重點<u>不在</u>中國古代經濟,<u>而在</u>中國現代經濟.

    [1] 氣質　　qìzhí　　　　　　temperament, qualities

2. 之 Adjective

- 投票<u>之</u>多

    例 (1): <u>之</u>大: 他說話聲音<u>之</u>大,誰也比不上.

    例 (2): <u>之</u>快: 他寫字的速度<u>之</u>快,連打字機也比不上.

3. ... 尚且 ... 何況 ... (呢)? — even ... much less ...

- 許多中年以上的人<u>尚且</u>忍耐不住 ... <u>何況</u>這無數的少年男女學生呢?

    例: 這種問題大學生<u>尚且</u>覺得難,<u>何況</u>是高中學生呢?
    (這種問題連大學生都覺得難 ...)

    NOTE: 不可以用'況且'

4. 不但不 (沒) ... 反而 ... — not only does (did) not ... but on the contrary ...

- 他們<u>不但不</u>能運用民氣,<u>反(而)</u>懼怕民氣了.

    例 (1): 我幫了他那麼多忙,他<u>不但沒</u>謝我,<u>反而</u>罵了我一頓.

    例 (2): 我本來以為我一定不喜歡寫毛筆字,沒想到寫了幾次以後,我不但不討厭反而愈來愈喜歡了.

例 (3): 我吃了那個醫生給我的葯以後,病不但沒好,反而愈來愈厲害了.

5. 甚至於(連)...都... – even

- 排隊游街,高喊著「打倒英,日強盜」,算不得救國事業;甚至於砍下手指寫血書...都算不得救國的事業.

  例 (1): 喝了酒以後他什麼都忘了,甚至於姓什麼叫什麼都不知道了.

  例 (2): 這個孩子是個天才,聰明的不得了,甚至於連大學課本都看的懂.

6. 即使...也(or 都,還)... – ...even if ... still (nevertheless) ...

- 即使吶喊也算是救國運動的一部分,你也不可忘記你的事業有比吶喊重要十倍百倍的.

  例 (1): 即使你是世界上最有錢的人有的時候也會不快樂.

  例 (2): 即使我父母不給我錢,我也要到中國去.

討論

1. 胡適對學生用罷課來干預[1]政治的態度是什麼?
2. 在這篇文章裏,胡適對當時的政府有沒有批評[2]?
3. 什麼是'民氣'?胡適認為'民氣'可不可靠?有沒有力量?
4. "大海上翻了船,最要緊的是救出我自己."請討論這句話.
5. 五十年代末期,[3] 共產黨激烈[4]批判[5]胡適思想,指出胡適麻痺[6]青年對政治的熱忱,[7] 要他們不過問[8]政治.這樣的批評你覺得公平[9]嗎?

    [1] 干預   gānyù   interfere, meddle

2	批評	pīpíng	criticism
3	末期	mòqī	last stage, final years
4	激烈	jīliè	intense, sharp, fierce
5	批判	pīpàn	criticize and judge
6	麻痺	mábì	benumb, blunt
7	熱忱	rèchén	enthusiasm, zeal
8	過問	guòwèn	concern oneself with, bother about
9	公平	gōngpíng	fair, just

The Sources of Leadership Talent
領袖人才的來源

Here, Hu Shi demonstrates the central importance he attaches to education. For him, the nation could only acquire leaders through providing quality education. When he wrote, China, a nation with thousands of years of recorded history, and a civilization with a long tradition of valuing education, did not have even one university with a history of more than thirty years. Thus Hu Shi appeals for educational reform. It was only through a thorough reform of Chinese education and attitudes about education, that the nation could produce a crop of talented leaders.

This essay was first published in *Independent Critic*, 12:2-5 (August 7, 1932). It was later included in *Collected Essays of Hu Shi*, IV, 494-99.

領袖人才的來源

北京大學教授孟森先生前天寄了一篇文字來，題目是論「士大夫」。(見獨立十二期)他下的定義是「『士大夫』者，以自然人為國負責，行事有權，敗事有罪，無神聖之保障，為誅殛所可加者也。」雖然孟先生說的「士大夫」，從狹義上

The Sources of Leadership Talent

領袖	lǐngxiù	a leader, a leading figure
人才	réncái	a person of talent, a person of ability, a talent
來源	láiyuán	source, origin; to originate (from, in, with, etc.), to stem from
教授	jiàoshòu	professor
孟森	Mèng Sēn	人名
篇	piān	Numerary Adjunct for compositions, poems, etc.
文字	wénzì	a piece of writing; written language; writing (as regards form or style)
論	lùn	to discuss, comment on, appraise, or evaluate; discussion, theory, system of thought
士大夫	shìdàifū	literati and officialdom (in old China)

見	jiàn	*vide* (referring reader to a text or parts of a text)
獨立	Dúlì	the name of a magazine
期	qī	a period, a date, a limit of time, a fixed date — used to identify issues of a periodical
下定義	xià dìngyì	to define, to give a definition 定義: definition
者	zhě	used after the subject of an equative sentence, indicating that certain explanation is expected
負責	fùzé	to bear responsibility, to be responsible 負: to carry on the back, to bear; 責: responsibility, duty
行事有權	xíngshìyǒuquán	辦事有權力 行事: to handle matters, to act, to proceed, to execute (a plan, an order); conduct, behavior; 權: 權力, power, authority
敗事有罪	bàishì yǒuzuì	作事失敗了就有罪 敗事: to fail in handling matters, to spoil or bungle a matter; 罪: crime, sin, guilt
無	wú	沒有
神聖	shénshèng	sacred, holy, divine
之	zhī	(lit.) 的
保障	bǎozhàng	protection, guarantee, security; to protect, to safeguard
誅殛	zhūjí	誅: to kill, to execute; 殛: to put to death
可加	kějiā	(something) may be put on (a person)
狹義	xiáyì	a narrow sense

說，好像是限於政治上負大責任的領袖；然而他又包括孟子說的「天民」一級不得位而有絕大影響的人物，所以我們可以說，若用現在的名詞，孟先生文中所謂「士大夫」應該可以叫做「領袖人物」，省稱為「領袖」。孟先生的文章是他和我的一席談話引出來的，我讀了忍不住想引伸他的意思，討論這個領袖人才的問題。

　　孟先生此文的言外之意是嘆息近世居領袖地位的人缺乏真領袖的人格風度，既拋棄了古代「士大夫」的風範，又不知道外國的「士大夫」的

限於	xiànyú	to be confined to, to be limited to
然而	ránér	可是，但是
包括	bāokuò	to include, to comprise
孟子	Mèngzǐ	Mencius
天民	tiānmín	有道德，作事合乎天理 (héhūtiānlǐ, in accord with the moral principles of Heaven) 的老百姓
級	jí	level, rank, grade; (at school) any division by year, class
得位	déwèi	得到官位, to succeed in obtaining an official position
絕大	juédà	extremely great, extremely big 絕: without match, peerless, unparalleled, unique, the utmost
任務	rènwù	personage or figure (usually re-

		ferring to famous persons)
若	ruò	要是, 如果
名詞	míngcí	term, (in grammar) noun
中	zhōng	裏頭
所謂	suǒwèi	so-called
省稱爲	shěngchēngwéi	簡單的叫 (作)
席	xí	Numerary Adjunct for a talk (with someone)
引出來	yǐnchūlái	to draw forth, to lead to
忍不住	rěnbúzhù	cannot help (doing something), cannot stand it any longer 忍: to endure, to bear, to forbear, to repress; 住: Resultative Verb ending meaning "fixity," "security"
引伸	yǐnshēn	to extend in meaning, to expound
此	cǐ	(lit.) 這
言外之意	yánwàizhīyì	言下之意, hidden meaning between the lines, implications, overtones
嘆(歎)息	tànxí	to sigh in lamentation, lament 嘆: to sigh in wonderment, to exclaim
近世	jìnshì	recent times, modern times
居	jū	to dwell, reside, inhabit, or occupy
缺乏	quēfá	to be short of, to lack, to be deficient in
人格	réngé	character, personality
風度	fēngdù	manner, poise, bearing, decorum
既 ... 又 ...	jì ... yòu ...	both ... and ... ; ... as well as ...
拋棄	pāoqì	to abandon, to relinquish, to give up
風範	fēngfàn	model, paragon

流風遺韻，所以成了一種不足表率人羣的領袖。他發願要搜集中國古來的士大夫人格可以做後人模範的，做一部「士大夫集傳」；他又希望有人搜集外國士大夫的精華，做一部「外國模範人物集傳」。這都是很應該做的工作，也許是很有效用的教育教材。我們知道新約裏的幾種耶穌傳記影響了無數人的人格；我們知道布魯達克（Plutarch）的英雄傳影響了後世許多的人物。歐洲的傳記文學發達的最完備，歷史上重要人物都有很詳細的傳記，往往有一篇傳記長至幾十萬言的，也往往有一個人的傳記多至幾十種的。這種傳記的翻譯，倘使有審慎的選擇和忠實明暢的譯筆，

流風遺韻	liúfēngyíyùn	流傳下來的人格和風範
成	chéng	to become, to constitute
不足	bùzú	不夠
表率	biǎoshuài	to serve as an example or paragon; example, paragon
人羣	rénqún	a crowd, throng, or multitude (of people)
發願	fāyuàn	to vow to achieve an objective
搜集	sōují	to seek and gather, to collect
古來	gǔlái	since ancient times
後人	hòurén	後來的人
模範	móxfàn	an exemplary person or thing, model, fine example
部	bù	Numerary Adjunct for a film, a machine, a volume of written work, etc.
集傳	jízhuàn	collected biographies
精華	jīnghuá	quintessence, essentials, the cream or choicest parts

有效用	yǒuxiàoyòng	effective and useful 效用: effectiveness, usefulness, use
教育	jiàoyù	education, to educate
材料	cáiliào	raw material, data, material (for teaching, study, writing an article, etc., for all building purposes); ingredients of a preparation (food, medicine, etc.)
新約	Xīnyuē	the New Testament
耶穌	Yēsū	Jesus (transliterated)
傳記	zhuànjì	biography
無數	wúshù	countless, innumerable 數: number
布魯達克	Bùlǔdákè	Plutarch (*ca.* 46- *ca.* 120), a Greek biographer
英雄	yīngxióng	a hero, a great man
後世	hòushì	later generations
發達	fādá	developed, flourishing
完備	wánbèi	complete with everything, having no deficiency 完: whole, complete, perfect, intact; 備: completeness, perfection
歷史	lìshǐ	history
詳細	xiángxì	in every detail and particular, detailed, nothing omitted
長至	chángzhì	長到, to be as long as
言	yán	字, words
倘使	tǎngshǐ	(lit.) 假如, 要是, 如果
審慎	shěnshèn	careful, cautious
選擇	xuǎnzé	choice, selection, option; to choose, to select, to opt for
忠實	zhōngshí	reliable or truthful (reports, etc.), loyal and faithful
明暢	míngchàng	fluent or smooth (said of the style of writing)
譯筆	yìbǐ	"translator's pen" — translator's skill, the quality or style of a translation

應該可以使我們多知道一點西洋的領袖人物的嘉言懿行,間接的可以使我們對於西方民族的生活方式得一點具體的了解。

中國的傳記文學太不發達了,所以中國的歷史人物往往只靠一些乾燥枯窘的碑版文字或史家列傳流傳下來;很少的傳記材料是可信的,可讀的已很少了;至於可歌可泣的傳記,可說是絕對沒有。我們對於古代大人物的認識,往往只全靠一些很零碎的軼事瑣聞。然而我至今還記得我做小孩子時代讀的朱子小學裏面記載的幾個可愛的

使	shǐ	to cause, to make, to enable
西洋	Xīyáng	the West
嘉言懿行	jiāyán yìxíng	fine words and virtuous deeds (worthy of emulation)
間接	jiànjiē	indirect; indirectly
民族	mínzú	a nation, a people, an ethnic group
方式	fāngshì	mode, manner, way (of doing things)
具體	jùtǐ	concrete (as opposed to abstract), tangible
乾燥	gānzào	dry, arid — dull, uninteresting
枯窘	kūjiǒng	dried up (said of one's inspiration), to be devoid of inspiration, to run out of ideas to write about
碑版文字	bēibǎn wénzì	an inscription on a stone tablet 碑版: a stone tablet
列傳	lièzhuàn	collected biographies, a collection of biographies 列: to arrange in a line, to enumerate
流傳	liúchuán	to transmit or be transmitted

		from person to person, generation to generation, to spread, to circulate, to hand down
可信	kěxìn	"can (or may) be believed" — believable
可讀	kědú	"can (or may) be read" — worth reading
可歌可泣	kěgēkěqì	"can sing about and weep over" — very moving, very touching
零碎	língsuì	fragmentary, fractional, piecemeal; fragments, fractions, odds and ends, bits and pieces
軼事	yìshì	anecdote (not included in history) 軼: to be lost, to be scattered
瑣聞	suǒwén	bits of news, scraps of information 瑣: trivial, petty
至今	zhìjīn	到現在
朱子	Zhūzǐ	Zhu Xi 朱熹 (1131-1200), alias Yuanhui 元晦 or Huian 晦庵, a great scholar of the Song dynasty; he is famous for his commentary on the Confucian classics, considered a standard exposition 子: ancient title of respect for a learned or virtuous man
小學	Xiǎoxué	book attributed to Zhu Xi
記載	jìzǎi	to record; a written record 載: (said of vehicles) to carry (loads) — to record
如	rú	like, as, as if
汲黯	Jí Àn	(died 112 B.C.), a loyal and outspoken minister of the Han dynasty (206 B.C.-220 A.D.)
陶淵明	Táo Yuānmíng	(372-427), one of China's great poets, also known as Tao Qian
之流	zhīliú	的一流, those of the same class 流: class, rate, grade

人物，如汲黯陶淵明之流。朱子記陶淵明，只記他做縣令時送一個長工給他兒子，附去一封家信，說：「此亦人子也，可善遇之。」這寥寥九個字的家書，印在腦子裏，也頗有很深刻的效力，使我三十年來不敢輕用一句暴戾的辭氣對待那幫我做事的人。這一個小小例子可以使我承認模範人物的傳記，無論如何不詳細，只須剪裁的得當，描寫的生動，也未嘗不可以做少年人的良好教育材料，也未嘗不可介紹一點做人的風範。

但是傳記文學的貧乏與忽略，都不夠解釋為

縣令	xiànlìng	county magistrate (official title in old China)
長工	chánggōng	a regular laborer on a farm, a farm hand
附去	fùqù	to send along with, to attach
亦	yì	(lit.) 也
人子	rénzǐ	(lit.) 人的孩子
善遇	shànyù	(lit.) 好好的對待 遇：對，對待
之	zhī	(lit.) third person objective case — him, her, it, them, this, that, these, those
寥寥	liáoliáo	很少
書	shū	信
印	yìn	to print, to stamp, to imprint
腦子	nǎozi	the brain; brains, mental capability, the faculty of memory
頗	pǒ	很
深刻	shēnkè	"to carve deep" — deep, profound (meaning, impression); penetrating, poignant, incisive (analysis or views)

效力	xiàolì	effect, efficacy; to devote (one's energy or life) to, to render (a service)
輕用	qīngyòng	隨便用
暴戾	bàolì	ruthless and tyrannical, cruel and fierce
辭氣	cíqì	speech and demeanor
對待	duìdài	to treat (a person kindly, cruelly, etc.)
承認	chéngrèn	to admit, to acknowledge, to recognize (a fault, a truth, a nation or regime)
如何	rúhé	(lit.) 怎麼樣
剪裁	jiǎncái	"to cut (or clip) with scissors" — to cut clothing material for a garment, to prune a piece of writing, to edit
得當	dédàng	合適, 適當, apt, appropriate, proper
描寫	miáoxiě	"to draw (or trace) and write" — to describe, to depict, to portray; description, depiction
生動	shēngdòng	vivid, lively, lifelike
未嘗	wèicháng	(used before another negative expression to form a positive statment) not necessarily; (used before a positive expression) have not, did not, never
少年	shàonián	early youth, juvenile, boy or girl of that age
良好	liánghǎo	好, 很好
但是	dànshi	可是
貧乏	pínfá	deficiency, lack, insufficiency; wanting, deficient, insufficient; destitute
與	yǔ	跟, 和
忽略	hūlüè	oversight, neglect; to overlook, to neglect, to lose sight of

什麼近世中國的領袖人物這樣稀少而又不高明。領袖的人才決不是光靠幾本「士大夫集傳」就能鑄造成功的。「士大夫」的稀少,只是因為「士大夫」在古代社會裏自成一個階級,而這個階級久已不存在了。在南北朝的晚期,顏之推說:「吾觀禮經,聖人之教,箕帚匕箸,咳唾唯諾,執燭沃盥,皆有節文,亦為至矣。但〔禮經〕既殘缺非復全書,其有所不載,及世事變改者,學達

稀少	xīshǎo	少, few, rare, little, scarce
高明	gāomíng	clever, brilliant, wise, superior; expert, master, qualified person
決	jué	(used before a negative expression) definitely, certainly, under any circumstances
光	guāng	只, 就
鑄造	zhùzào	to melt or cast metal, to mint coins, to coin — to make, to produce, to educate
成功	chénggōng	to succeed; successful; success
階級	jiējí	a (social) class, a rank
已	yǐ	已經
存在	cúnzài	to exist, to be present; existence, presence, being
南北朝	Nán Běi Cháo	Southern (420-589) and Northern (386-581) Dynasties
晚期	wǎnqī	later period
顏之推	Yán Zhītuī	(531- ?), a famous writer-official
吾	wú	(lit.) 我
觀	guān	看
禮經	Lǐjīng	*The Book of Rites*, a Confucian classic
聖人	shèngrén	a sage, a saint

		聖: holy, sacred
教	jiào	teaching, education
箕	jī	a dust basket, a dust pan (by extension may be used as a verb)
帚	zhǒu	a sweeping broom (may be used as a verb)
匕	bǐ	a spoon (may be used as a verb)
箸	zhù	chopsticks (may be used as a verb)
咳	ké	to cough
唾	tò	to spit
唯	wéi	to say yes to a superior, to echo others
諾	nuò	to say yes to a superior, to echo others
執燭	zhízhú	(給長輩) 拿著燭火
沃盥	wòguàn	(給長輩) 倒水盥洗 (guànxǐ, to wash)
皆	jiē	(lit.) 都
節文	jiéwén	requirements of decorum, rules of politeness, ceremonies for courtesy, etiquette
為	wéi	to be
至	zhì	(indicating a superlative) — the greatest, the most
矣	yǐ	interjection indicating the end of a phrase or sentence
但	dàn	但是, 可是
既	jì	已經, already, given the fact that
殘缺	cánquē	incomplete, fragmentary
非復	fēifù	不再是, not any longer
其	qí	a particle which equals "noun + 的" and is used to form a clausal phrase
載	zài	記載, to record
及	jí	(lit.) 跟, 和
世事	shìshì	世界上的事情

君子自爲節度，相承行之。故世號『士大夫風操』。而家門頗有不同，所見互稱長短。然其阡陌亦可自知。（顏氏家訓風操第六）」在那個時代，雖然經過了魏晉曠達風氣的解放，雖然經過了多少戰禍的摧毀，「士大夫」的階級還沒有完全毀滅，一些名門望族都竭力維持他們的門閥。帝王的威權，外族的壓迫，終不能完全消滅這門閥自衛

學達君子	xuédájūnzǐ	有學識的君子 君子: a man of virtue, a man of noble character, a perfect and true gentleman
自爲節度	zìwéijiédù	(lit.) (they) act by themselves with restraint and due consideration (of circumstances)
相承行之	xiāngchéngxíngzhī	(lit.) 一代接着一代實行它
故	gù	所以
世號	shìhào	designated (called) ... from generation to generation
風操	fēngcāo	style, character, and behaviour
家門	jiāmén	family, household
互稱長短	hùchēngchángduǎn	A 説 B 有什麼長處（優點），什麼短處（缺點），B 也説 A 有什麼長處和短處
然	rán	然而, 可是
阡陌	qiānmò	a road leading north and south and a road leading east and west; path between rice fields — the main principle or gist
可知	kězhī	可以知道, may be known
顏氏家訓	Yánshì jiāxùn	"Yan Family's Precepts" — a work by Yan Zhitui dealing

		with the discipline of one's own mind and the family
魏	Wèi	the Wei Dynasty (220-265) of the Three Kingdoms Period
晉	Jìn	the Jin (Chin) Dynasty (265-420)
曠達	kuàngdá	unrestrained, free
風氣	fēngqì	"wind and air" — general mood, atmosphere; common or established practices, conventions
戰禍	zhànhuò	the calamities of war
摧毀	cuīhuǐ	destruction; to destroy, smash or wreck
毀滅	huǐmiè	to destroy and exterminate
名門望族	míngmén wàngzú	a famous family and renowned clan
竭力	jiélì	"to exhaust one's strength" — to do one's utmost
維持	wéichí	to maintain, preserve, keep, or sustain; to guard and support
門閥	ménfá	high family standing, a family of power and influence 閥: a powerful and influential person, family, clique
帝王	dìwáng	the emperor, the king, the throne
威權	wēiquán	prestige, power, authority
外族	wàizú	alien or foreign clans, families, tribes, peoples or nations
壓迫	yāpò	to press hard, to oppress, to pressure, to force; oppression, pressure
終	zhōng	in the end, after all, in the long run, at last, finally
消滅	xiāomiè	to annihilate, to exterminate, to destroy; to die out
自衞	zìwèi	自己保衞 (bǎowèi, to defend, safeguard) 自己

的階級觀念。門閥的爭存不全靠聲勢的煊赫，子孫的貴盛。他們所依靠的是那「士大夫風操」，即是那個士大夫階級所用來律己律人的生活典型。即如顏氏一家，遭遇亡國之禍，流徙異地，然而顏之推所最關心的還是「整齊門內，提撕子孫，」所以他著作家訓，留作他家子孫的典則。隋唐以後，門閥的自尊還能維持這「士大夫風操」至幾百年之久。我們看唐朝柳氏和宋朝呂氏司馬氏的家訓，還可以想見當日士大夫的風範的保存是全靠那種整齊嚴肅的士大夫階級的教育的。

觀念	guānniàn	concept, idea, view, sense
聲勢	shēngshì	(a display of) prestige, power, and influence
煊赫	xuānhè	ablaze — brilliant, glorious, illustrious, very impressive
子孫	zǐsūn	descendants, posterity, offspring
貴盛	guìshèng	distinguished and prosperous
倚靠	yǐkào	靠, to depend on, to rely on, to count on
即是	jíshì	就是, namely, that is
律己	lǜjǐ	to discipline oneself
律人	lǜrén	to discipline other people
典型	diǎnxíng	an archtype, a model, a pattern
即如	jírú	就(好)像, just (or exactly, precisely) as, just like
氏	shì	family, clan; an individual with the surname that precedes
遭遇	zāoyù	to meet with, to encounter or run up against (problems, disasters, etc.)

亡國	wángguó	fall of a nation, national doom; conquered nation, subjugated nation; to conquer a nation, to subjugate a nation, to let a nation perish 亡: to lose, to perish
禍	huò	calamity, disaster, misfortune, evil
流徙	liúxǐ	to exile 流: to flow, to move, to wander, to stray; 徙: 搬, to move (from one place to another)
異地	yìdì	外地, 別的地方
整齊	zhěngqí	to set in order or to subject to orderly control; orderly, in good order, tidy, neat, well-arranged
門內	ménnèi	家裏頭
提撕	tíxī	to give guidance and help to, to make wary, vigilant, alert, or watchful
著作	zhùzuò	to write; work, book, writings
典則	diǎnzé	standard, criterion
隋	Suí	the Sui Dynasty (581-618)
唐	Táng	the Tang Dynasty (618-907)
自尊	zìzūn	self-respect, self-esteem, self pride
至...之久	zhì...zhījiǔ	到...那麼久
宋朝	Sòngcháo	the Song Dynasty (960-1279)
想見	xiǎngjiàn	to visualize, to infer, to gather
當日	dāngrì	"on that very day" 一 那時, at that time, then
保存	bǎocún	preservation, safekeeping; to preserve, conserve, keep, or safeguard
嚴肅	yánsù	serious, solemn, austere

然而這士大夫階級終於被科舉制度和別種政治和經濟的勢力打破了。元明以後，三家村的小兒只消讀幾部刻板書，念幾百篇科舉時文，就可以有登科作官的機會；一朝得了科第，像紅鸞禧戲文裏的丐頭女婿，自然有送錢投靠的人來擁戴他去走馬上任。他從小學的是科舉時文，從來沒有夢見過什麽古來門閥裏的「士大夫風操」的教育與訓練，我們如何能期望他居士大夫之位要維持士大夫的人品呢？

　　以上我說的話，並不是追悼那個士大夫階級的崩壞，更不是希冀那種門閥訓練的復活。我要

終於	zhōngyú	finally, at last, in the end
被	bèi	by (used with the passive voice to introduce the agent of an action, usually implies negative outcome)
科舉制度	kējǔ zhìdù	the civil service examination system of old China
打破	dǎpò	to smash to pieces, to break
元	Yuán	the Yuan Dynasty (1260-1368)
明	Míng	the Ming Dynasty (1368-1644)
三家村	sānjiācūn	a small village
只消	zhǐxiāo	只須, to have only to, to need only
刻板	kèbǎn	monotonous, dull, stereotyped
時文	shíwén	a peculiar style of writing adopted by candidates for the civil service examination in old China known as "eight-legged"

		writing (八股文)
登科	dēngkē	to pass the civil service examination in traditional China
一朝	yìzhāo	once, in one day, in one short day
科第	kēdì	科舉
像	xiàng	如, such as, as, like
紅鸞喜	Hóngluánxǐ	the title of a play
戲文	xìwén	drama script, theatrical writing
丐頭	gàitóu	the leader of beggars
女婿	nǚxù	son-in-law
投靠	tóukào	to go and seek refuge with somebody
擁戴	yōngdài	to support a leader or ruler
走馬上任	zǒumǎshàngrèn	to travel to a place to assume a new post
		走馬: to gallop or trot along on horseback;
		上任: to take up an official post, to assume office
夢見	mèngjiàn	to see in a dream, to dream about
訓練	xùnliàn	training; to train
期望	qīwàng	to expect, to hope
人品	rénpǐn	moral standing, moral quality, character, personality
以上	yǐshàng	above (a given point or line)
追悼	zhuīdào	to commemorate (the dead), to mourn a person's death
		追: to chase after, to pursue;
		悼: to recall, to reminisce
崩壞	bēnghuài	collapse; to collapse, to disintegrate, to break down
希冀	xījì	希望
復活	fùhuó	revival, resurrection; to come back to life, to revive, to resurrect

指出的是一種歷史事實。凡成為領袖人物的，固然必須有過人的天資做底子，可是他們的知識見地，做人的風度，總得靠他們的教育訓練。一個時代有一個時代的「士大夫」，一個國家有一個國家的範型式的領袖人物。他們的高下優劣，總都逃不出他們所受的教育訓練的勢力。某種範型的訓育自然產生某種範型的領袖。

這種領袖人物的訓育的來源，在古代差不多全靠特殊階級（如中國古代的士大夫門閥，如日本的貴族門閥，如歐洲的貴族階級及教會。）的特殊訓練。在近代的歐洲則差不多全靠那些訓練領袖人才的大學。歐洲之有今日的燦爛文化，差不多全是中古時代留下的幾十個大學的功勞。近代文明有四個基本源頭：一是文藝復興，二是十六七世紀的新科

指出	zhǐchū	to point out, to indicate
事實	shìshí	fact, reality, truth
凡 ...	fán ...	every (any, all) ...
成為	chéngwéi	to become, to turn into, to come to be
固然 ... 可是 ...	gùrán ... kěshì ...	no doubt (it is true, indeed, surely, certainly, to be sure) ... , but ...
過人	guòrén	to surpass other people, to excel
天資	tiānzī	natural endowments, inborn talent or intellectual capacity

底子	dǐzi	foundation, grounding, groundwork
知識	zhīshì	knowledge; pertaining to learning or culture, intellectual
見地	jiàndì	insight, judgment
總得	zhǒngděi	after all (one) must ...
範型	fànxíng	pattern, model, example
式	shì	type, model, style
高下優劣	gāoxià yōulie	superiority and inferiority, high and low quality
逃不出	táobùchū	cannot escape from
某	mǒu	a certain (person or thing)
訓育	xùnyù	訓練跟(和)教育
產生	chǎnshēng	to produce (something intangible, versus 生產), to give rise to, to cause, to bring about
特殊	tèshū	特別, special, unusual, unique
貴族	guìzú	the nobility, a noble, an aristocrat
教會	jiàohuì	the church
則	zé	就, then, in this case
今日	jīnrì	今天, 現在
燦爛	cànlàn	brilliant, glorious, resplendent
中古時代	Zhōnggǔ shídài	the (European) Middle Ages
功勞	gōngláo	merit, meritorious deeds, credit, contribution
文明	wénmíng	civilization
基本	jīběn	basic, fundamental, main, essential; root, foundation, or base
源頭	yuántóu	head or source (of a stream)
文藝復興	wényì fùxīng	the (European) Renaissance 文藝: 文學跟藝術, literature and art; 復興: a revival, a return to prosperity; to revive, to resurge, to rejuvenate
世紀	shìjì	century

學，三是宗教革新，四是工業革命。這四個大運動的領袖人物，沒有一個不是大學的產兒。中古時代的大學誠然是幼稚的可憐，然而意大利有幾個大學都有一千年的歷史；巴黎，牛津，康橋都有八九百年的歷史；歐洲的有名大學，多數是有幾百年的歷史的；最新的大學，如莫斯科大學也有一百八十多年了，柏林大學是一百二十歲了。有了這樣長期的存在，才有積聚的圖書設備，才有集中的人才，才有繼長增高的學問，才有那使人依戀崇敬的「學風」。至於今日，西方國家的領袖人物，那一個不是從大學出來的？即使偶有三五個例外，也沒有一個不是直接間接受大學教育的深刻影響的。

在我們這個不幸的國家，一千年來，差不多沒有一個訓練領袖人才的機關。貴族門閥是崩壞

科學	kēxué	science
宗教革新	zōngjiào géxīn	religious reformation or innovation
		宗教: religion;
		革新: reformation, innovation; to reform, innovate, or renovate
工業革命	gōngyè gémìng	industrial revolution
運動	yùndòng	a social movement, a campaign, a drive; physical exercises, sports; motion, movement
產兒	chǎnér	a newborn infant
誠然	chéngrán	certainly, surely, to be sure,

		indeed
幼稚	yòuzhì	immature, naïve, unsophisticated
可憐	kělián	pitiable, pitiful; to have pity on, to pity; meagre, wretched, miserable
義大利	Yìdàlì	Italy
牛津	Niújīn	Oxford
劍橋	Jiànqiáo	Cambridge
莫斯科	Mòsīkē	Moscow
柏林	Bólín	Berlin
長期	chángqí	很長的時期
積聚	jījù	to accumulate, to gather, to build up
圖書	túshū	maps, charts, and books
設備	shèbèi	facilities, equipment, installation
集中	jízhōng	to put together, to concentrate, to amass, to focus, to centralize
繼長增高	jìzhǎngzēnggāo	不斷的(地)成長增高
依戀	yīliàn	to be reluctant to leave, to feel regret at parting from
崇敬	chóngjìng	to regard with esteem, to honor, to revere
學風	xuéfēng	school discipline, style of study
至於	zhìyú	(一直)到; as for
即使...也...	jíshǐ...yě...	就是...也..., even if (though)...still (nevertheless)...
偶	ǒu	偶然, accidentally, by chance; accidental, fortuitous
例外	lìwài	an exception
直接	zhíjiē	directly; direct
不幸	búxìng	misfortune, adversity; unfortunate; unfortunately
機關	jīguān	office, organ, body, organization, institution; a machine; intrigue, scheme, stratagem, plot

了，又沒有一個高等教育的書院是有持久性的，也沒有一種教育是訓練「有為有守」的人才的。五千年的古國，沒有一個三十年的大學！八股試帖是不能造領袖人才的，做書院課卷是不能造領袖人才的，當日最高的教育，——理學與經學考據——也是不能造領袖人才的。現在這些東西都快成了歷史陳迹了，然而這些新起的「大學」，東鈔西襲的課程，朝三暮四的學制，七零八落的設備

高等教育	gāoděng jiàoyù	higher education 高等: high or adanced in grade or rank
書院	shūyuàn	school (in former times), academy of classical learning
持久	chíjiǔ	to last long; lasting, enduring, durable
一性	-xìng	suffix for making an abstract noun with the preceding noun or adjective — the quality, nature, or character of ...
有為有守	yǒuwéiyǒushǒu	有些事(他)作,有些事(他)守住原則 (shǒuzhù yuánzé, to hold the right principles — and not do)
古國	gǔguó	有很長的歷史的國家
八股	bāgǔ	the "eight-legged" essay (rigid style of literary writing during the era of the civil service examinations)
試帖	shìtiě	test in the civil service examinations
造	zào	to make, to create
課卷	kèjuàn	student's paper, student's work
理學	lǐxué	a school of learning in the Song and Ming Dynasties devoted to the study of the Confucian clas-

經學	jīngxué	sics with a rational approach / learning devoted to the study of the classics
考據	kǎojù	textual criticism, textual research
陳跡	chénjī	relics, vestiges 陳: old, stale, preserved for a long time; 跡: mark, trace, remains, ruins, vestige
東…西…	dōng … xī …	"east … west …" — (from) here … (from) there … (with verbs or nouns inserted to indicate "here and there," or "everywhere," or "inconstancy", or "disorganization")
東鈔(抄)西襲	dōngchāoxīxí	to plagiarize here and there 鈔: to copy, to transcribe, to plagiarize; 襲: to plagiarize, to appropriate, to follow the pattern of, to carry on as before
東家宿而西家餐	dōngjiāsù ér xījiācān	在不同的人家住跟吃飯－老是換地方
課程	kèchéng	curriculum
朝…暮…	zhāo … mù …	"in the morning … in the evening …" — with nouns or verbs inserted to indicate "very fast," or "all day long," or "fickleness," or "unpredictability"
朝三暮四	zhāosānmùsì	inconsistent, whimsical
朝秦暮楚	zhāoQín mùChǔ	"to support and serve the Qin state in the morning and the Chu state in the evening" — quick to switch sides, fickle, inconstant, capricious
學制	xuézhì	an educational system
七…八…	qī … bā …	"seven … eight …" — with verbs or nouns inserted to indicate "many" or "many and in disorder"

，四成五成的經費，朝秦暮楚的校長，東家宿而西家餐的教員，十日一雨五日一風的學潮，——也都還沒有造就領袖人才的資格。

　　丁文江先生在中國政治的出路（獨立第十一期）裏曾指出「中國的軍事教育比任何其他的教育都要落後」，所以多數的軍人都「因為缺乏最低的近代知識和訓練，不足以擔任國家的艱鉅。」其實他太恭維「任何其他的教育」了！茫茫的中國，何處是訓練大政治家的所在？何處是養成執法不阿的偉大法官的所在？何處是訓練財政經濟專家學者的所在？何處是訓練我們的思想大師或教

七零八落	qīlíngbāluò	scattered here and there, in confusion 零: fraction; fractional; 落: few and far-spaced, loose and scattered, to stand apart
四成五成	sìchéngwǔchéng	forty or fifty percent 成: one tenth
經費	jīngfèi	expenditure, funds, budget
學潮	xuécháo	student strike, campus upheaval
造就	zàojiù	to bring (through education, training) to a certain level of attainment
資格	zīgé	qualification, prerequisite, requirement
丁文江	Dīng Wénjiāng	人名
中國政治的出路	Zhōngguó zhèngzhìde chūlù	書名, "The Way Out for China's Politics"
曾	céng	ever, once, to have had the experience of
軍事	jūnshì	military, military affairs
任何	rènhé	any, whatever, whichever

足以	zúyǐ	to be enough, to be sufficient to
擔任	dānrèn	to shoulder, to bear, to take charge of, to assume the position of (said of a high or important position)
艱鉅	jiānjù	difficulty, hardship; difficult, hard, arduous, laborious, formidable
恭維(惟)	gōngwéi	to pay compliments, to flatter
茫茫	mángmáng	boundless and indistinct
何處	héchù	(lit.) 甚麼地方
所在	suǒzài	place, location
養成	yǎngchéng	to discipline and train (a person of ability), to bring up (qualified personnel), to cultivate (good habits), to develope (bad habits); also used as a noun
執法不阿	zhífǎbùē	to enforce or execute the law without fawning, to uphold the law strictly, to stick to the legal principles without letup 執: to grasp, to hold, to maintain or uphold, to execute; 法: law; 阿: to favor
偉大	wěidà	great, lofty
法官	fǎguān	a judge (at court), a judicial official
財政	cáizhèng	financial administration, finance
專家	zhuānjiā	expert, specialist 專: focussed on one thing, for a particular person, thing, occasion, purpose, etc.; 家: a specialist (in any branch of art or science)
學者	xuézhě	a scholar, a learned person
思想	sīxiǎng	to think, to ponder; thinking, thought, mentality, ideological inclination, ideology

育大師的所在？

　　領袖人物的資格在今日已不比古代的容易了。在古代還可以有劉邦劉裕一流的梟雄出來平定天下，還可以像趙普那樣的人妄想用「半部論語治天下」。在今日的中國，領袖人物必須具備充分的現代見識，必須有充分的現代訓練，必須有足以引起多數人信仰的人格。這種資格的養成，在今日的社會，除了學校，別無他途。

　　我們到今日才感覺整頓教育的需要，真有點像「臨渴掘井」了。然而治七年之病，終須努力

大師	dàshī	a great master, a master
劉邦	Liú Bāng	founder of the Han Dynasty (r. 206-195 B.C.)
劉裕	Liú Yù	founder of the Liu Song (or former Song) Dynasty, reigned 420-422
梟雄	xiāoxióng	an unscrupulous, fierce and ambitious person 梟: an owl, a legendary bird said to eat its own mother — brave, capable, and unscrupulous
平定	píngdìng	to quell, suppress, or put down (a rebellion, etc.); calm down (said of an emotion, feeling, etc.); settled (said of a situation, etc.)
趙普	Zhào Pǔ	(922-992), a high-ranking official in the courts of the first two emperors of the Song Dynasty
妄想	wàngxiǎng	to desire wildly; an absurd desire, a fancy, a daydream; daydreaming

論語	Lúnyǔ	the Confucian *Analects*, a collection of discourses, maxims, and aphorisms of Confucius, compiled in the fourth century B.C.
治	zhì	to rule or govern (a nation, etc.), to cure or heal (a disease, etc.)
具備	jùbèi	to have all complete, to have all ready to possess, to be provided with
充分	chōngfèn	ample, full, sufficient; fully, completely, thoroughly
見識	jiànshi	experience, knowledge; to widen one's knowledge, to enrich one's experience
引起	yǐnqǐ	to give rise to, to cause, to trigger
信仰	xìnyǎng	to believe in, to have faith in; (religious or political) belief, faith or conviction
別無他途	biéwútātú	(lit.) 沒有其他路(法子)
感覺	gǎnjué	to feel, to sense, to perceive, to become aware; feeling, perception, sensation
整頓	zhěngdùn	to rectify, to put in order, to put to right a poorly-managed organization, system, etc., to reorganize
臨渴掘井	línkějuéjǐng	"to begin digging a well while one is thirsty" — to do something too late, fail to make timely preparation 臨: on the point of, near to, during, at, whilst; 掘: to dig; 井: a well
治七年之病	zhì qīniánzhībìng	醫好七年(很久)的病
終	zhōng	after all, in the long run, in the end

求三年之艾。國家與民族的生命是千萬年的。我們在今日如果真感覺到全國無領袖的苦痛,如果真感覺到「盲人騎瞎馬」的危機,我們應當深刻的認清只有咬定牙根來澈底整頓教育,穩定教育,提高教育的一條狹路可走。如果這條路上的荊棘不掃除,虎狼不驅逐,奠基不穩固;如果我們還想讓這條路去長久埋沒在淤泥水潦之中,——那麼,我們這個國家也只好長久被一班無知識無操守的渾人領導到沉淪的無底地獄裏去了。

三年之艾	sānniánzhīài	乾了三年的艾草 艾: moxa (used in traditional Chinese medicine)
盲	máng	瞎, blind
危機	wéijī	a danger point, a critical point, a precarious moment, a crisis
認清	rènqīng	認識清楚
咬定牙根	yǎodìngyágēn	"to set the teeth firmly," "to clench one's teeth" — to endure pain or hardship with determination, to persevere
澈底	chèdǐ	thorough, complete, thoroughgoing
穩定	wěndìng	to stabilize, to steady; stable, steady
狹	xiá	窄, narrow
荊棘	jīngjí	thistles and thorns, brambles
掃除	sǎochú	to sweep away, to wipe out, to remove; cleaning, cleanup
虎	hǔ	tiger
狼	láng	wolf

驅逐	qūzhú	to expel, to drive out, to get rid of
奠基	diànjī	to lay a foundation
穩固	wěngù	firm, solid, stable
埋沒	máimò	to bury, to cover up (with earth, snow, etc.), to bury (one's talents, etc.), to conceal from recognition 埋: to bury (with earth); 沒: to sink (in water) (note pronunciation)
淤泥	yūní	silt, sludge
水潦	shuǐliǎo	a puddle
只好	zhǐhǎo	to have no alternative but, cannot help but
一班	yìbān	a class of (people), a group of (people)
操守	cāoshǒu	discretion in conduct, attention to moral principle, (personal) integrity 操: to hold, to grasp, to handle, to operate, to exercise, to drill; 守: to observe, to abide by, to keep watch, to guard
渾人	húnrén	an unreasonable fellow 渾: muddy
領導	lǐngdǎo	to lead, to guide; leader
沉淪	chénlún	to sink into (vice, degradation, depravity, etc.)
地獄	dìyù	"the underground prison" — hell, Hades

句型

1. 既 ... 又 ... — both ... and ...

- 既拋棄了古代「士大夫」的風範,又不知道外國「士大夫」的流風遺韻.

    例: 他既不聰明又不用功,所以老是考不好.
    (他不但不聰明而且不用功 ...
    他又不聰明又不用功 ...)

2. ... 也未嘗不可 (以) ... — it is not necessarily impossible or impermissible

- 這一個小小例子 ... 無論如何不詳細,只須剪裁的得當,描寫的生動,也未嘗不可以做少年人的良好教育材料,也未嘗不可介紹一點做人的風範.

    例 (1): 無論東西多貴,只要是值得買的,有用的,多花一點錢也未嘗不可.
    (... 多花錢雖然不好,但是在特殊[1]的情況下,花錢是可以的.)(在這兒,這個特殊的情況指的是:買值得買的,有用的東西.)
    例 (2): "我反對上課的時候說笑話." "我覺得上課的時候為了讓學生有興趣,說些笑話也未嘗不可."
    (" ... 有興趣,也未嘗不可以說些笑話.")
    例 (3): 雖然你的心臟[2]不好,但是每天喝一小杯也未嘗不可.

    [1] 特殊   tèshū   special
    [2] 心臟   xīnzàng   heart

3. 只消 ... 就可以 ... — to need only ...

- 元明以後,三家村的小兒只消讀幾部刻板書,念幾百篇科舉時文,就可以有登科作官的機會.

    例 (1): 在中國城吃飯很便宜,只消幾塊錢就可以吃飽了.
    例 (2): 學開車很容易,只消多練習幾次,就可以開得很好了.

4. 之 (所以) v ... (全) 都是 ... 的功勞 (錯) — (consequence) results from (or can be attributed to) (cause)

■ 歐洲之有今日的燦爛文化,差不多全是中古時代留下的幾十個大學的功勞.

例 (1): 他之所以有今天的成就都是他太太的功勞.
例 (2): 他之所以能學好中文,都是老師們的功勞.
例 (3): 小王之所以到現在還沒畢業都是他自己的錯.

討論

1. 在這篇文章裏所說的"領袖,"究竟是指[1]那一類[2]人?
2. 胡適說西方的領袖人才都是從大學出身[3]的,你同意嗎?
3. 在胡適看來,中國最大的問題是什麼?
4. 教育是不是解決中國問題最有效的辦法?
5. "此亦人子也,可善遇之"這句話表現一種怎樣的人格?

[1] 指	zhǐ	point to, refer to
[2] 類	lèi	kind, type
[3] 出身	chūshēn	come (from a certain background)

On Immortality
不朽

Our eighth selection presents Hu Shi's thinking on the critical question of the individual's effect on society. Briefly put, Hu believed that the good men do lives after them but so does evil. All things done by men affect the tide of history, and their acts, good or bad, carry infinitely into the future. This is true of both the hero and the ordinary man. This essay reflects Hu's individualism — the notion that all men have a unique, permanent value to society. Although the Communists were later to claim that Hu was against the masses and favored "rule by experts," the views expressed here clearly point to Hu's affirmation of the value of the individual.

This essay was first published in *New Youth* (Xīn qīngnían 新青年), 6.2 (February 1919). It was later included in *Collected Essays of Hu Shi*, iv, 975-88.

不朽

─我的宗教─

不朽有種種說法,但是總括看來,只有兩種說法是眞有區別的。一種是把「不朽」解作靈魂不滅的意思。一種就是春秋左傳上說的「三不朽」。

(一)神不滅論:宗教家往往說靈魂不滅,死後須受末日的裁判:做好事的享受天國天堂的快樂,做惡事的要受地獄的苦痛。這種說法,幾千年來不但受了無數愚夫愚婦的迷信,居然還受了許多學者的信仰。但是古今來也有許多學者對於靈魂是否可離形體而存在的問題,不能不發生疑問

On Immortality

不朽	bùxiǔ	immortal, immortality
宗教	zōngjiào	religion
總括看來	zǒngkuò kànlái	放在一起來看
		總括: to sum up, to put together
區別	qūbié	分別, difference, distinction; to differentiate, to distinguish
解作	jiězuò	解成, to explain as
靈魂	línghún	soul, spirit
不滅	bùmiè	imperishable, indestructible
春秋	Chūnqiū	*The Spring and Autumn Annals*, attributed to Confucius
左傳	Zuǒzhuàn	*The Tso Commentary* on the

		Spring and Autumn Annals
神	shén	精神, soul, spirit
論	lùn	a theory, a system of thought; to discuss, to debate
末日	mòrì	day of Judgment, the last day
裁判	cáipàn	a verdict or judgment by law; a judge, a referee; to judge
享受	xiǎngshòu	to enjoy, to indulge oneself in (some pleasant pursuit); enjoyment
天國	tiānguó	the Kingdom of Heaven
天堂	tiāntáng	heaven, paradise
惡	è	壞
地獄	dìyù	hell, Hades
苦痛	kǔtòng	痛苦, suffering, pain
無數	wúshù	countless, innumerable 無:沒有; 數: number, amount
愚夫愚婦	yúfūyúfù	the ignorant multitude, the masses 愚: foolish, stupid; 夫:男人; 婦:女人
迷信	míxìn	blind faith, blind worship, superstitious belief; to believe blindly
學者	xuézhě	a scholar, a learned person
信仰	xìnyǎng	(religious or political) belief; to believe in
古今來	gǔjīnlái	from ancient times until today, through the ages, since time immemorial
是否	shìfǒu	是不是
離	lí	離開
形體	xíngtǐ	the human body which has a form or shape (as contrasted to the spirit which is invisible)
存在	cúnzài	to exist, to be present
疑問	yíwèn	question, doubt

。最重要的如南北朝人范縝的神滅論說：「形者神之質，神者形之用。……神之於質，猶利之於刀；形之於用，猶刀之於利。……捨利無刀，捨刀無利。未聞刀沒而利存，豈容形亡而神在？」宋朝的司馬光也說：「形既朽滅，神亦飄散，雖有剉燒舂磨，亦無所施。」但是司馬光說的「形既朽滅，神亦飄散，」還不免把形與神看作兩件事，不如范縝說的更透切。范縝說人的神靈即是形體的作用，形體便是神靈的形質。正如刀子是

如	rú	像, like, as
南北朝	NánBěicháo	Southern and Northern Dynasties (420-589)
范縝	Fàn Zhěn	人名
形	xíng	形體, 有形的東西
者	zhě	(lit.) used after the subject of an equative sentence, indicating that certain explanation is intended
之	zhī	的
質	zhì	matter, substance
用	yòng	practical use, practical application
之於	zhīyú	(lit.) 對於, with regard to
猶	yóu	(lit.) 如, 像
利	lì	sharpness (said of blade, etc.)
捨	shě	to give up, to abandon, to discard
未	wèi	沒有, to have never (followed by a verbal element)
聞	wén	聽, 聽說
沒	mò	to go into hiding, obscurity or oblivion, to sink, to drown (note pronunciation)

存	cún	存在
豈容	qǐróng	how can it be permitted that ... , how can it be possible that ... 豈: an interrogative particle implying a conflicting or dissenting view or answer
亡	wáng	to perish; dead, lost
宋朝	Sòngcháo	the Song Dynasty (960-1279)
司馬光	Sīmǎ Guāng	人名 (1019-1086), a scholar-official of the Song Dynasty
既	jì	既然已經
朽滅	xiǔmiè	decayed and perished
亦	yì	也
飄散	piāosàn	dispersed and flying about 飄: to move with the wind, to drift; 散: scattered, dispersed
雖	suī	雖然
銼	cuò	a steel file
燒	shāo	to burn
舂	chōng	a pestle (for husking grain); to pound rice to remove the grain, to husk rice by pounding
磨	mó	to rub, to grind
施	shī	用, to apply, to implement
不免	bùmiǎn	unavoidable; unavoidably
與	yǔ	跟, 和, and (a connective, used between nominal elements)
看作	kànzuò	看成, to regard as, to consider as, to treat as
不如	bùrú	比不上
透切	tòuqiè	penetrating and incisive
神靈	shénlíng	精神靈魂, spirit and soul
即是	jíshì	就是, is exactly
作用	zuòyòng	uses, functions, usefulness
便是	biànshì	就是, 即是
形質	xíngzhì	form and substance
正如	zhèngrú	exactly like, just like, just as

形質，刀子的利鈍是作用；有刀子方才有利鈍，沒有刀子便沒有利鈍。人有形體方才有作用：這個作用，我們叫做「靈魂」。若沒有形體，便沒有作用了，便沒有靈魂了。范縝這篇神滅論出來的時候，惹起了無數人的反對。梁武帝叫了七十幾個名士作論駁他，都沒有什麼真有價值的議論。其中只有沈約的難神滅論說：「利若遍施四方，則利體無處復立；利之為用正存一邊毫毛處耳。神之與形，舉體若合，又安得同乎？若以此譬為盡耶，則不盡；若謂本不盡耶，則不可以為譬也。」這一段是說刀是無機體，人是有機體，故不能彼此相比。這話固然有理，但終不能推翻「

利鈍	lìdùn	sharpness and bluntness (said of a knife)
方才	fāngcái	才, only then, not until
便	biàn	就
若	ruò	要是, 如果
惹起	rěqi	to incite, to provoke
反對	fǎnduì	to object, to oppose; objection
梁武帝	Liáng Wǔ Dì	Emperor Wu of Liang (r. 502-549)
名士	míngshì	a celebrated scholar
論	lùn	argumentation, a treatise, discourse
駁	bó	to refute, to rebut
有價值	yǒujiàzhí	valuable
議論	yìlùn	argument, comments, debate, discussion; to discuss
其中	qízhōng	among, in the midst, within, therein, of them, of those, among which

沈約	Shěn Yuē	人名 (441-513), a poet-scholar of the Southern Dynasties
難	nàn	to blame, to reproach (note pronunciation)
遍	piàn	everywhere, throughout, all over
四方	sìfāng	the four directions (east, west, north and south); in every direction
則	zé	就
處	chù	地方
復	fù	再
毫毛	háomáo	fine hair on human skin; hair-breadth, extremely small space
耳	ěr	a final particle meaning "only," "merely"
以…爲…	yǐ … wéi …	(lit.) 把…當作…
此譬	cǐpì	(lit.) 這個比方
耶	yé	a final particle for a question
謂	wèi	(lit.) 説
以爲譬	yǐwéipì	(lit.) to take (something) as a metaphor or analogy
無機體	wújītǐ	inorganic matter
有機體	yǒujītǐ	organic matter
故	gù	(lit.) 所以
彼此	bǐcǐ	互相, mutually, reciprocally, each other, one another
相比	xiāngbǐ	比
固然…但…	gùrán … dàn …	it is true (surely, certainly, no doubt) … but …
有理	yǒulǐ	有道理, reasonable, logical, justifiable; to have justice on one's side
終	zhōng	finally, at last, after all, in the long run
推翻	tuīfān	to overturn (a theory, principle), to overthrow (a government)

神者形之用」的議論。近世唯物派的學者也說人的靈魂並不是什麼無形體，獨立存在的物事，不過是神經作用的總名；靈魂的種種作用都即是腦部各部分的機能作用；若有某部被損傷，某種作用即時廢止；人年幼時腦部不曾完全發達，神靈作用也不能完全，老年人腦部漸漸衰耗，神靈作用也漸漸衰耗。這種議論的大旨，與范縝所說「神者形之用」正相同。但是有許多人總捨不得把靈魂打消了，所以咬住說靈魂另是一種神秘玄妙的物事，並不是神經的作用。這個「神秘玄妙」的物事究竟是什麼，他們也說不出來，只覺得總應該有這麼一件物事。既是「神秘玄妙」，自然不能用科學試驗來證明他，也不能用科學試驗來駁倒他。既然如此，我們只好用實驗主義(Prag-

近世	jìnshì	recent times, modern times
唯物派	wéiwùpài	the school of materialism 唯: only, alone; 物: matter, material, substance; 派: a school (of philosophy, art)
獨立	dúlì	independent; independence
物事	wùshì	物, matter, thing, being
神經	shénjīng	nerve
總名	zǒngmíng	a generic term
腦部	nǎobù	the brain (as a part of the human body)
機能	jīnéng	function
某	mǒu	a certain (thing or person)
損傷	sǔnshāng	to harm, to damage, to injure; losses, casualties

即時	jíshí	馬上, 立刻, immediately, at once
廢止	fèizhǐ	to discontinue
年幼	niányòu	young of age
曾	céng	ever, once, to have had the experience of
發達	fādá	developed, advanced
衰耗	shuāihào	weakening and deterioration; to weaken and deteriorate
大旨	dàzhǐ	the main point, the chief purpose, meaning, objective
相同	xiāngtóng	一樣
總	zǒng	總是, 老是
打消	dǎxiāo	to strike out, to cancel, to give up (an intention, idea, notion)
咬住	yǎozhù	to bite firmly; to insist
另	lìng	another
神秘	shénmì	mysterious, mystical
玄妙	xuánmiào	profound, abstruse, subtle
究竟	jiūjìng	到底, after all, in the long run
科學	kēxué	science
試驗	shìyàn	an experiment; to experiment, to try out or test
證明	zhèngmíng	to prove, certify, testify, attest to, or confirm; proof, evidence, testimony, a certificate
駁倒	bódǎo	to defeat in a debate 倒: a Resultative Verb Ending meaning "falling," or "collapse"
既然如此	jìránrúcǐ	既然像這樣, 既然是這樣
只好	zhǐhǎo	cannot help but, have no alternative but
實驗主義	shíyàn zhǔyì	pragmatism (philosophy stressing practical consequences and values as standards by which concepts are to be analyzed and their validity determined), experimentalism 實驗: to experiment, to test; experiment, test

matism)的方法,看這種學說的實際效果如何,以爲評判的標準。依此標準看來,信神不滅論的固然也有好人,信神滅論的也未必全是壞人。即如司馬光范縝赫胥黎一類的人,說不信靈魂不滅的話,何嘗沒有高尚的道德?更進一層說,有些人因爲迷信天堂,天國,地獄,末日裁判,方才修德行善,這種修行全是自私自利的,也算不得眞正道德。總而言之,靈魂滅不滅的問題,於人生行爲上實在沒有什麼重大影響;既沒有實際的影響,簡直可說是不成問題了。

(二)三不朽說:左傳說的三種不朽是:①立德

學說	xuéshuō	a theory
實際	shíjì	practical, actual; actual situation, actuality
效果	xiàoguǒ	effect and result, efficacy
如何	rúhé	像甚麼,是甚麼,怎麼樣
以為	yǐwéi	當作, to take something to be, to regard something as
評判	píngpàn	to criticize, to pass judgment
標準	biāozhǔn	standard, criterion
依	yī	照, in accordance with, in compliance with
此	cǐ	這個
信	xìn	相信,信仰
未必	wèibì	不一定
全是	quánshì	完全是,都是
即如	jírú	就像, just as, just like
赫胥黎	Hèxūlí	Huxley
類	lèi	種, a kind, type, category
何嘗	hécháng	how could (it be the case?)

高尚	gāoshàng	noble, exalted, respectable, lofty
道德	dàodé	morality, ethics; moral, ethical
進一層	jìnyīcéng	to advance further
		層: a component part in a sequence, a level
修德	xiūdé	修養品德
行善	xíngshàn	做好事
修行	xiūxíng	修養品德, to practice Buddhist or Taoist rules
自私自利	zìsīzìlì	selfish, thinking of nothing but one's own gain; selfishness
算不得	suànbùdé	not to be counted or regarded as
真正	zhēnzhèng	真的
總而言之	zǒngéryánzhī	to sum up, in short, in a word
		總: to gather, to collect, to assemble
人生	rénshēng	human life, life
行為	xíngwéi	behaviour, conduct, acts
實在	shízài	really, truly, certainly; 其實, in fact, as a matter of fact; (said of a person) trustworthy, honest, dependable; (said of work) well-done, done carefully; (said of an object) concrete, tangible
重大	zhòngdà	important, significant, serious, grave
檢直	jiǎnzhí	簡直, simply, outright
不成問題	bùchéng wèntí	unquestionable
		成: to complete, to achieve, to accomplish, to become
説	shuō	學説, a theory
立德	lìdé	to achieve virtue
		立: to establish, to build, to set up;
		德: morality, virtues

的不朽，②立功的不朽，③立言的不朽。「德」便是個人人格的價值，像墨翟耶穌一類的人，一生刻意孤行，精誠勇猛，使當時的人敬愛信仰，使千百年後的人想念崇拜。這便是立德的不朽。「功」便是事業，像哥侖布發現美洲，像華盛頓造成美洲共和國，替當時的人開一新天地，替歷史開一新紀元，替天下後世的人種下無量幸福的種子。這便是立功的不朽。「言」便是語言著作，像那詩經三百篇的許多無名詩人，又像陶潛杜

立功	lìgōng	to render distinguished service, to achieve distinction 功: merit, achievement
立言	lìyán	to leave worthy writings to posterity 言: speech, words
個人	gèrén	the individual (as contrasted with the group); oneself; personal; personally
人格	réngé	character, personality
墨翟	Mò Dí	Mo-tze (ca. 501- ca. 416 B.C.), a great philosopher of the Warring States period
耶穌	Yēsū	Jesus
刻意	kèyì	painstakingly, sedulously, (to do something) with intensive attention in order to achieve perfection or great success
孤行	gūxíng	to do something alone
精誠勇猛	jīngchéng yǒngměng	with the utmost faith, dedication, courage, and vehemence 精: keen, sharp, dedicated, intensive; 誠: sincere; sincerity, good

		faith; 勇: brave, fearless, heroic; 猛: brave, fierce
使	shǐ	(a causative verb) to make, cause, enable
當時	dāngshí	在那個時候, at that time, then, in those days
敬愛	jìngài	to respect and love
想念	xiǎngniàn	to give thought to (a person), to long for, to yearn for
崇拜	chóngbài	to revere, to venerate, to adore, to idolize
事業	shìyè	enterprise, undertaking, career, pursuit
哥倫布	Gēlúnbù	Christopher Columbus (1446?-1506)
美洲	Měizhōu	the American continent (north and south) 洲: continent
華盛頓	Huáshèngdùn	George Washington (1732-1799)
造成	zàochéng	to create, to build up, to cause to happen
共和國	gònghéguó	a republic
開紀元	kāijìyuán	to usher in a new epoch 紀元: epoch, era
後世	hòushì	later generations
種下	zhòngxià	to sow, to plant
無量	wúliàng	無數, countless, immeasurable 量: quantity
幸福	xìngfú	blissful, blessed; happiness and well-being, bliss
種子	zhǒngzǐ	seed
語言	yǔyán	language, speech
著作	zhùzuò	writing, written work; to write
詩經	Shījīng	*The Book of Odes*, one of the five Confucian classics
篇	piān	Numerary Adjunct for compositions, poems
無名	wúmíng	沒有名子, anonymous, unknown
陶潛	Táo Qián	(372-427), 晉朝大詩人

甫、莎士比亞、易卜生一類的文學家,又像柏拉圖、盧騷、彌兒一類的哲學家,又像牛敦、達爾文一類的科學家,或是做了幾首好詩使千百年後的人歡喜感歎;或是做了幾本好戲使當時的人鼓舞感動,使後世的人發憤興起;或是創出一種新哲學,或是發明了一種新學說,或在當時發生思想的革命,或在後世影響無窮。這便是立言的不朽。總而言之,這種不朽說,不問人死後靈魂能不能存在,只問他的人格,他的事業,他的著作有沒有永遠存在的價值。即如基督教徒說耶穌是上帝的兒子,他的神靈永永存在,我們正不用駁這種無憑據的神話,只說耶穌的人格,事業,和教訓都可以

杜甫	Dù Fǔ	(712-770), 唐朝大詩人
莎士比亞	Xiāoshìbǐyà	William Shakespeare
易卜生	Yìbǔshēng	Henrik Ibsen (1828-1906)
文學家	wénxuéjiā	man of letters, literary man, literateur
		文學: literature;
		家: specialist (in art or science)
柏拉圖	Bólātú	Plato
盧騷	Lúsāo	Jean Jacques Rousseau (1712-1778)
彌兒	Míer	John Stuart Mill (1806-1873), British philosopher and political economist
哲學家	zhéxuéjiā	a philosopher
		哲學: philosophy
牛敦	Niúdūn	Sir Isaac Newton (1642-1727)
達爾文	Dáěrwén	Charles (Robert) Darwin (1809-1882)

歡喜	huānxǐ	高興
感歎	gǎntàn	to respond with feeling (emotion) and to sigh over
戲	xì	a drama, a play
鼓舞	gǔwǔ	to rouse, stir up, excite, or spur on
感動	gǎndòng	to affect, move, or touch (mentally and emotionally)
發憤	fāfèn	to be roused to action, to be spurred
興起	xīngqǐ	to rise, to launch
創出	chuàngchū	to establish, to create, to found
思想	sīxiǎng	thinking, thought, ideology; to think, to ponder
革命	gémìng	revolution
無窮	wúqióng	endless, limitless, boundless, inexhaustible, interminable
永遠	yǒngyuǎn	forever, eternally, perpetually
基督教	Jīdūjiào	Christianity (particularly referring to the Protestants) 基督: Jesus Christ; 教: religion
教徒	jiàotú	a religious believer
上帝	shàngdì	The Supreme Ruler, God
永永	yǒngyǒng	永遠
憑據	píngjù	basis for belief or supposition, ground, reason, proof, evidence 憑: basis, proof, evidence; to lean on, to rely on, to depend on; 據: proof, evidence; to occupy, to take possession of; according to, on the basis of
神話	shénhuà	a myth
教訓	jiàoxùn	admonitions, teachings; a moral, a lesson; to admonish, to exhort
何必	hébì	why should? why must? why is it necessary?

不朽,又何必説那些無謂的神話呢?又如孔教會的人每到了孔丘的生日,一定要舉行祭孔的典禮,還有些人學那「朝山進香」的法子,要趕到曲阜孔林去對孔丘的神靈表示敬意!其實孔丘的不朽全在他的人格與教訓,不在他那「在天之靈」。大總統多行兩次丁祭,孔教會多行兩次「朝山進香」,就可以使孔丘格外不朽了嗎?更進一步説,像那三百篇裏的詩人,也沒有姓名,也沒有事實,但是他們都可以説是立言的不朽。爲什麼呢?因爲不朽全靠一個人的眞價值,並不靠姓名事實的流傳,也不靠靈魂的存在。試看古今來的多少大發明家,那發明火的,發明養蠶的,發明繰絲的,發明織布的,發明水車的,發明舂米的水碓的,發明規矩的,發明秤的,……雖然姓名不傳,事實湮沒,但他們的功業永遠存在,他們也

無謂的	wúwèide	senseless, meaningless
孔教會	Kǒngjiàohuì	信孔子的教會
孔丘	Kǒng Qiū	formal name of Confucius
舉行	jǔxíng	to hold (a meeting, a ceremony, a rally, a party, an examination, etc.); to take place
祭	jì	to honor by a rite or sacrifice, to offer sacrifices to, to worship
典禮	diǎnlǐ	ceremony, rite
朝山進香	cháoshānjìnxiāng	to go on a pilgrimage, and offer incense to Buddha 朝: to make a pilgrimage to, to have an audience with (a king, emperor); 進: to offer, to present;

		香: incense, spice, balm
趕到	gǎndào	to hurry to, to arrive in haste
曲阜	Qūfù	the birthplace of Confucius, in present-day Shandong province
孔林	Kǒnglín	the tomb of Confucius in Shandong
敬意	jìngyì	respect, regard
在...不在...	zài ... búzài ...	to lie in ... and not (to lie) in ...
天	tiān	天上, heaven
總統	zǒngtǒng	president (of a nation)
行	xíng	to practice, to perform the act of, to carry out
丁祭	dīngjì	to worship, to offer sacrifices to
格外	géwài	exceptionally, extraordinarily
三百篇	Sānbǎipiān	詩經 (totaling about 300 pieces)
流傳	liúchuán	to be transmitted (to be handed down) from person to person or from generation to generation; transmitting; transmission
發明	fāmíng	to invent, devise or innovate; invention
蠶	cán	silkworm
繅絲	sāosī	to draw silk from cocoons
織布	zhībù	to weave cloth
水碓	shuǐduì	a rice-polishing device using water power
規矩	guīju	(originally) a pair of compasses and a carpenter's square — rules, established practice, custom; well-behaved, well-disciplined
秤	chèng	a weighing scale
湮沒	yānmò	to fall into oblivion, be neglected, be forgotten 湮: to fall into oblivion, to bury in oblivion; 沒: to sink, to drown, to be submerged, to go into oblivion or obscurity
功業	gōngyè	meritorious deeds

就都不朽了。這種不朽比那個人的小小靈魂的存在,可不是更可寶貴,更可羨慕嗎?況且那靈魂的有無還在不可知之中,這三種不朽——德,功,言,——可是實在的。這三種不朽可不是比那靈魂的不滅更靠得住嗎?

以上兩種不朽論,依我個人看來,不消說得,那「三不朽說」是比那「神不滅說」好得多了。但是那「三不朽說」還有三層缺點,不可不知。第一,照平常的解說看來,那些真能不朽的人只不過那極少數有道德,有功業,有著述的人。還有那無量平常人難道就沒有不朽的希望嗎?世界上能有幾個墨翟耶穌,幾個哥侖布華盛頓,幾個杜甫陶潛,幾個牛敦達爾文呢?這豈不成了一種「寡頭」的不朽論嗎?第二,這種不朽論單從積極一方面着想,但沒有消極的裁制。那種靈魂的不朽論既說有天國的快樂,又說有地獄的苦楚,是積極消極兩方面都顧着的。如今單說立德可以不朽,不立德又怎樣呢?立功可以不朽,有罪惡又怎樣呢?第三,這種不朽論所說的「德,功

寶貴	bǎoguì	to value, to treasure, to cherish; valuable, precious
羨慕	xiànmù	to envy, to covet, to admire
況且	kuàngqiě	furthermore, moreover, besides
靠得住	kàodezhù	reliable, dependable, able to be

		trusted
以上	yǐshàng	the above, the foregoing, the above-mentioned; above, over, more than
不消說得	bùxiāoshuōde	needless to say
缺點	quēdiǎn	a defect, shortcoming, weakness or drawback
平常	píngcháng	ordinary, common; ordinarily, generally, usually, as a rule
解說	jiěshuō	explanation, interpretation; to explain orally, to comment, to appease, to resolve (a dispute)
少數	shǎoshù	small number, few, minority
著述	zhùshù	writing, a written work; to write, to author, to compile
豈不	qǐbù	wouldn't it result in ... ? 豈: an interrogative particle implying a conflicting or dissenting view or response — how, what
寡頭	guǎtóu	oligarchical 寡: little, few, rare
單	dān	solely, only, simply
積極	jījí	active, positive, persistent; actively, positively, persistently
着想	zhuóxiǎng	to consider (from a certain perspective)
消極	xiāojí	passive, negative, pessimistic; passively, negatively, pessimistically (antonym of 積極)
裁制	cáizhì	to restrain, to restrict, to limit
既 ... 又 ...	jì ... yòu ...	又 ... 又 ...
苦楚	kǔchǔ	痛苦, pain, suffering
顧	gù	to mind, to care for, to look after, to concern oneself about
如今	rújīn	現在
罪惡	zuìè	sin, evil, crime, vice, guilt

，言，」三件，範圍都很含糊。究竟怎樣的人格方才可算是「德」呢？怎樣的事業方才可算是「功」呢？怎樣的著作方才可算是「言」呢？我且舉一個例。哥侖布發現美洲固然可算得立了不朽之功，但是他船上的水手火頭又怎樣呢？他那隻船的造船工人又怎樣呢？他船上用的羅盤器械的製造工人又怎樣呢？他所讀的書的著作者又怎樣呢？……舉這一條例，已可見「三不朽」的界限含糊不清了。

因為要補足這三層缺點，所以我想提出第三種不朽論來請大家討論。我一時想不起別的好名字，姑且稱他做「社會的不朽論」。

(三)社會的不朽論：社會的生命，無論是看縱剖面，是看橫截面，都像一種有機的組織。從縱剖面看來，社會的歷史是不斷的；前人影響後人

範圍	fànwéi	sphere, scope, range
含糊	hánhú	(said of a statement) vague, ambiguous, confusing; (said of attitudes, manners) befuddled, uncertain
且	qiě	just, for the time being
舉例	jǔlì	to give examples
算得	suàndé	can be counted or regarded as
水手	shuǐshǒu	a sailor, a mariner
火頭	huǒtóu	the person responsible for the start of a fire, a cook
造	zào	作, to make, do, build or manufacture

羅盤	luópán	a compass
器械	qìxiè	machine, machinery
著作者	zhùzuòzhě	著作的人, one who authors a piece of writing, a book, etc.
界限	jièxiàn	outer limit, border
不清	bùqīng	不清楚
補足	bǔzú	to make complete or whole, to make up for a deficit 補: to repair, mend, supplement or make up; 足: sufficient, enough, full, adequate
提出	tíchū	to put forward (a proposal), to advance (a theory), to make (a suggestion), to raise (a question)
一時	yìshí	for a moment, for a time
姑且	gūqiě	for the time being
A 稱 B 作 ...	A chēng B zuò ...	A calls B ...
生命	shēngmìng	life
縱剖面	zòngpōumiàn	vertical or longitudinal section 縱: from north to south, vertical, longitudinal, lengthwise; 剖: to cut, rip, or tear open; 面: side, aspect, surface, (in math) a plane surface
橫截面	héngjiémiàn	a cross-section 橫截: to cut across; 橫: from east to west or vice versa, horizontal, lateral; 截: to cut, to section, to truncate
組織	zǔzhī	an organization, a formation, (in biology) tissue, texture; to organize, to form, to constitute
不斷	búduàn	unceasing, uninterrupted, continuous, constant 斷: to break, cut apart, or sever

，後人又影響更後人；沒有我們的祖宗和那無數的古人，又那裏有今日的我和你？沒有今日的我和你，又那裏有將來的後人？沒有那無量數的個人，便沒有歷史，但是沒有歷史，那無數的個人也決不是那個樣子的個人：總而言之，個人造成歷史，歷史造成個人。從橫截面看來，社會的生活是交互影響的：個人造成社會，社會造成個人：社會的生活全靠個人分工合作的生活，但個人的生活，無論如何不同，都脫不了社會的影響；若沒有那樣這樣的社會，決不會有這樣那樣的我和你；若沒有無數的我和你，社會也決不是這個樣子。來勃尼慈（Leibnitz）說得好：「這個世界乃是一片大充實，（Plenum, 爲眞空 Vacuum 之對。）其中一切物質都是接連着的。一個大充實裏面有一點變動，全部的物質都要受影響，影響的程度與物體距離的遠近成正比例。世界也是如此。每一個人不但直接受他身邊親近的人的影響，並且間

祖宗	zǔzōng	ancestors, forefathers
古人	gǔrén	古時候的人
今日	jīnrì	今天, 現在
無量數	wúliàngshù	無量, 無數, countless
決	jué	一定
交互	jiāohù	each other, mutual, reciprocal
分功合作 (分工合作)	fēngōnghézuò	to share and cooperate (in a task) 分功: to divide the work; 合作: to cooperate with one another

脫不了	tuōbùliǎo	cannot leave, escape from or get out of (note pronunciation)
來勃尼慈	Láibóníci	Gottfried Wilhelm von Leibnitz (1646-1716), German philosopher, writer, and mathematician
乃是	nǎishì	是, 就是
片	piàn	Numerary Adjunct for any flat object, such as a piece of bread, a slice of meat, a tile, a snowflake, a lake, an open field, a plain, etc.
充實	chōngshí	plenum; substantial, rich; to substantiate, enrich, replenish, strengthen, or improve
為	wéi	是
真空	zhēnkōng	vacuum
對	duì	an opposite
一切	yīqiè	所有的
全部	quánbù	whole, complete, total, all
物質	wùzhí	(in physics) matter
受影響	shòuyǐngxiǎng	to be influenced, to be affected
程度	chéngdù	degree, extent, stage, state or condition; standard, required qualifications or attainments, general achievement in academic studies
物體	wùtǐ	(in physics) a body, substance, or object
距離	jùlí	distance
正比例	zhèngbǐlì	direct proportion opposite: 反比例, inverse proportion
如此	rúcǐ	像這樣
不但 ... 並且 ...	búdàn ... bìngqiě ...	not only ... but also ...
直接	zhíjiē	direct, first hand; directly opposite: 間接 (see below)
身邊	shēnbiān	one's vicinity, one's immediate surroundings
親近	qīnjìn	to be near or intimate with

接又間接的受距離很遠的人的影響。所以世間的交互影響，無論距離遠近，都受得着的。所以世界上的人，每人受着全世界一切動作的影響。如果他有周知萬物的智慧，他可以在每人的身上看出世間一切施爲，無論過去未來都可看得出，在這一個現在裏面便有無窮時間空間的影子。」（見Monadology第六十一節）

從這個交互影響的社會觀和世界觀上面，便生出我所說的「社會的不朽論」來。我這「社會的不朽論」的大旨是：「我這個『小我』不是獨立存在的，是和無量數小我有直接或間接的交互關係的；是和社會的全體和世界的全體都有互爲影響的關係的；是和社會世界的過去和未來都有因果關係的。種種從前的因，種種現在無數『小我』和無數他種勢力所造成的因，都成了我這個『小我』的一部分。我這個『小我』，加上了種

間接	jiānjiē	indirect; indirectly opposite: 直接 (see above)
受得着	shòudezháo	able to get, receive, be subjected to
動作	dòngzuò	action, movement
周知	zhōuzhī	to know completely, fully, or thoroughly 周: circumference, full circle; complete, universal, all around

萬物	wànwù	a myriad of objects — all things under the sun, all creatures in the world, all matters in the universe
智慧	zhìhuì	wisdom, intelligence
施爲	shīwéi	action, behavior, conduct 施: to do, to act; 爲: to do, to act
過去	guòqù	what has passed — the past
未來	wèilái	what has not yet come — the future
無窮	wúqióng	endless, limitless, boundless, infinite, inexhaustible, interminable 窮: to exhaust; exhausted; the extreme, the farthest
空間	kōngjiān	space
影子	yǐngzi	shadow, (figuratively) trace
見	jiàn	to perceive, to examine, to consult
節	jié	passage, paragraph, section
觀	guān	a view, a concept; to see, to observe, to view
小我	xiǎowǒ	(lit.) the little self — the individual, the ego, the self opposite: 大我 (see below)
互爲影響	hùwéiyǐngxiǎng	互相影響, A 影響 B, B 也影響 A
因果關係	yīnguǒguānxi	relationship of cause and effect, causality 因: 原因; 果: 結果
種種	zhǒngzhǒng	all kinds or types of
他種	tāzhǒng	別種
加上	jiāshàng	to add, plus

種從前的因，又加上了種種現在的因，傳遞下去，又要造成無數將來的『小我』。這種種過去的『小我』，和種種現在的『小我』，和種種將來無窮的『小我』，一代傳一代，一點加一滴；一線相傳，連綿不斷；一水奔流，滔滔不絕：——這便是一個『大我』。『小我』是會消滅的，『大我』是永遠不滅的。『小我』是有死的，『大我』是永遠不死，永遠不朽的。『小我』雖然會死，但是每一個『小我』的一切作為，一切功德罪惡，一切語言行事，無論大小，無論是非，無論善惡，一一都永遠留存在那個『大我』之中。那個『大我』，便是古往今來一切『小我』的紀功碑，彰善祠，罪狀判決書，孝子慈孫百世不能

傳遞	chuándì	to transmit, to deliver, to transfer
代	dài	generation, era, dynasty
點	diǎn	dot, point, drop
滴	dī	water drop
一線相傳	yīxiànxiāngchuán	to transmit through an unbroken line
連綿不斷	liánmiánbúduàn	in endless succession, continuously
奔流	bēnliú	(said of water) to flow swiftly; swift flow, torrent 奔: to move quickly, to run
滔滔不絕	tāotāobùjué	flowing smoothly and endlessly 滔滔: torrential, surging; 不絕: 不斷

大我	dàwǒ	(lit.) the big self, the larger community with which one identifies — the universe, the public, the state, the society, the nation opposite: 小我 (see above)
消滅	xiāomiè	to destroy, extinguish, or exterminate
作爲	zuòwéi	conduct, behavior, action
行事	xíngshì	conduct, behavior, the way of dealing with people or things
是非	shìfēi	對(或)錯
善惡	shàn'è	好(或)壞
留存(在)	liúcún (zài)	to stay and exist (in)
之中	zhīzhōng	的中間
古往今來	gǔwǎngjīnlái	from ancient times till today, through the ages, since time immemorial
紀功碑	jìgōngbēi	a stone tablet erected in memory of a worthy deed 紀功: to record an accomplishment
彰善祠	zhāngshàncí	a temple or hall built to publicize and encourage the good 彰: to manifest, to display, to make known
罪狀判決書	zuìzhuàng pànjuéshū	a written statement containing charges and verdicts 罪狀: nature of an offense or crime, charges in an indictment; 判決: verdict, sentence; 書: writing, document
慈孫	císūn	a kind, affectionate grandson
百世	bǎishì	a period of a hundred generations — a very long time

改的惡謚法。這個『大我』是永遠不朽的,故一切『小我』的事業,人格,一舉一動,一言一笑,一個念頭,一場功勞,一樁罪過,也都永遠不朽。這便是社會的不朽,『大我』的不朽。」

那邊「一座低低的土牆,遮着一個彈三絃的人。」那三絃的聲浪,在空間起了無數波瀾;那被衝動的空氣質點,直接間接衝動無數旁的空氣質點;這種波瀾,由近而遠,至於無窮空間;由現在而將來,由此剎那以至於無量剎那,至於無窮時間:——這已是不滅不朽了。那時間,那「低低的土牆」外邊來了一位詩人,聽見那三絃的聲音,忽然起了一個念頭;由這一個念頭,就成了一首好詩;這首好詩傳誦了許多人;人讀了這詩,各起種種念頭;由這種種念頭,更發生無量數的念頭,更發生無數的動作,以至於無窮。然而那「低低的土牆」裏面那個彈三絃的人又如何知道他所發生的影響呢?

一個生肺病的人在路上偶然吐了一口痰。那口痰被太陽晒乾了,化為微塵,被風吹起空中,

謚法	shìfǎ	the system of conferring posthumous titles
一舉一動	yìjǔyídòng	every movement and every action, behavior
一言一笑	yìyányíxiào	every word and every smile (or laugh), behavior
念頭	niàntou	想法
場	chǎng	Numerary Adjunct for an event which occupies a period of time

功勞	gōngláo	meritorious deeds
椿	zhuāng	Numerary Adjunct for affairs or matters
罪過	zuìguò	fault, sin
座	zuò	Numerary Adjunct for something relatively big and fixed, such as a mountain, a bridge, a bronze statue, etc.
遮	zhē	to screen, cover, shade, shield, conceal, or shut off
彈	tán	to play (a string instrument, piano or organ)
三弦	sānxián	a Chinese musical instrument with three strings played by fingers
聲浪	shēnglàng	the sound wave
起	qǐ	to give rise to
波瀾	bōlán	waves or billows
衝動	chōngdòng	to excite, to stir
質點	zhídiǎn	(in physics) a particle
由	yóu	從
至於	zhìyú	to arrive at, to reach; to the extent of; as to, as for
刹那	shànà	*ksana*, a moment, an instant, a twinkling
傳誦	chuánsòng	to pass from mouth to mouth, to be admired and appreciated by all, popular
然而	ránér	可是
肺病	fèibìng	lung ailment, tuberculosis
偶然	ǒurán	accidentally, by chance
吐痰	tǔtán	to spit phlegm, to spit
口	kǒu	a measure word, a mouthful of
晒乾	shàigān	to dry in the sun 晒: to expose to sunlight, to dry in the sun
化為	huàwéi	to change into, turn into, to transfrom into
微塵	wēichén	fine dust

東西飄散,漸吹漸遠,至於無窮時間,至於無窮空間。偶然一部份的病菌被體弱的人呼吸進去,便發生肺病,由他一身傳染一家,更由一家傳染無數人家。如此展轉傳染,至於無窮空間,至於無窮時間。然而那先前吐痰的人的骨頭早已腐爛了,他又如何知道他所種的惡果呢?

一千五六百年前有一個人叫做范縝說了幾句話道:「神之於形,猶利之於刀;未聞刀沒而利存,豈容形亡而神在?」這幾句話在當時受了無數人的攻擊。到了宋朝有個司馬光把這幾句話記在他的資治通鑑裏。一千五六百年之後,有一個十一歲的小孩子,——就是我,——看通鑑到這幾句話,心裏受了一大感動,後來便影響了他半生的思想行事。然而那說話的范縝早已死了一千五百年了!

二千六七百年前,在印度地方有一個窮人病死了,沒人收屍,屍首暴露在路上,已腐爛了。那邊來了一輛車,車上坐着一個王太子,看見了這個腐爛發臭的死人,心中起了一念;由這一念,展轉發生無數念。後來那位王太子把王位也拋了,富貴也拋了,父母妻子也拋了,獨自去尋思一個解脫生老病死的方法。後來這位王子便成了一個教主,創了一種哲學的宗教,感化了無數人

病菌	bìngjūn	germ, bacteria, virus
體弱	tǐruò	physically weak and feeble
呼吸	hūxī	to inhale and exhale, to breathe; breathing
傳染	chuánrǎn	to infect
展(or 輾)轉	zhǎnzhuǎn	to pass through many hands, persons, or places; indirectly
骨頭	gútou	bones
腐爛	fǔlàn	to rot or decay, to disintegrate or decompose
攻擊	gōngjí	to attack, to assault
資治通鑑	Zīzhìtōngjiàn	title of a 294-volume chronicle by Sima Guang 司馬光 (1019-1086), covering a period of 1,362 years down to the Five Dynasties period (907-960)
半生	bànshēng	half of one's life span
印度	Yìndù	India
窮人	qióngrén	沒有錢的人
收屍	shōushī	to collect dead bodies
屍首	shīshǒu	a corpse, remains
暴露	pùlù (bàolù)	to expose or be exposed
王太子	wángtàizǐ	a crown prince
發臭	fāchòu	to exude a foul odor 發: to exude, to become; 臭: smelly, foul, stinking
王位	wángwèi	throne, crown
拋	pāo	to throw away, to abandon, to give up
富貴	fùguì	wealth and high position
尋思	xúnsī	to ponder, to consider, to meditate (in search of an answer or a solution)
解脫	jiětuō	to free oneself from worldly worries, to get rid of shackles
教主	jiàozhǔ	founder of a religion
感化	gǎnhuà	to influence and to reform (people)

。他的影響勢力至今還在；將來即使他的宗教全滅了，他的影響勢力終久還存在，以至於無窮。這可是那腐爛發臭的路斃所曾夢想到的嗎？

以上不過是略舉幾件事，說明上文說的「社會的不朽」，「大我的不朽」。這種不朽論，總而言之，只是說個人的一切功德罪惡，一切言語行事，無論大小好壞，一一都留下一些影響在那個「大我」之中，一一都與這永遠不朽的「大我」一同永遠不朽。

上文我批評那「三不朽論」的三層缺點：(一)只限於極少數的人，(二)沒有消極的裁制，(三)所說「功，德，言，」的範圍太含糊了。如今所說「社會的不朽」，其實只是把那「三不朽論」的範圍更推廣了。既然不論事業功德的大小，一切都可不朽，那第一第三兩層短處都沒有了。冠絕古今的道德功業固可以不朽，那極平常的「庸言庸行」，油鹽柴米的瑣屑，愚夫愚婦的細事，一言一笑的微細，也都永遠不朽。那發現美洲的哥侖布固可以不朽，那些和他同行的水手火頭，造船的工人，造羅盤器械的工人，供給他糧食衣服銀錢的

即使	jíshǐ	even if
終久	zhōngjiǔ	after all, in the long run, in the end
路斃	lùbì	one who dies on the roadside; to die on the roadside
夢想	mèngxiǎng	to dream of
略舉	lüèjǔ	to cite or enumerate (a few

		things, etc., as examples or illustrations)
		略: brief, slight, small in extent or amount;
		舉: to cite or enumerate
說明	shuōmíng	to explain, clarify, or expound; explanation, instruction, caption
上文	shàngwén	the above text, the foregoing statement
一一	yīyī	one by one, one after another
一同	yìtóng	一塊
批評	pīpíng	to criticize; criticism, comment
限於	xiànyú	to be limited to; owing to the limitation of
推廣	tuīguǎng	to propagate, to popularize
短處	duǎnchù	shortcomings, defects, faults, weak points
冠絕古今	guànjuégǔjīn	to reign supreme through all ages
		冠: cap — first rate
固	gù	固然
庸言	yōngyán	a trite remark, a cliché, a commonplace word
		庸: mediocre, common
庸行	yōngxíng	a commonplace deed, a regular course of action
油鹽柴米	yóuyáncháimǐ	(cooking) oil, salt, firewood, and rice — daily necessities
瑣屑	suǒxiè	petty, small, trivial, trifling
細事	xìshì	trifling matters
微細	wēixì	small, minute, trifling
發見	fāxiàn	發現
同行	tóngxíng	to travel together
供給	gōngjǐ	to supply, to furnish, to provide, to equip
糧食	liángshí	foodstuff, provisions, grains for human consumption
銀錢	yínqián	money

人，他所讀的書的著作家，生他的父母，生他父母的父母祖宗，以及生育訓練那些工人商人的父母祖宗，以及他以前和同時的社會，……都永遠不朽。社會是有機的組織，那英雄偉人可以不朽，那挑水的，燒飯的，甚至於浴堂裏替你擦背的，甚至於每天替你家掏糞倒馬桶的，也都永遠不朽。至於那第二層缺點，也可免去。如今說立德不朽，行惡也不朽；立功不朽，犯罪也不朽；「流芳百世」不朽，「遺臭萬年」也不朽；功德蓋世固是不朽的善因，吐一口痰也有不朽的惡果。我的朋友李守常先生說得好：「稍一失腳，必致遺留層層罪惡種子於未來無量的人，—即未來無

以及	yǐjí	跟, 和
生育	shēngyù	to give birth to (children) and rear (them)
訓練	xùnliàn	to train; training
英雄	yīngxióng	hero
偉人	wěirén	a great man
挑水的	tiāoshuǐde	a water-bearer 挑: to carry things with a pole on one's shoulder
燒飯的	shāofànde	a cook, one who prepares meals 燒: to cook, to heat up (water), to bake (bricks)
甚至於	shènzhìyú	even to the extent of
浴堂	yùtáng	a bathhouse
擦背的	cābèide	one who scrubs peoples' backs (in a bathhouse, etc.) 擦: to scrub (a back), to mop

		(a floor), to rub, to scratch, to strike (a match)
掏糞	tāofèn	to dredge a cesspool
倒馬桶	dàomǎtǒng	to empty a chamber pot
免去	miǎnqù	to avoid
行惡	xíngè	to do evil deeds
犯罪	fànzuì	to commit a crime, an offense, or a sin
流芳百世	liúfāngbǎishì	to hand down a fine reputation through generations, to be honored by all generations 流: to flow, to move; 芳: fragrant; fragrance; (fig.) a fine reputation
遺臭萬年	yíchòuwànnián	"to leave a stink for ten thousand years" — to go down in history as a byword of infamy 遺: to leave behind (either intentionally or unintentionally)
功德蓋世	gōngdégàishì	(one's) merit and virtue are without match 蓋: to cover; 蓋世: to surpass one's generation, to reign supreme in one's time
稍	shāo	slightly, a little
一	yī	once
失腳	shījiǎo	to slip, to lose one's footing, (fig.) to make a mistake
必	bì	一定
致	zhì	to cause to come, to bring about, to occasion or result in, to achieve
遺留 ...(於)	yíliú ... (yú)	to leave behind, to hand down ... to
層層	céngcéng	one layer after another, layer upon layer — in endlessly large numbers
即	jí	就是, is exactly, namely

量的我,─永不能消除,永不能懺悔,」這就是消極的裁制了。

中國儒家的宗教提出一個父母的觀念,和一個祖先的觀念,來做人生一切行為的裁制力。所以說,「一出言而不敢忘父母,一舉足而不敢忘父母。」父母死後,又用喪禮祭禮等等見神見鬼的方法,時刻提醒這種人生行為的裁制力。所以又說,「齋明盛服,以承祭祀,洋洋乎如在其上,如在其左右。」又說,「齋三日,則見其所為齋者;祭之日,入室,僾然必有見乎其位;周還出戶,肅然必有聞乎其容聲;出戶而聽,愾然必有聞乎其嘆息之聲。」這都是「神道設教」,見神見鬼的手段。這種宗教的手段在今日是不中用了。還有那種「默示」的宗教,神權的宗教,崇拜偶像的宗教,在我們心裏也不能發生效力,不能裁制我們一生的行為。以我個人看來,這種「社會的不朽」觀念很可以做我的宗教了。我的宗教的教旨是:「我這個現在的『小我』,對於那永遠不朽的『大我』的無窮過去,須負重大的責

消除	xiāochú	to eliminate, to get rid of
懺悔	chànhuǐ	to repent one's sin
儒家	rújiā	the Confucian school of thought, Confucianists
觀念	guānniàn	a concept, an idea or view
祖先	zǔxiān	祖宗
出言	chūyán	to give forth a word, to utter a

		word, to speak
舉足	jǔzú	to take steps
喪禮	sānglǐ	funeral rites
祭禮	jìlǐ	sacrificial rites
等等	děngděng	and so forth, et cetera
見神見鬼	jiànshén jiànguǐ	看見神看見鬼
時刻	shíkè	always, constantly, continuously
提醒	tíxǐng	to remind
齋明盛服	zhāimíngshèngfú	to purify oneself by observing rules of abstinence and dress
祭祀	jìsì	to offer sacrifices (to)
洋洋乎	yángyánghū	(lit.) overflowing, swelling (as the sound of music, etc.)
如	rú	好像
齋	zhāi	to purify oneself by observing rules of abstinence
入室	rùshì	進到屋裏
僾然	àirán	彷彿 (fǎngfú: like, similar to), 好像
出戶	chūhù	走出屋子
肅然	sùrán	reverently
聞	wén	聽
愾然	kàirán	full of wrath
嘆(歎)息	tànxí	to sigh
神道設教	shéndàoshèjiào	用宗教的法子來教育(人民)
手段	shǒuduàn	means (as opposed to ends), a devious way of dealing with people or things
中用	zhōngyòng	to be useful
默示	mòshì	to hint, to signal silently
神權	shénquán	religious authority, to rule by divine right
偶像	ǒuxiàng	idol
效力	xiàolì	effect, efficacy; to render a service to
教旨	jiàozhǐ	the main purport of a religion
負	fù	to bear, to sustain, to carry on the back

任；對於那永遠不朽的『大我』的無窮未來，也須負重大的責任。我須要時時想着，我應該如何努力利用現在的『小我』，方才可以不辜負了那『大我』的無窮過去，方才可以不遺害那『大我』的無窮未來？」

辜負	gūfù	to let down, to be unworthy of, to fail to live up to, to disappoint
遺害	yíhài	to leave a harmful influence on

句型

1. 既然如此 ... 只好 ... －　since it is so ... have no choice but ...

- 既然如此,我們只好用實驗主義的方法 ...

    例 (1): "我們明天去看電影好不好?" "不行,我沒有空." "既然如此,那我們只好改天再去了."

    例 (2): "我餓死了,一塊兒去吃飯好不好?" "我還不餓,我剛吃過東西." "既然如此,那我只好一個人去了."

2. 不問 ... 只問 ... －　not ask (care) ... but ask (care) ...

- 這種不朽說,不問人死後靈魂能不能存在,只問他的人格 ...

    例 (1): 買東西的時候我向來不問東西貴還是便宜,只問品質[1] 好不好

    例 (2): 交朋友的時候,我不問他家裏有沒有錢,只問他是不是好人.

    [1] 品質　　　　pǐnzhì　　　　quality

3. A 跟 (和,與) B 成正比 (例) －　A is in direct proportion to B
   A 跟 (和,與) B 成反比 (例) －　A is in inverse proportion to B

- 影響的程度與物體距離的遠近成正比例.

    例 (1): 他賺的錢跟他花的錢成正比,所以他總是錢不夠用.

    例 (2): 美國的進口跟出口成反比.

討論

1. 簡單的說一說范縝的 "神滅論," 他用刀與利的譬喻[1] 來說明精神與物質互相依存[2] 的關係,你同意嗎?

2. 什麼是中國傳統的³"三不朽"？胡適對"三不朽"有什麼批評？

3. 什麼是"大我"？什麼是"小我"？"大我"與"小我"有什麼關係？

4. 胡適主張⁴好的可以不朽,壞的也一樣可以不朽,你同意嗎？

5. 胡適寫這篇文章,主要的目的⁵是什麼？

¹ 譬喻	pìyù	analogy
² 依存	yīcún	depend on (something or somebody) for existence
³ 傳統的	chuántǒngde	traditional
⁴ 主張	zhǔzhāng	advocate, maintain
⁵ 目的	mùdì	purpose, goal

A Preliminary Discussion of Literary Reform
文學改良芻議

We conclude our selections with excerpts from one of Hu Shi's most famous essays, written in 1917 while he was still a student at Columbia University. In this essay Hu Shi issues his now famous call for language reform. He proposed that all writing in Chinese be in the vernacular, in *baihua* (白話), rather than in the classical language called *wenyan* (文言). This was the opening shot in the literary revolution, the effects of which are seen still even in the present day. His appeal, and those of others, had a profound effect on the vernacular language movement in China. Yet, curiously enough, Hu Shi chose to write this essay in the classical language, perhaps hoping to reach, by using this medium, those in China who could be instrumental in promoting such reform. This essay is an important document in the intellectual history of China.

This essay was first published in *New Youth*, 2.5 (January 1917). It was later included in *Collected Essays of Hu Shi*, i, 7-23.

文學改良芻議

吾以爲今日而言文學改良，須從八事入手。八事者何？

一曰，須言之有物。
二曰，不摹倣古人。
三曰，須講求文法。
四曰，不作無病之呻吟。
五曰，務去爛調套語。
六曰，不用典。
七曰，不講對仗。
八曰，不避俗字俗語。

一曰須言之有物

吾國近世文學之大病，在於言之無物。吾所謂「物」，非古人所謂「文以載道」之說也。吾

A Preliminary Discussion of Literary Reform

芻議	chúyì	a preliminary discussion
吾	wú	我
以爲	yǐwéi	認爲, 想
言	yán	談
入手	rùshǒu	下手, to put one's hand to, to begin with, to proceed from
者	zhě	used as a particle to indicate a pause; used with an adjective, a

		verb, or a verbal phrase to form a noun meaning "that which," "those who," etc.; used to sum up the things which have been mentioned in the preceding text
何	hé	(是)甚麼?
曰	yuē	是說
言之有物	yánzhīyǒuwù	所談的或所寫的有思想,有內容
摹倣	mófǎng	模倣, to imitate
無	wú	沒有
之	zhī	a particle corresponding to the vernacular "的"; used to replace someone or something and serving as an object in a sentence
呻吟	shēnyín	痛苦時發出的聲音;發出痛苦的聲音
務	wù	務必,一定得
去	qù	除去,去掉
爛調	làndiào	(now usually written 濫調), hackneyed tune, worn out theme
套語	tàoyǔ	formulaic, conventional expressions
用典	yòngdiǎn	to use allusions (to history, classics, etc.)
講	jiǎng	講求, to stress, to be particular about
對仗	duìzhàng	verbal parallelism, antithesis
避	bì	to avoid, to shun
俗字	súzì	a common, non-literary word
俗語	súyǔ	a common, non-literary expression
非	fēi	不是
文以載道	wényǐzàidào	"Literature is to carry (bear) doctrines" — literary didacticism
說	shuō	說法,學說,理論

所謂「物」，約有二事：

一、情感　情感者，文學之靈魂。文學而無情感，如人之無魂，木偶而已，行尸走肉而已。

二、思想　吾所謂「思想」，蓋兼見地、識力、理想三者而言之。思想不必皆賴文學而傳，而文學以有思想而益貴；思想亦以有文學的價值而益貴也。

二曰不摹倣古人

文學者，隨時代而變遷者也。一時代有一時代之文學：周、秦有周、秦之文學，漢、魏有漢、魏之文學，唐、宋、元、明有唐、宋、元、明之文學。此非吾一人之私言，乃文明進化之公理也。凡此諸時代，各因時勢風會而變，各有其特長；吾輩以歷史進化之眼光觀之，決不可謂古人之文學皆勝於今人也。

今日之中國，當造今日之文學，不必摹倣唐

約	yuē	大約,大概
情感	qínggǎn	emotion, feeling
靈魂	línghún	soul
如	rú	好像
木偶	mùǒu	wooden figure, puppet
而已	éryǐ	罷了, that is all, there is nothing more
行屍走肉	xíngshīzǒuròu	a walking corpse
蓋	gài	大概, approximately, about
兼	jiān	to have, do or combine more than two things concurrently

見地	jiàndì	insight, judgment
識力	shílì	power of discernment
皆	jiē	都
賴	lài	依賴, 靠
傳	chuán	to transmit, to pass on, to spread
以	yǐ	used as a particle corresponding to the vernacular "因爲," "拿,用," "爲了"
貴	guì	可貴, valuable
亦	yì	也
變遷	biànqiān	變化, 改變
私言	sīyán	personal opinion or view
乃	nǎi	是
進化	jìnhuà	evolution
公理	gōnglǐ	大家公認的道理, generally acknowledged truth
凡	fán	every, any, all
此	cǐ	這
諸	zhū	all, various
時勢	shíshì	the trend of the times
風會	fēnghuì	(usually unpredictable) changes or happenings of the times
其	qí	a particle corresponding to the vernacular "他的" or "它的;" used to refer to a person or thing meaning "他," "它," etc.
特長	tècháng	strong point, special feature, specialty
吾輩	wúbèi	我們
眼光	yǎnguāng	vision, view, perspective
觀	guān	看, 觀察
謂	wèi	說
勝於	shèngyú	to be superior to, to excel
當	dāng	應當, 應該
造	zào	作, to produce, to make

、宋，亦不必摹倣周、秦也。

吾每謂今日之文學，其足與世界「第一流」文學比較而無愧色者，獨有白話小說一項。此無他故，以此種小說皆不事摹倣古人，而惟實寫今日社會之情狀，故能成真正文學。

三曰須講文法

今之作文作詩者，每不講求文法之結構。夫不講文法，是謂「不通」。

四曰不作無病之呻吟

今之少年往往作悲觀，其取別號則曰「寒灰」，「無生」，「死灰」；其作爲詩文，則對落日而思暮年，對秋風而思零落，春來則惟恐其速去，花發又惟懼其早謝：此亡國之哀音也。其流弊所至，遂養成一種暮氣，不思奮發有爲，服勞報國，但知發牢騷之音，感喟之文。

足	zú	够
與	yǔ	跟,和
第一流	dìyīliú	first rate
愧色	kuìsè	a look of shame
獨有	dúyǒu	只有
項	xiàng	item, matter
他故	tāgù	其他的緣故,別的原因
事	shì	attend to, devote (oneself) to
惟	wéi	只,就
實寫	shíxiě	to describe (people and things) as they really appear to be
情狀	qíngzhuàng	情形,狀態

故	gù	所以
每	měi	每每, 往往, 常常
結構	jiégòu	structure, construction
夫	fú	a particle used to introduce the author's comment on a given subject (note pronunciation)
不通	bùtōng	"to be impassable" — to be illogical, ungrammatical, meaningless, or not showing good sense
悲觀	bēiguān	pessimistic
取	qǔ	to adopt, to choose
別號	biéhào	別名, an alias, a second name
寒灰	hánhuī	寒: 冷; 灰: ash, dust
無生	wúshēng	沒有生命
作爲	zuòwéi	作, 寫
思	sī	想
暮年	mùnián	晚年, 老年
零落	língluò	withered and fallen
速去	sùqù	很快的離去
發	fā	to come or bring into existence, to give forth
懼	jù	怕
早謝	zǎoxiè	(of flowers, leaves) to wither early
哀音	āiyīn	a mournful sound
流弊	liúbì	long accumulated evil effect
至	zhì	到
遂	suì	就
養成	yǎngchéng	to form, to acquire, to cultivate
暮氣	mùqì	gloomy mood, defeatist attitude, apathy
奮發有爲	fènfāyǒuwéi	to exert oneself and work hard
服勞報國	fúláobàoguó	to render service for one's country
牢騷	láosāo	discontent, complaint
感喟	gǎnkuì	to feel moved and sigh

五曰務去爛調套語

今之學者，胸中記得幾個文學的套語，便稱詩人。其所爲詩文，處處是陳言爛調。其流弊所至，遂令國中生出許多似是而非、貌似而實非之詩文。

吾所謂務去爛調套語者，別無他法，惟在人人以其耳目所親見親聞所親身閱歷之事物，一一自己鑄詞以形容描寫之；但求其不失眞，但求能達其狀物寫意之目的，即是工夫。

六曰不用典

今分典爲廣狹二義，分論之如下：

一、廣義之典非吾所謂典也。廣義之典約有五種：

（甲）古人所設譬喻，其取譬之事物，含有普通意義，不以時代而失其效用者，今人亦可用之。

（乙）成語　成語者，合字成辭，別爲意義。其習見之句，通行已久，不妨用之。

學者	xuézhě	educated people
胸中	xiōngzhōng	"in one's chest (bosom)" — in one's heart, in one's mind
稱	chēng	稱…爲…, to call, to address
陳言	chényán	stale expressions
令	lìng	使, 讓
似是而非	sìshìérfēi	好像對,可是(其實)不對
貌似而實非	màosìérshífēi	表面上像,可是其實不像

耳目	ěrmù	耳朵和眼睛
親見	qīnjiàn	親眼看見
親聞	qīnwén	親耳聽見
親身	qīnshēn	personally, first hand; personal
閱歷	yuèlì	to see, hear, or do for oneself, to experience; experience
一一	yīyī	one by one, one after another
鑄詞	zhùcí	to coin or invent a new word or phrase
形容	xíngróng	描寫, to describe
失真	shīzhēn	to lack fidelity, not to be true to the original
達	dá	達到, to reach, to attain (a goal)
狀物	zhuàngwù	形容事情或東西
寫意	xiěyì	描寫思想感情
目的	mùdì	purpose, goal, objective
即是	jíshì	就是
工夫	gōngfu	skill
分...為...	fēn...wéi...	to divide ... into ...
狹	xiá	窄, narrow
義	yì	意義, meaning, sense
分	fēn	分別地, separately
論	lùn	討論
如下	rúxià	as follows
設	shè	to establish, to set up
譬喻	pìyù	analogy, simile or metaphor
含有	hányǒu	to contain
效用	xiàoyòng	effectiveness, usefulness
成語	chéngyǔ	set phrase, idiomatic expression
辭	cí	phrase, verbal expression
別為意義	biéwéiyìyì	表示別種不同的意思
習見	xíjiàn	常見
通行	tōngxíng	commonly practiced, current
已久	yǐjiǔ	已經很久了
不妨	bùfáng	there is no harm in (doing something), it does not hurt to (do something)

(丙)引史事　引史事與今所議論之事相比較，不可謂爲用典也。

(丁)引古人作比　此亦非用典也。

(戊)引古人之語　此亦非用典也。

二、狹義之典，吾所主張不用者也。吾所謂用「典」者，謂文人詞客不能自己鑄詞造句以寫眼前之景、胸中之意，故借用或不全切、或全不切之故事陳言以代之，以圖含混過去：是謂「用典」。

七曰不講對仗

排偶乃人類言語之一種特性；故雖古代文字，如老子、孔子之文，亦間有駢句。至於後世文學末流，言之無物，乃以文勝；今日而言文學改良，當「先立乎其大者」，不當枉廢有用之精力於微細纖巧之末：此吾所以有廢駢廢律之說也。

八曰不避俗語俗字

以今世歷史進化的眼光觀之，則白話文學之爲中國文學之正宗，又爲將來文學必用之利器，

引	yǐn	引用, to quote, to cite
史事	shǐshì	歷史上發生的事
議論	yìlùn	討論
相	xiāng	互相, each other, one another
文人詞客	wénréncíkè	men of letters
切	qiè	to the point, appropriate, fitting
代	dài	代替, to replace, to substitute

圖	tú	for 打算, 想要
含混過去	hánhùnguòqu	to get by under false pretenses
排偶	páiǒu	parallelism, the use of parallel structure in language
言語	yányǔ	language, especially spoken language
老子	Lǎozǐ	604-531 B.C., a renowned philosopher and founder of Taoism
孔子	Kǒngzǐ	Confucius
間	jiàn	偶而, occasionally
駢句	piánjù	parallel sentences
至於	zhìyú	到了
末流	mòliú	the later and decadent stage of a school of thought, literature, etc.
文	wén	(in this context) form, technique
先立乎其大者	xiānlìhūqídàzhě	先建立它的重要的部份
枉廢	wǎngfèi	(now usually written 枉費) to spend in vain, to be of no avail
微細纖巧	wēixìxiānqiǎo	very small and delicate
末	mò	end, tip — nonessentials, minor details
廢	fèi	to abolish, to abandon
駢	pián	駢文, rhythmical prose characterized by parallelism and ornateness
律	lǜ	律詩, a poem of eight lines, each containing five or seven characters, with strict rules about tones, rhymes, and verbal parallelism
正宗	zhèngzōng	orthodox school (of literature, thought, etc.); orthodox
利器	lìqì	sharp weapon — efficient tool, instrument, etc.

可斷言也。以此之故，吾主張今日作文作詩，宜採用俗語俗字。與其用三千年前之死字，不如用二十世紀之活字；與其作不能行遠不能普及之秦、漢、六朝文字，不如作家喻戶曉之水滸、西遊文字也。

民國六年一月。

斷言	duànyán	to say or state with certainty
宜	yí	應當
採用	cǎiyòng	to adopt (a suggestion, new technique, etc.), to use, to employ
與其 A 不如 B	yǔqí A bùrú B	"It's better to B than A," "B rather than A"
世紀	shìjì	century
行遠	xíngyuǎn	to go far
普及	pǔjí	to reach everywhere; universal, available to all
家喻戶曉	jiāyùhùxiǎo	每一家都知道 喻：知道； 曉：明白，曉得
水滸	*Shuǐhǔ*	水滸傳,一本白話小說,作者是施耐庵 (ca. 1290-ca. 1365)
西遊	*Xīyóu*	西遊記, a very popular vernacular novel, telling the adventures of a Buddhist monk and his three disciples on their way to India

句型

1. 與其 ... 不如 ... — would rather

- 與其作不能行遠不能普及之秦,漢,六朝文字,不如作家喻戶曉之水滸,西遊文字也.

    例 (1): 人活在世界上,與其不自由,不如死.

    例 (2): 與其躺在床上睡不着覺,不如起來看書.

討論

1. "文學改良芻議"是白話運動的宣言,然而這篇文章卻是用文言文寫的,這個矛盾說明了甚麼現象?
2. 現代人寫文章摹倣古人會造成甚麼問題?
3. 對胡適提出的八點主張,你有沒有不同意的?

Selected Bibliography

Grieder, Jerome B. *Hu Shih and the Chinese Renaissance.* Cambridge, Mass.: Harvard University Press, 1970.

Hu Shi (Hu Shih) 胡適. *Changshi ji* 嘗試集 (A collection of experiments). Taipei: Hu Shi jinianguan 胡適紀念館, 1971. First published, Shanghai: Yadong tushuguan 亞東圖書館, 1920.

Hu Shi. *The Chinese Renaissance.* Chicago: University of Chicago Press, 1934. Reprinted with introduction by Hyman Kublin. New York: Paragon Book Reprint Corp., 1963.

Hu Shi. *Hu Shi de riji* 胡適的日記 (The diary of Hu Shi). Ed. by Zhongguo shehui kexueyuan jindaishi yanjiusuo, Zhonghua minguoshi yanjiushi 中國社會科學院近代史研究所中華民國史研究室. Hong Kong: Zhonghua shuju 中華書局, 1985.

Hu Shi. *Hu Shi laiwang shuxin xuan* 胡適來往書信選 (Selected collection of correspondence from and to Hu Shi). Ed. by Zhongguo shehui kexueyuan jindaishi yanjiusuo, Zhonghua minguoshi yanjiushi. Hong Kong: Zhonghua shuju, 1983.

Hu Shi. *Hu Shi lunxue jinzhu* 胡適論學近著 (Hu Shi's recent writings on scholarship). Shanghai: Shangwu yinshuguan 商務印書館, 1935.

Hu Shi. *Hu Shi wencun* 胡適文存 (Collected essays of Hu Shi). 2 vols. Shanghai: Yadong Tushuguan, 1921.

Hu Shi. *Hu Shi wencun, erji* 胡適文存二集 (Collected essays of Hu Shi, second collection). 2 vols. Shanghai: Yadong Tushuguan, 1924.

Hu Shi. *Hu Shi wencun, sanji* 胡適文存三集 (Collected essays of Hu Shi, third collection). 4 vols. Shanghai: Yadong Tushuguan, 1930.

Hu Shi. *Sishi zishu* 四十自述 (A self-account at forty). Taipei: Yuandong tushu gongsi 遠東圖書公司, 1959. First published, Shanghai: Yadong tushuguan, 1933.

Tang Degang (Tong Te-kong) 唐德剛. *Hu Shi zayi* 胡適雜憶 (Miscellaneous reflections on Hu Shi). Taipei: Zhuanji wenxue chubanshe 傳記文學出版社, 1979.

Yu Yingshi (Yü Ying-shih) 余英時. "Zhongguo jindai sixiangshi shang de Hu Shi" 中國近代思想史上的胡適 (Hu Shi in the modern intellectual history of China). In Hu Songping 胡頌平 ed., *Hu Shizhi xiansheng nianpu changbian chugao* 胡適之先生年譜長編初稿 (The first draft of Hu Shi's comprehensive chronological biography). 10 vols.; vol. 1, pp. 1-74. Taipei: Lianjing chuban shiye gongsi 聯經出版事業公司, 1984.

Zhou Mingzhi (Chou Min-chih) 周明之. *Hu Shi and Intellectual Choice in Modern China*. Ann Arbor, Michigan: The University of Michigan Press, 1984.

www.ingramcontent.com/pod-product-compliance
Lightning Source LLC
Chambersburg PA
CBHW051208290426
44109CB00021B/2379